THE MORNING AFTER

THE
MORNING
AFTER

*Sexual Politics
at the End of the Cold War*

CYNTHIA ENLOE

UNIVERSITY OF CALIFORNIA PRESS
BERKELEY   LOS ANGELES   LONDON

University of California Press
Berkeley and Los Angeles, California

University of California Press, Ltd.
London, England

© 1993 by
The Regents of the University of California

Library of Congress Cataloging-in-Publication Data

Enloe, Cynthia H., 1938–
   The morning after: sexual politics at the end of the Cold
War / Cynthia Enloe.
       p.   cm.
   Includes bibliographical references (p.   ) and index.
   ISBN 0-520-08335-0 (alk. paper).—ISBN 0-520-08336-9
(pbk. : alk. paper)
       1. Sex role.   2. Man-woman relationships.   3. Feminist
theory.   4. Cold War.   5. Post-communism.   I. Title.
   HQ1233.E55   1993
   305.3—dc20   92-43416
                                                       CIP

9 8 7 6 5 4 3 2

The paper used in this publication meets the minimum
requirements of American National Standard for Information
Sciences—Permanence of Paper for Printed Library Materials,
ANSI Z39.48-1984.♾

For Clark University students past and present

Contents

Illustrations

Introduction

"Now that the war is over, Esmeralda has had her IUD removed." What? I read the sentence again.

Esmeralda is a Salvadoran woman who spent many of her young adult years as a guerrilla in the Farabundo Martí National Liberation Front, the FMLN. She pounded out tortillas and washed her boyfriend's clothes as well as wielding a gun.[1] Now it was the "morning after." Not of an illicit affair, but of a Cold War–fueled civil war. Her country's strife had been brought to an end by a peace accord signed by government men and opposition men up in New York, under the watchful eye of the men from Washington. So Esmeralda was going to hand her gun over to United Nations peacekeepers and try to remake her life. One of her first postwar acts was to have her IUD taken out. During the war her guerrilla tasks had made it seem politically irresponsible to get pregnant. But now she was being urged by men in the political leadership to imagine her postwar life as one devoted to being a good mother.

Some Salvadoran women, however, had quite a different vision of postwar relationships between their country's women and men. They were imagining an end to police rape and domestic violence. Men's violence against women had escalated under the pressures of a civil war fueled by classic Cold War anxieties. These women were organizing to ensure that the peace accords, even if not designed by women on either side, would create economic opportunities for women more diverse than the conventional peacetime roles of wife and mother. Some of these Salvadoran women were investing their postwar energies in printing T-shirts that declared *"Soy Feminist!"* (I am a Feminist!)[2]

Esmeralda was sending up warning signals. Wars—hot and cold— are like love affairs. They don't just end. They fizzle and sputter; some-times they reignite. Mornings after are times for puzzling, for sorting things out, for trying to assess whether one is starting a new day or continuing an old routine. The civil wars in Central America and the global Cold War, which intensified so many local conflicts during the last forty years, have not come to a neat end. They must have ending pro-cesses, ones not as elegant or as conclusive as, say, an operatic grande finale. These messier processes may go on for years, even generations. And they aren't predictable, although many groups and regimes have done their best to dictate the paths such endings will take.

In summer 1992, North Americans and Europeans lost interest in Central America and turned their fickle attention to Yugoslavia, which was experiencing the end of the Cold War as an outbreak of virulent nationalisms. Meanwhile, the most popular American movie was one shedding new light on a little-known corner of a war that ended a generation ago. As people shook their heads in despair at the Croats, Bosnians, and Serbs shooting each other, "A League of Their Own" was packing the cinemas to tell a lighthearted version of the reimposition of conventional femininity and masculinity in the United States at the end of World War II. Only now, five decades after VE- and VJ-Day, were American audiences—with help from Geena Davis's batting and Ma-donna's fielding—learning that women played professional baseball with talent and verve before delighted fans while the male players were overseas. And only now were most moviegoers learning what recipe of men's profit motives and women's self-deprecation went into making those women hang up their cleats, making way for the remasculinization of America's pastime. Just thinking about the movie as one strolled out of the theater into the soft summer evening air extended that war's "postwar era." For a postwar era lasts as long as people affected by a conflict employ that painful or exhilarating experience to assess their own current relationships and aspirations.

So, too, the post–Cold War era: while the 1989 revolutions in Eastern Europe are being recorded as the end of the Cold War, the rivalry between the superpowers and their allies which defined loyalty and subversion for so many people in so many countries didn't simply end when Vaclav Havel appeared on a Prague balcony or when Berliners shook hands through the dismantled wall. The Cold War is having a multitude of endings. Most of those endings aren't hosted by government officials or filmed by television crews.

The configuration of ideas and behavior on which we bestowed the shorthand label "the Cold War" existed because many people far from the public spotlight were willing to see, or were pressed into seeing, the world—and their neighbors—in a particular way. Thus, to end that Cold War is to make myriad transformations in the ways people live their ordinary lives. Whom can I trust? What are my loyalties? Are there alternatives to the government's expectations of me? The Cold War began and was sustained as people individually came to have certain answers to these questions. The Cold War is genuinely ending only as people come to have fresh answers to the old questions.

These questions will not have the same meanings for women as they do for men. The Cold War depended on a deeply militarized understanding of identity and security. Militarization relies on distinct notions about masculinity, notions that have staying power only if they are legitimized by women as well as men. And the ending to a particular war cannot undo decades of deeper militarization. For instance, it is true that in the November 1992 presidential election in the U.S., the Gulf War victory seems to have had surprisingly little effect on voters' choices. A mere 25 percent of voters interviewed on election day said that the Gulf War "mattered" to them as they tried to decide whether to cast their ballots in favor of the incumbent who had led the country in that war or his principal challenger, who had never made defense policy decisions or served in the military. Most of the minority who told exit pollsters that that war *had* mattered to them voted for George Bush.[3] And yet many Americans may now be imagining their post–Gulf War military to be more admirable than any of their civilian institutions.

Even among military veterans interviewed by the pollsters, Bill Clinton garnered the most votes: 41 percent, compared with George Bush's 38 percent and Ross Perot's 21 percent.[4] This was despite Clinton's status as the only nonveteran of the three, despite his opposition to the Vietnam War and his reluctant support of the Gulf War, and despite his campaign pledge to lift the existing ban on gay men and lesbians serving in the military. The veterans' electoral percentages may suggest that many men who have performed military duty (only 5 percent of American veterans are women, although their proportions are growing) do not now make "veteran" a central part of their political identities. Pollsters may categorize these men as veterans, but when they weigh their own electoral choices, they think of themselves as African-American or as Californian or as elderly. A second, perhaps more remote interpretation is that, as veterans, many American men are rethinking the role of military solutions and of militarized values in their country's future.

Does this election behavior, which helped produce the Clinton presidency, mean that Americans—at least the 55 percent of adults who voted—can be thought of as demilitarized? There are other tests of demilitarization, other straws in the wind to watch: the willingness of American voters to vote for women congressional candidates who refuse to define national security in terms of military strength; the willingness of American elected legislators themselves, men and women, to challenge defense officials and intelligence security experts publicly; the willingness of Bill Clinton and his advisers to resist opting for military solutions as a way of proving the nonveteran president's masculine trustworthiness; the willingness of Americans to confront their economic problems without blaming the Germans and the Japanese for their past reluctance to spend extraordinary amounts of public funds on defense and without pressing the Japanese or the Germans to rearm in the 1990s in the name of competitive "fairness"; the willingness of defense contractors and women living in towns now dependent on military bases to imagine life with seriously reduced armed forces; the willingness of young men to imagine service in United Nations peacekeeping forces as being as much a guarantor of their fragile manliness as service in a U.S. Army unit in Saudi Arabia or a U.S. Air Force jet flying over Libya; the willingness of young women to feel as much first-class citizens when working in a city's housing agency as when flying a helicopter for the navy. The list of tests of demilitarization is longer. It is longer because the militarization of the last three generations of Americans has been so deep and so subtle that we scarcely yet know how to map its gendered terrain.

A lot of women and men in Poland, Chile, South Africa, and France never served in their governments' militaries; yet between 1945 and 1989 their lives were also militarized. The militarization which sustained Cold War relationships between people for forty years required armed forces with huge appetites for recruits; it also depended on ideas about manliness and womanliness that touched people who never went through basic training. It may prove harder to uproot those ideas than it was to dismantle a wall. This book is about the varieties of masculinity and femininity that it took to create the Cold War and the sorts of transformations in the relationships between women and men it will take to ensure that the ending processes move forward.

The evidence coming in so far suggests that the end of superpower rivalry is not in itself guaranteeing an end to the militarization of masculinity on which it thrived. On the other hand, masculinity is not abstract, nor is it monolithic. Feminists have shown in their research and in their campaigns for reform that ideas about what constitutes acceptable behavior by men can share patriarchal tendencies and yet vary in surprising ways across cultures. Patriarchy does not come in "one size fits all."

In fact, tourists, traveling executives, overseas troops, aid technocrats, migrant workers—everyone who moves between cultures watches for signs of what constitute appropriate ways to be manly in different societies. Sometimes men try to mimic those forms of masculinity; at other times they view the alternatives with contempt and go home with a renewed sense of the superiority of their own home-grown formulas for being "real men." So it's not just anthropologists who compare masculinity across cultures. But rarely are these comparisons used as springboards for investigating the big questions of international politics: Will the end of the Cold War mean fewer wars? Will the United Nations breed a less violent form of security?

What has been happening since the Gulf War, for instance, to the ideas of Kuwaiti men and women about appropriate masculine behavior? The answer may be quite different from what has been happening to those of Japanese men and women since that same war, as they have plunged into a debate over sending Japanese troops overseas. In Kuwait, a year after the Iraqi retreat, the reestablished monarchy was encouraging Kuwaiti men to train with U.S. soldiers in joint military maneuvers for the sake of national revitalization. At the same time that these maneuvers were taking place, reports were circulating that many Kuwaiti men had been taking out their postwar frustrations by sexually assaulting Kuwaiti women and Asian domestic servants.[5] What sorts of new masculinity have Kuwaiti men been learning from their American mentors? Meanwhile, in Japan, the ruling Liberal Democrats have pushed through a reluctant parliament a bill legalizing the deployment of Japanese troops abroad—to Cambodia, as United Nations peacekeepers—for the first time since the end of World War II. The rationale was not to make war but to keep peace as members of UN teams, so that Japanese male officials can demonstrate to U.S. and European male officials that they have come of age politically. Simultaneously, however, media watchers reported that the biggest increases in Japanese magazine sales were occurring among monthlies like *Popeye,* aimed at young men who wanted to learn not about rifles or jets but about "how to live happily in big cities."[6]

So trying to make sense of the processes that are ending the Cold War—or prolonging it under new guises—can't be accomplished by painting the world with broad brushstrokes. It requires a curiosity that pays attention to differences as well as similarities. And it is an enterprise that rewards those who take seriously the experiences of ordinary women and men, who follow the breadcrumbs leading from national and international elite decisions back to the daily lives of people who seem to wield little political influence.

This book is inspired not by pessimism but by curiosity. And curiosity can make one cautious. It doesn't seem quite time yet to pronounce that the Cold War is over. Not if by the Cold War one means a densely woven web of relationships and attitudes that have sustained not only large and lethal militaries but also ideas about enemies, about rivalries. There is too much still to keep an eye on. There is too much still to figure out. And a lot of what needs watching and explaining has to do with how women and men—alone and together—act out their relationships with militarism.

Some of the ideas spelled out in the chapters that follow were first posed when the Cold War was still under full sail. I have rethought them in light of the events of the last three years. Other chapters I was prompted to write initially by people who had the insight to see the need for a conference or for a collection that would tackle some of the post–Cold War puzzles occupying so many of us inside and outside academia. Thus, although these chapters now read quite differently than they once did, I would like to thank the editors and conference organizers who prompted me to think about just how the dynamics between masculinity and femininity constructed the Cold War and today are directing its sputtering end: Beth Hess and Myra Marx Ferree; John Gillis; Ann Holder, Margaret Cerullo, and Marla Erlien; Cynthia Peters; Saundra Sturdevant; Amy Virship; Kate Tentler; Connie Sutton; and Elizabetta Addis, Valeria Russo, and Lorenza Sebesta.

Among those friends and colleagues who have generously acted as guides to militarizing and demilitarizing cultures about which I still know all too little are Lois Wasserspring, Dessima Williams, Seira Tamang, Beverly Grier, Elaine Salo, Jacqueline Cock, Nira Yuval-Davis, Marie Aimée Helie-Lucas, Nishkala Suntharalingam, Melissa Gilbert, Octavia Taylor, Seungsook Moon, Saralee Hamilton, Lynn Wilson, Alison Cohn, Kathleen Barry, Elizabetta Addis, Fadia Faquir, Ximena Bunster, Eva Isaksson, Zena Sochor, Keith Severin, Ann Smith, Jan Pettman, Julie Wheelwright, and Lilo Klug. I have had the good fortune to be able to try out hunches about wartime and postwar American society with Sharon Krefetz, Sally Deutsch, John Blydenburgh, Mark Miller, Pronita

Gupta, Alison Bernstein, Jackson Katz, and Carol Cohn. My under-standing of the continuing twists and turns that the U.S. military is taking as it adjusts—or tries to avoid adjusting—to new sexual and racial politics has been deepened by conversations with Mary Katzen-stein, Linda Grant DePauw, Doreen Lehr, Mary Wertsch, Richard Moser, Cortez Enloe, Stephanie Atkinson, Edwin Dorn, and Gary Lehr-ing. I am indebted to the congressional staff of Representative Beverly Byron for supplying me with transcripts of hearings and Pentagon re-ports. My writing coaches continue to be Gilda Bruckman, Serena Hils-inger, Laura Zimmerman, Madeline Drexler, and Ellen Cooney. Pat Miles more than once, thank goodness, caught me on the verge of making too-simple assumptions about why people act the way they do.

There is a whole new, burgeoning field of research and teaching now recognized as Gender and International Relations. It has informed much of this book. The fact that the field is named, is visible, and is influencing so many people trying to chart the post–Cold War world is due in no small measure to the energy and irreverent intelligence of a small handful of women scholars, among whom I am especially indebted to Ann Tickner, Spike Peterson, and Sandra Whitworth.

Candida Lacey talked through much of this book with me from its beginning. And, as she has done so splendidly for the past seven years, she showed me how to write with readers in mind. Philippa Brewster is a primary reason why I keep trying to push out from shore these fragile crafts called books.

Naomi Schneider, editor for the University of California Press, ener-gized me with her enthusiasm. Her lively vision of what university press publishing can be ensures that an author working with her doesn't think she has to choose among scholarly care, political commitment, and a good read. William Murphy and Sarah Anderson of the Press tracked down photo credits. Production editor and copyeditor Erika Büky and Liz Gold asked just the right questions before it was too late. I am grateful, too, to the two anonymous reviewers who contributed their suggestions for revision.

Joni Seager has done a much better job of making sense of military involvement in environmental crises than I'm afraid I have done in making sense of how environmental neglect has affected women's and men's continuing relationships with militaries. We desperately need to do both.[7] Her ideas—and her talent for telling it like it is with passion and humor—have influenced these pages from start to finish.

To the students at Clark University I owe special thanks. Any writer who is lucky enough to teach knows that students make the best critics. They insist that ideas hold water, that they go someplace, that they have a bearing on real lives. Students who have worked with me in political science and women's studies courses at Clark have been generous. But they don't let me get away with much. What more could a writer want?

Chapter One

Are UN Peacekeepers Real Men?

AND OTHER POST−COLD WAR PUZZLES

It's so clear she's a mother. It's so obvious that she expects him to listen to her, as should any son. No matter that he is facing her with a rifle in hand in a phalanx of soldiers.

When I first looked at the photograph of a Russian woman facing troops, what I thought of was not what it takes to foil a military coup. I did not wonder at the crumbling of the Soviet state. No, my mind conjured up memories of my own mother scolding my best playmate, Alfie Ross, for using a double negative. Five-year-old me was thoroughly mortified.

With a second glance I tried to banish these memories of childhood embarrassment. My own mother had been trying to roll back the tides of bad grammar. This Russian woman was trying to end the Cold War. Still, each woman acted out of a sense of her maternal authority. The Russian woman seemed to be emboldened by her maternalism to chastise a young soldier to stop wielding military might against his society's fledgling democracy. For journalists, the image was irresistible: the frumpy Slavic woman facing down sleek modern weaponry, as if she were its equal. Funny—the image verged on being funny. The photograph was not intended, I suspected, to convey a serious message. It was not imagined by the photographer or the photographer's editor as help-

ing readers around the world understand precisely how the rivalry between the great powers, which had defined an entire generation, was
being unraveled, strand by strand.

But what if one took this Russian woman seriously? Perhaps one
would be able to make more sense, not only of the failure of the Soviet
coup, but also of the creation of this thing we now so glibly refer to as
the post–Cold War world.

Motherhood was an embattled strategic turf during the Cold War,
just as it had been during hotter conflicts on both sides of the Iron
Curtain. Stalinists promoted patriotic motherhood through the Communist Party's Soviet Women's Committee. None of the major players or
their allies during the four decades of Cold War rivalry could have
enlisted sufficient numbers of conscripts or voluntary soldiers without a
large measure of support from mothers. When not only Russian but also
Estonian and Lithuanian mothers began to withdraw that support, the
Red Army was in deep political trouble. This withdrawal had begun
several years before the moment immortalized by the photographer
during the August coup. As early as 1989, in fact, numbers of Soviet
women had begun to organize a campaign for a very different military
system. The woman wielding her maternal authority in front of coup-
supporting soldiers thus wasn't a lone, idiosyncratic figure. Stretched out
behind her, although not captured on celluloid, was a grass-roots movement of mothers with their own emergent analysis of Cold War militarism.[1]

In the mid-1980s, a British film team produced a documentary series,
Comrades, portraying the lives of ordinary Soviet citizens. One hour was
devoted to an elderly Russian woman who was on trial for theft, another
followed a Muslim craftsman who lovingly repaired Islamic mosaics in
Soviet Asia, and a third showed an Estonian fashion designer defying the
inefficient textile industry in an effort to turn out styles to match those
of European couturiers. But it was the episode devoted to a young
Russian conscript that today seems most revealing. For "Soldier Boy,"
the British filmmakers interviewed the mother and father of the teenage
conscript.[2] The woman whose fuzzy-cheeked son was about to leave

home for the first time was nervous. But she was also filled with a mixture of loss and pride. Her son was about to join a popularly esteemed state institution, one associated in the past with saving the country from Nazi invasion and in the present with protecting it from American threat. By joining this institution, he was graduating from boyhood to manhood. A mother who tried to hold on to her son would not only be unpatriotic, robbing the military of its needed soldiery, but would also be a bad mother, robbing a boy of his chance to achieve masculinized adulthood.

The filmmakers weren't able to follow the young man beyond basic training. But it would not be surprising if he had been sent to Afghanistan; Soviet troops were still mired in that guerrilla war when the documentary was being shot. Nor was the crew able to return to interview the mother after her son returned—if he returned. Perhaps she would have told them of her new worries, maybe now mixed with anger, prompted by stories slowly filtering back from Afghanistan. These were not stories of enemy atrocities. They were stories of cruelty within the ranks of the Red Army itself: harsh hazing rituals carried out by older soldiers against younger conscripts or by men of one ethnic group against men of another ethnic group, with officers participating or standing passively by.

Some mothers began to collect the stories, to add up the suicides, to challenge officials' sanguine explanations. In 1989, some of the women whose sons had been officially listed as missing in action began to form their own groups, independent of the official organizations designed to channel the anxieties of soldiers' mothers. The first objective of these groups was to extract more information about their sons' fates from the government. It was the unresponsiveness and even contempt with which officials greeted these requests that sparked more radical thinking and activist grass-roots organizing among increasing numbers of women. After a large demonstration outside the Soviet Chamber of Deputies in March 1989, the organizers founded the Committee of Soldiers' Mothers. A year later, it changed its name to *Materinskoe Serdise,* "Mother's Heart." Although the exact size of its membership remained unknown, the organization began to receive telephone calls and letters from parents throughout the Soviet Union anxious to know more about the where-abouts and well-being of their sons serving in the military.[3]

These women were redefining motherhood. Being a good Soviet mother and being a Soviet patriot no longer seemed mutually reinforc-ing. The mothers began to forge a radically new portrait of the state's military. No longer did it seem the patriotic defender of Soviet society, the transformer of boys into mother-free men. It seemed more of an inhumane machine devouring the sons of mothers. The Gorbachev re-gime, trying to extricate itself from Afghanistan while instituting politi-cal reforms at home, was particularly vulnerable to this emergent mater-nal dissent. It was not only the military that had to be mollified but also the maternal organizations, which were wearing a new mantle, a new legitimacy. An official investigatory commission was created. Its 1991 report confirmed the women's claim. The authors estimated that for the past fifteen years an average of eight thousand Soviet soldiers had died annually in service: 50 percent from suicide, 20 percent from beatings or other inflicted injuries, 10 percent from accidents, and only 20% in the line of duty.[4]

In the wake of the abortive August coup, women organizing out of their identities as mothers of soldiers became even more assertive. In October 1991, a group of 250 women from fifty-six towns in Russia held a hunger strike outside Moscow's White House to demand that the state-sponsored All-Union Congress of Parents of Servicemen not be privileged as the sole organization representing soldiers' families. A few days later, representatives of the mothers of soldiers movement, as it was now being labeled, surrounded the defense minister and insisted that they be allowed inside the congress. When he turned his back on them and drove off, they pushed their way into the meeting hall, only to be evicted by police.[5]

The ending of any war is a complicated process. It is not an event: the signing of a peace accord, the decommissioning of a missile. It is a long series of steps, with each step shaping the steps that follow, yet no step automatically succeeding the ones that came before it. And the war-ending process is gendered. Many of the steps require the redefining of

Fig. 1. Air raid drill, New York, 1951. (FPG International)

long-held notions of femininity and masculinity as well as the abandonment of government policies intended to sustain particular relationships
between men and women and between men or women and the state. The
Cold War has had distinct attributes, but in its dissolution it is no
different from the Crimean War or World War II.

We will be able to chart more accurately the gendered processes that
are at work in constructing the post–Cold War world if we can describe
exactly what it is that needs to be dismantled. What were the gendered
relationships on which the Cold War relied for its creation and forty-
five-year-long perpetuation?

The regimes that were essential to perpetuating the Cold War had to
convince their citizenries that the world was a dangerous place. Their
citizens had to behave as if surrounded by imminent danger. Having
internalized an acute sense of danger, citizens would be more likely to

accept the heavy taxation and the underfunding of health, housing, and education that came with high military spending. Being persuaded that danger lurked, citizens would be more willing to leave secrecy unquestioned, to leave conscription and wiretapping unchallenged. The more convincingly danger was portrayed, the more vulnerable was any campaign for social change to accusations of subversion. Calling for a reduction of a factory's toxic emissions, working to spread literacy among poor urban women, organizing the harvesters of agricultural crops—all would be more easily imagined as threats to the state and to the social order itself if the world could be thought of as fraught with diffuse danger.

But of course women and men do not experience danger in identical ways. In most of the societies that were drawn into the Cold War, men were thought to be manly insofar as they did not shy away from danger and perhaps even flirted with it as they protected the nation's children and women. Women, on the other hand, were considered those most vulnerable to danger. Only a foolish woman, a woman who ignored the dictates of femininity, behaved as though she was not endangered, as though a man's protection was irrelevant. If she went out alone at night, if she hitchhiked or traveled far from home without a masculine shield, she deserved what she got. Likewise, women could be persuaded to support their governments' efforts to organize against the Cold War threat. Any man was socialized into the gendered culture of danger in part by the women who would look to him to provide protection, to be the brave one.

This gendering of danger has been dissected, and its myths exposed, chiefly by women in India, Great Britain, Mexico, the United States, Brazil, and elsewhere who have created movements against violence toward women and against government efforts to control women's sexuality. But the lessons are pertinent to making sense of the Cold War. For example, feminist researchers have uncovered a 1958 report by a presidential commission assessing the U.S. Military Assistance Program which urged national security strategists to think about Third World women's fertility. As the Cold War rivalry spiraled, the report explained that high birth rates were due to women's uncontrolled fertility. These rates were producing population growth in countries of strategic importance to the U.S.—such as Egypt, Mexico, Brazil, and Indonesia—that would destabilize their regimes and make them dangerously susceptible to Communist subversion.[6] During the next two decades, women in many countries imagined to be strategically important in the U.S.–Soviet rivalry would find that they were sharing their beds not only with their husbands but also with U.S. national security officials.

Many Brazilian women who organized against their country's anti-Communist military government in the 1970s and 1980s came to the conclusion that militarized anti-Communism and domestic violence against women needed to be critiqued in the same breath, for the construction of the worldview that placed danger at its core relied on gendered danger as well.[7] Male bonding among policymakers privy to state secrets, recruiting military "manpower," and keeping checks on women-led social reform movements—all were part of a web woven to perpetuate the Cold War, each thread of which required women to relate to danger in a markedly different way than was required of men.

It was no coincidence, therefore, that the "feminine mystique" gained such political potency in the United States in the 1950s, at the very time when the government was taking steps to roll back the allegedly anomalous gender changes wrought by World War II. Pressing women—especially white, middle-class women—back into the domestic sphere went hand in hand with promoting consumerist capitalism; the feminine mystique became as solid a pillar of the U.S. version of Cold War culture as did its remasculinized military. Both were part of the "American way of life" that would protect U.S. citizens from the lures of Communism. Perhaps it is not surprising, then, that scores of women voluntarily offered their services to Washington's new civil defense bureaucracy.[8] Homosexuality, latchkey children, women in combat—all, U.S. Cold War cultural strategists warned, could undermine the country's capacity to meet the global threat. Smuggling FBI agents into U.S. Army women's softball teams in the 1950s in order to track down alleged lesbians, therefore, was just one small policy brick laid on the American side of the rising Cold War wall.[9]

From this vantage point, perhaps the political career of Phyllis Schlafly seems more coherent. She initially appeared on the political scene in the 1960s as a supporter of U.S. senator and presidential candidate Barry Goldwater, an outspoken advocate of a national security policy propelled by fervent anti-Communism. But by the 1980s Phyllis Schlafly was best known not for her foreign policy views but for her sharp attacks on the Equal Rights Amendment and other feminist goals. At first glance, Schlafly's public career might appear fractured; Act One appears to have had little to do with Act Two. But it may in fact have been all of a piece: it was her belief in militarization in the face of Soviet threat that convinced her that any movement trying to revise traditional relationships between women and men was a threat to U.S. national security. Thus, allowing women soldiers to volunteer for combat positions would not maximize the military's access to talent; rather, it would erode the gendered cultural shield which was America's best defense against the dual threats of Communism and the Soviet Union. Cold War militarization required that men be able to kill for their country and that women be prohibited from killing for their country. Each part of the formula sustained the other.[10]

Vaclav Havel, the eloquent Czech playwright turned president, in his essays and prison letters to his wife, Olga, spelled out how the post–1968 Czechoslovakian regime deliberately pushed its citizens toward domestic coziness and consumerism. Havel believed that his country's nervous Communist Party leadership promoted domesticity as a strategy for ensuring the political quiescence it needed from its citizens in order for the country to be a reliable junior partner in the Warsaw Pact. "People are thinking today far more of themselves, their homes and their families. It is there that they find rest, there that they can forget all the world's folly . . . they make life agreeable for themselves, building cottages, looking after their cars, taking more interest in their food and clothing. . . ."[11]

While Havel himself only hints at the different implications for women and for men of this Cold War–perpetuating strategy, in reality it was a national security formula, which translated into a change in gender roles—not for Czech women as much as for Czech men. Domestication already was the culturally approved norm for women. A double burden had been carried by women of Warsaw Pact countries ever since the 1950s, when their governments instituted the Soviet-encouraged economic policy of mobilizing women to join the labor force without altering the domestic division of labor. Even if they had paid employment, Czech women's first priority was to provide a home for their husbands and children.[12] Thus, in the name of Cold War perpetuation, it was Vaclav more than Olga who felt the government's pressure to retire from the public square, the cafe, and the parliament.

.   .   .   .   .

Vaclav and Olga Havel. Betsy and Oliver North. Ethel and Julius Rosenberg. Winnie and Nelson Mandela. Alexander Sakharov and Elena Bonner. Imelda and Ferdinand Marcos.

The Cold War was a thicket of gendered relationships that had to be either reshaped or entrenched. Often those gendered politics of national security were played out under the glow of public celebration or the harsh light of public scrutiny. Usually they occurred within ordinary households. Women tried to figure out whether being a good mother meant waving a tearful though proud goodbye to a son going off to do his military service or hiding him from the army's recruiters. Men tried to suppress fears of emasculation when denied public roles in their country's political life or else took a manly pride in being allowed into the inner sanctum of their state's national security bureaucracy. Government officials devised occasionally uneasy relationships with church officials so that they could collaborate in the entrenchment of patriarchal family values. American girls dressed their Barbies in the latest doll fashion, an Air Force dress uniform, while their Yugoslav cousins stifled yearnings for degenerate Barbies of their own.[13] The Cold War could not have lasted four decades without a myriad of such daily acts and decisions by women and men.

The Cold War, then, is best understood as involving not simply a contest between two superpowers, each trying to absorb as many countries as possible into its own orbit, but also a series of contests within each of those societies over the definitions of masculinity and femininity that would sustain or dilute that rivalry.

Investigations of women's relationships to militarism have been pouring forth during the last decade. Those concerned with women in Third World countries have shown the most explicit curiosity about the Cold War's gendered dynamics because government-articulated anti-Communism—in Guatemala, the Philippines, and Chile, for example—has so clearly shaped notions of the subversive woman. Furthermore, external tugs from both sides of the Iron Curtain have affected military counterinsurgency doctrines, development priorities, and guerrilla resources in these countries. Studies of Soviet, Eastern European, Western European, and North American women's relationships to military institutions and militaristic ideas, on the other hand, have seemed less informed by curiosity about the Cold War, which was more likely to be taken as a given. This attitude was certainly evident in my own earlier work. Thus, there remains plenty of work to be done in unraveling the relationships between the metapolitics of Communism/anti-Communism and U.S.–Soviet rivalries and the micropolitics of women's relationships to other women, to men, and to the state. But the material is there.

Masculinity, by contrast, is a territory only recently opened for exploration. We have acres of bookshelves of course, filled with studies of men in the Cold War. But that is quite a different topic. A biography of Konrad Adenauer or an institutional history of the KGB may be crammed with information about both famous and anonymous men, yet leave the reader intellectually starved for an analysis of masculinity. We may know the career tracks, partisan alliances, and policy justifications of politicians and bureaucrats who sustained great power rivalries, yet be in the dark when puzzling about how, exactly, those men's sometimes tenuous holds on their own masculine identities served to choreograph their interactions with other officials or their foreign policy inclinations.

To explore the complexities of masculinity in the history of the Cold War calls for more than curiosity about men. It requires curiosity about women as well. For masculinity is constructed out of ideas about femininity, its alleged opposite. Men in real life learn about and accept or resist their culture's ideas about what is natural in male behavior by relying on (while still controlling) women, by fantasizing about women, and by working to separate themselves from women. Where are the women? This is a question that can reveal the major players in the creation and the perpetuation of the Cold War to be more than merely idiosyncratic heroes or villains, more than just personifications of their bureaucratic posts. It is a question that reminds us that the people on the podium or around the conference table are not women. It is a question that makes us see men as people who have been socialized—not always successfully—into particular gender assumptions and who have had bestowed on them distinct privileges, authorities, and limitations.

Thus, to take an interest in masculinity is not to turn the searchlight away from women. In fact, the overlooked as well as celebrated ways in which masculinity has functioned in international politics since the 1940s are best understood if we give the women affected by the male actors' behavior a voice—and if we listen to them. Thus, explorations of women's relationships to militarization should be seen as treasure troves of information about the ways in which men's ideas about their own and other men's manliness have been created. Luise White's much-praised history of colonized Kenyan women in prostitution, for instance, can inform us about African and British men's sexual expectations during both world wars.[14] Similarly, Victoria De Grazia's study of Mussolini's policies intended to control women can provide us with fresh insights into Fascist efforts to militarize men's identities.[15]

That masculinity is socially constructed, often with the help of self-consciously honed public policy, has been hard for many people to accept. Much political energy has been invested for many years in persuading us to believe that men "naturally" feel what they feel, do what they do, and become what they become. There are serious beginnings in exploring how and why masculinity is constructed, however: some in works of social theorizing, others in historical case studies.[16] Still, there is a danger that this new attention to masculinity could reinvigorate patriarchy. Those who have been uncomfortable with the serious attention paid to women with the advent of feminist journalism and of women's studies might reach out to the burgeoning literature on masculinity the way a panicked swimmer would embrace an alligator: it's not the ideal lifesaver, but it might keep you afloat until the sea calms down.

It is a misplaced hope. For the significant work now being done on masculinity is not a repopulating of the political landscape with men in the name of postmodernism. Rather, those conducting the valuable investigations of masculinity start from the essential feminist discovery that we can make sense of men's gendered reactions only if we take women's experiences seriously. Indeed, the more we have learned about the deliberate efforts to circumscribe women's behavior, the more we have exposed the human decision making that undergirds much of masculinity. We don't yet have feminist-informed studies of such male-dominated institutions as the United Nations Security Council or the Central Intelligence Agency. But the day when we will may not be far off. Already we have a Canadian feminist's analysis of the International Labor Organization.[17] And there are North American, European, and Japanese feminist scholars energetically at work right now charting the masculinist assumptions that have guided the distinctively post–World War II profession of international relations research.[18]

.   .   .   .   .

The 1989 revolutions in Eastern Europe brought about the dismantling of the Warsaw Pact and a surge of demilitarization. But although Polish, Czech, Hungarian, East German, and Romanian women played central roles in the grass-roots organizing that made the eventual upheavals possible, this demilitarization was not guided by feminist insights into the causes of militarization.[19] In a mirror image of Western anti-Communist regimes' needing the symbol of the overworked, "unfeminine" Soviet or Polish woman to justify their Cold War policies, the Communist regimes had depended on feminism's being so tainted by its association with Western bourgeois individualism that no woman in their own nations would be inspired by feminist analyses or aspirations. Without the image of the self-absorbed, materialistic, man-hating Western feminist to combat, the restlessness of women in Eastern Europe

might have translated into gender-conscious political action much earlier. Olga Havel might have become famous in her own right rather than
as an imprisoned playwright's loyal wife. But, unlike the revolutions in
Eritrea and Nicaragua, most of those in Eastern Europe were informed
by only the faintest glimmers of organized feminist consciousness. Thus,
men were not challenged to rethink their own masculinist presumptions
about power or public life until after the Communist regimes had crumbled.

East Germany initially appeared to provide a contrast. Cities such as
Berlin, Dresden, and Weimar were the sites of feminist organizing in
1989.[20] It often appeared ahead of male-led organizing because the regime was preoccupied with monitoring the masculinized coffee houses
and universities and thus was caught unprepared for the political activism that flowed out of the theaters and the churches, sites of women's
organizing. During those turbulent autumn months, women's groups
presented detailed platforms, built diverse umbrella organizations, and
mobilized thousands of women in public rallies. For a while they
couldn't be ignored by the male contestants for power. They wedged
their way into the bargaining rooms and into the transitional regime. But
even these consciously feminist women of East Germany couldn't direct
the course of the next stage, the government-to-government bargaining
sessions that ultimately produced German reunification. Whereas the
bringing down of the old regime had been a process shaped by struggles
between politicized women and men in East Germany, German reunification was a virtually all-male political process. Soon after, many East
German women joined many East German men in voting for Helmut
Kohl's Christian Democratic Party, with its promises of material well-
being and free markets. Those few feminists who warned that reunification without feminist guarantees could be a disaster for women were
seen as out of step. Even they might have found it hard to believe that,
within two years after reunification, 12 percent of single mothers in
eastern Germany would be among the ranks of the unemployed.[21]

Democratization and demilitarization have commonly been presumed
to serve women's interests. Demilitarization loosens the bond between

men and the state; thus, it should make the state more transparent and porous. Democratization simultaneously opens up the public spaces; thus, it should permit more voices to be heard and policy agendas to be reimagined. But such changes will take place only if the two processes are not designed in such a way as to reprivilege masculinity.

The democratic elections of 1990 in Eastern Europe revealed the tenacity of patriarchy. The results of these elections made invisible women's contributions to creating the conditions that made these elections possible:

- The percentage of women in Czechoslovakia's parliament dropped from 29.3 to 8.6.
- The percentage of women in Poland's parliament dropped from 20.2 to 13.5.
- The percentage of women in Hungary's parliament plummeted from 26.6 to 7.2.
- In the pre-reunification election of March 1990, the percentage of women in East Germany's parliament slipped from 33.6 to 20.5; parliamentary elections in December for a unified German legislature managed to return the same proportion of women, 20.5 percent.
- The percentage of women in Romania's parliament fell from 34.4 to 5.5.[22]

It is not that those Cold War legislatures in which Eastern European women had held a quarter or a third of the seats had wielded effective influence. They hadn't. But that may be the point. Demilitarization and democratization together infused these once drab and impotent bodies with new vitality and new power. Legislatures became places where one could give meaningful voice to public concerns. Even in Poland, where a conservative woman has been made prime minister, the legislative agenda—which assigns priority to restricting Polish women's freedom of reproductive choice—is being hammered out with little organized influence by Polish women.[23] If a man had never felt comfortable spending his waking hours fixing his car or building a garden shed, now he had

an alternative outlet for his energies. It was precisely because the legislatures were transformed by the end of the Cold War that they became, in
many men's eyes, worthy loci for reemergent civic activism. Legislatures
became thereby places too important to allow more than a handful of
women. Does the democratization of parliaments equal the defeminiza-
tion of parliaments?

While Eastern European nations' legislatures have been masculinized,
their popular cultures have been sexualized. As women have filed out of
the parliaments, they have walked into proliferating beauty contests,
franchised brothels, free-enterprise escort services, and joint-venture
overseas marriage services.[24] Nor have they done so necessarily against
their wills. Russian and Eastern European feminist social commentators
who have observed the postrevolutionary traumas of the last several
years explain that consumerism is being woven into the democratized
fabric of civic life in ways that co-opt many women in their own objec-
tification.

"Now there are calendars full of nude women everywhere in the
ministry." A Czech feminist who worked in her country's environmental
affairs ministry is describing the new bureaucratic culture of post-1989
Prague. Such sexist expressions were defined as pornography and prohibited under the old regime. But with the emergence of capitalism and
liberalism in the 1990s, nude women's photos on office walls have
become so commonplace that most women office workers feel they have
no space to object. "And imagine what it's like coming into a colleague's
office to discuss a policy. You sit down and have to put your cup of coffee
on a glass-topped coffee table which is displaying assorted cut-out photographs of nude women."[25] Some women even seem to be taking pleasure
in the widespread availability of pornography. The shriveled consumer
markets of the Cold War—the price paid for Cold War expenditures on
bloated armies and protected weapons factories—nurtured aspirations
among the double-burdened women that can only now be pursued: for
beauty, for pleasure, for financial security, for the marriageable man
with a good income and a two-car garage.

Filipina feminists allied with women working as prostitutes servicing

American sailors around Subic Bay naval base learned what Eastern European feminists trying to create a nascent women's movement today are learning (and what impatient American feminists still may have to learn): any woman hoping to sow the seeds of political consciousness must take other women's desires and even fantasies seriously. Those fantasies could throw light on how political priorities constructed in one era shape women's attitudes toward themselves and the men in their lives in the following era. Writing off as merely a victim of false consciousness a Russian woman who sends her name to a new marriage service for American men risks missing a chance to gain a new understanding of how the post–Cold War world is being constructed.

. . . . .

Like militarization, demilitarization is sexualized. Men returning from wars have sexual expectations. Fathering is one form of demilitarized citizenship. A year after victory but still in desert fatigues, proud men hold up their newborn babies. No women are inside the photographer's frame. But they are more than bit players in any country's demilitarization.

Other men return from war zones anxious about jobs, not just for their own well-being but with a sense of the male breadwinner's familial responsibilities. With the many-stranded winding-down of the Cold War, wars have been ending—often raggedly—in Angola, Nicaragua, El Salvador, Namibia, Cambodia, Afghanistan, Ethiopia, and Lebanon. Each of these wars was fueled by its own particular internal sparks—its class disparities, factional rivalries, and ethnicized oppressions. But each was prolonged and made more ferocious by American and Soviet infusions of direct and indirect aid and encouragement, sometimes to the regime and sometimes to the insurgents.

To end each of these Cold War–proxy wars, thousands of men must be persuaded to change their ideas of what is right and natural—and even pleasurable—to do as men. Militarized forms of manliness may be all that some of the younger Cambodian, Lebanese, or Ethiopian men have known. The precise recipes for militarized masculinity will differ, however. Each man's willingness to hand in his grenade launcher or his combat boots and to imagine a demilitarized role for himself in his society will depend on his own experiences as a vigilante, a death squad assassin, an army conscript, a unit commander, or a nighttime civil guard. Perhaps he has been humiliated by other men and thus sees demilitarization as a chance to regain his manly dignity. Or perhaps he has felt more important in his military role than he ever did as a shopkeeper or civil servant. He may have been embarrassed in front of his buddies when he vomited every time he saw a person being wounded. Or he may have felt energized by his new license to wield violent force. Perhaps he found emotional satisfaction in a rarely felt intensity of friendship among men. Or perhaps he felt lonely, deprived of the support and comfort formerly supplied by his wife or mother.

Just how a man (or adolescent boy) has experienced militarization and how willingly he sheds the habits and expectations of militarization will redound on the women he returns to. His new definition of his masculinity—or his refusal to redefine his identity—will be played out in his family life, in his interactions with women workmates, and in his exchanges with women who are perfect strangers.

Each of these women, in turn, will be counted on, as she always has been, to coax, absorb, sacrifice, and tutor. Some women, however, may not want to give up their jobs, may not want to have another child, may have grown used to having sex only on occasional leaves, or may not think donning a veil is a proper price for peace (in the home or in the government). These women may rebel against the sorts of expectations leaders will try to impose on them in the name of post–Cold War "political stabilization."

It can take years to demilitarize a society. Masculinity and femininity will be among the political territories where the struggles for demilitarization will have to be played out. Vietnamese women and men are still in the process of demilitarization, long after most Americans and Europeans have turned their attention elsewhere. During 1990–92 alone, 500,000 Vietnamese soldiers—overwhelmingly male—were demobilized.[26] Some had fought in the earlier war against the United States and its Saigon ally. Many were young boys then but were conscripted to fight the succeeding war in neighboring Cambodia. The conclusion of that conflict, due in large measure to the new cooperation between Washington and Moscow, has reunited husbands and wives after long separations. It has also thrown thousands of men onto the already strained Vietnamese labor market, causing the regime to feel nervous over the lack of jobs for men who believe they have made patriotic sacrifices. These scores of male veterans are searching for jobs at a time when Hanoi is cutting support to unprofitable state companies. Women's own waged work, as well as the continuing high birth rate, have thus become issues not simply of economic planning but also of demilitarization.

It is no coincidence that prostitution has spread. Local Women's Federation activists are expressing alarm. Vietnamese journalists estimate that there are now one hundred thousand women working as prostitutes in Ho Chi Minh City and another thirty thousand in Hanoi.[27] We often think that increasing numbers of women are pressed into prostitution because of militarization. But there are forms of demilitarization—such as in Russia or Vietnam—that can bring rising prostitution, as men look for new enterprises and as women are displaced from other forms of livelihood. In September 1991, the Hanoi newspaper *Lao Dong* reported that "hundreds of girls have been sold to brothels in Phnom Penh and southern China."[28] An American reporter assigned to Phnom Penh in early 1992 went to the disco at Le Royal Hotel, only to see "swarms of Vietnamese prostitutes descend on unaccompanied men." He offhandedly speculated that, "with lighter skins and more experience than Cambodian women, they dominate the market, and apparently find Phnom Penh more profitable than Saigon."[29]

These articles did not explore what these Vietnamese women had done before working as prostitutes, who had transported them to Cambodia or southern China, or who owned the brothels in which some of them worked. Prostitutes were mentioned either as features on the landscape or as indicators of economic stress. Women working as prostitutes may have much more to tell. They may help us to describe more accurately the ways in which women's and men's sexual relationships are being re-formed by Washington's and Moscow's rapprochement.

.   .   .   .   .

The post–Cold War era is a period in which many new militaries are being created: at least a dozen are being crafted in Africa alone. Eritreans and Namibians are creating new state forces. Planks of peace agreements and democracy pledges in Angola, Mozambique, South Africa, Togo, Rwanda, and Mali all include promises to reorganize the state's military, to demobilize some soldiers, and to retrain and resocialize others. Former Cold War sponsors are joining with lending agencies such as the World Bank to press for cuts in weapons purchases and defense expenditures which only a few years ago were justified in the name of development and security. Africa specialists in the U.S. State Department have called together academic researchers to share ideas about how best to steer nervous or reluctant African governments toward demobilization.[30] Suddenly the attitudes and behaviors of young African men about to lose their prestige or even their livelihoods have had to be imagined as serious foreign policy concerns. Would their mothers, wives, and sisters also be imagined in the discussions of African demilitarization? The impact of military downsizing on African women's marriages, their safety, their sexuality, and their farming need to be on State Department and World Bank agendas.

The breakups of the Soviet Union and Yugoslavia are spawning new, autonomous state forces. Lithuania, Latvia, and Estonia have begun creating their new militaries even while units of the old Soviet military still are barracked on their soil. While most of the Asian republics of the former USSR thus far are finding military association with the Russian-dominated Commonwealth of Independent States to be politically wise, the Armenians, Georgians, and Ukrainians have begun to fashion their own military institutions.

Meanwhile, the disintegration of Yugoslavia has produced new Slovenian, Croatian, and Bosnian state forces. And peace accords are requiring radical reformations of existing state defense institutions in El Salvador, South Africa, Cambodia, and Lebanon.

Every one of these new militaries will prompt government officials to make decisions about whether to recruit women, whether to inaugurate compulsory military service, how to instill discipline and enthusiasm in young men, and whether to acknowledge homosexuality in the ranks. These decisions are only the beginning. Governments creating new militaries will also make deliberate decisions about whether to manipulate masculinized ethnic stereotypes to enhance officers' authority, how to control soldiers' wives, whether to condone military prostitution—with what safeguards for male soldiers—and whether to turn a blind eye to wife battering within soldiers' homes.

As they reach these decisions, to which existing militaries will they look to provide models? Canada? Finland? The United States? India? It is important to record which groups are invited to sit around the policy-making table when these crucial decisions are made. Whose credentials will be deemed relevant—those of prostitutes? Of school teachers? Of mothers?

The large industrial states are reacting to the end of the rivalry between the great powers by forecasting substantial personnel reductions—"downsizing" is the American bureaucratic term. But cutting back on the number of soldiers a military needs is never a simple numerical operation. Will African-American women, who currently comprise 45 percent of all the women in the U.S. Army's rank and file, make up such a large percentage after the cuts? In the wake of the Los Angeles riots, will there be more pressures on the Pentagon to continue to serve as a major socializer of African-American men, even if this means organizing troop reductions so that more white soldiers are given early demobilization?[31]

If German leaders respond to calls to end male conscription and introduce an all-volunteer force, will women be allowed to enlist in greater numbers than they are now? What about Turkish-German men? And what will happen to the peculiar relationship of Scottish men to the British army if historic Scottish regiments are merged into less regionally

distinct units? If the Gurkha Brigade falls under the same British budget-
ary ax, will Nepali notions of masculinity undergo a profound transformation? A substantially reduced military is rarely just a smaller military.
Cuts in any military's personnel usually alter significantly its relationships to the women and men in the country's various social classes and
ethnic communities.

Not all of the militaries being created, redesigned, or proposed are
being tied to orthodox, sovereign nation-states. French and German
officials have proposed the formation of a new European defense force
under the aegis of the previously dormant WEU, the Western European
Union. Such a force has the attraction to some of being separate from
NATO and at arm's length from U.S. influence.

Simultaneously, the United Nations peacekeeping forces, drawn from
the militaries of its member states, are being looked upon by the governments of many industrialized and Third World countries as offering the
best hope for a genuinely post–Cold War, nonimperialist military. Others worry that so much preoccupation with the UN's new military
responsibilities will draw money and value away from the organization's
less glamorous, somewhat less masculinized development efforts. Like
any other institution, the United Nations is susceptible to masculinization and militarization.

Thus we are entering a period of global history when perhaps more
new militaries are being designed and launched than at any time since the
multiplication of new states during the decolonialization of the 1950s.
However, the point is not that militaries have been fixed institutions
during the Cold War and are only now being projected into uncertain
orbit. A military isn't like a Georgia O'Keeffe painting or an I. M. Pei
building—when it's done it's done. A military is forever in a state of
becoming—like a compost heap. The questions we must pose today to
understand just what is happening in the Ukraine or South Africa are
questions we should have been asking of any military in 1951 and 1985.
They are questions that come out of an awareness that any government
trying to use its military to sustain its domestic authority and its influence
with other states will attempt to use ideas about femininity and mascu-

linity as well as ideas about race and class to get the armed force it feels it can trust.

At this moment, then, someone in the corridors of Estonia's fledgling defense ministry is mulling over whether gay men and lesbians should be allowed into the country's new military. That decision is not a foregone conclusion. It never has been a foregone conclusion—not in any country's military since homosexuality became an object of explicit state manipulation in the twentieth century. So there will be memos, discussions, advice from psychologists, off-the-record anecdotes, and sly asides. Faxes will likely be sent to Brussels to ask NATO about the policies of its fifteen allies on homosexual soldiering. Back will come faxes saying that the Dutch and Canadians no longer see heterosexuality as a requisite for effective soldiering, while the Americans and British do, though with far less confidence than they did even five years ago. Of principal concern for designers of the Estonian military will no doubt be the question of whether permitting gay men and lesbians to soldier will enhance or jeopardize the new military in the eyes of the country's citizenry. Another matter for official debate will be whether a homosexual man lacks the sort of manly qualities presumed to be needed to wield a gun, follow orders, risk physical danger, and support fellow soldiers under stress. Lesbians will be considered quite differently. If the Estonian bureaucratic discussions sound at all like those in the United States, Canada, and elsewhere, then Baltic concern over lesbians will be voiced in terms of their being "too" compatible, not incompatible, with soldiering.

In the London headquarters of the once-somnolent WEU, another official is having to figure out how to respond to the official referred to as Mrs. Baarveld-Schlaman. She is formally titled the vice-chairman of the WEU's Defense Committee, so she cannot be dismissed cavalierly. Mrs. Baarveld-Schlaman has submitted a formal report that surveyed the status of women in the union's member forces and found it wanting. She and her committee have looked forward to the mid-1990s, when in all probability a number of WEU forces that now rely on male conscription—such as France, Germany, and Italy—will have forsaken that personnel formula and moved toward volunteerism. At that point, she predicts, there will be more appreciation for the skills, educational attainments, and commitment that women can bring to soldiering. She and her colleagues urge the entire WEU not to drag its feet until that day arrives, but instead to take the initiative now to lower the barriers which are keeping the proportion of women in the military well below 10 percent throughout Western Europe. If the WEU is to play a more active role in post–Cold War security arrangements, it cannot afford to deprive itself of such potentially valuable "manpower." Nor can it afford to be so far out of step with changes in all other sectors of European socioeconomic life.[32]

Portugal, with one of the most patriarchal of Western European militaries, is moving in the direction the report recommends. In 1992, the Portugese defense ministry cautiously opened the officer corps to women. Joana Costa Reis, a twenty-five-year-old student of modern languages, was one of the first applicants for the fifteen slots. She thought officer training would allow her to pursue her interests in camping, survival skills, and guns. She was joined by twenty-three-year-old Rosa Maria Santos, who quit her job in order to pursue a career in the army.[33] At about the same time, Japan's Self-Defense Agency admitted thirty-nine women cadets into the National Defense Academy. Upon graduation, they will become the first women officers in Japan's military.[34]

The creation and reorganization of so many military institutions are occurring at a time when gay men and lesbians are more vocal and better organized politically in a wider array of countries than ever before. Militaries have never conducted their discussions about the sorts of sexuality they deemed best suited for soldiering under such a public gaze. Not that there is agreement among gay and lesbian activists in any country over whether military service offers a chance for homosexuals to gain first-class citizenship. What is true, however, is that discussions of such topics among gay men and lesbians have served to underscore for everyone the state-sanctioned artificiality of the heterosexualized soldier.[35]

Similarly, the question of how and when to use women to compensate for shortages of the kinds of men the government trusts with its weaponry can no longer be addressed within the safe confines of ministerial offices. Women officers in NATO have their own organizations. Civilian feminists, women legislators, and civil rights lawyers in the United States, Canada, and Scandinavia monitor closely their governments' responses to sexual harassment and discrimination in promotions as well as any refinements in the definition of combat. As among gay men and lesbians, however, there is no consensus among feminists about how women should regard military service. Some feminists in each of these countries see the state's military as a potential site for economic advancement and for political legitimation and never use the concept of militarism to gauge that military's impact on the social order. Other feminists start with questions about militarism. They begin their assessment of their country's military with a wary belief that a military is essentially a patriarchal institution, even if it occasionally sees fit to enlist women into its fold.[36] As each new country joins the ranks of nonconscription militaries and as governments are tempted to reach out to at least a small sector of women, these debates will grow more common. They are already going on in Italy.[37]

The form of military force that is inspiring perhaps the greatest hope is the United Nations peacekeeping force. It inspires optimism because it seems to perform military duties without being militaristic. And its troops at first glance appear to escape the distorting dynamics of militarism because they may not depend so heavily on patriarchal masculinity. According to one UN official, who observed UN peacekeeping soldiers in Namibia in the 1980s, local women seemed to view men soldiering under the UN's banner as less alienating, more approachable, and perhaps more trustworthy than men soldiering for any of the several rival governments. This official reported that she witnessed a higher proportion of marriages between UN soldiers and local women than she believed had occurred between, for instance, American soldiers and local women in Korea.[38]

To date we in fact know amazingly little about what happens to a male soldier's sense of masculine license when he dons the blue helmet or armband of the United Nations peacekeeper. The contents of formal agreements, or "codes of conduct," between the United Nations Secretary and specific host officials are kept secret. This makes it difficult, for instance, for women in a host country to find out what suppositions about male peacekeeping soldiers' sexuality are written into the code's provisions for health and policing. The crucial question may be whether soldiering for a state calls forth different notions of masculinity than soldiering for a nonstate international agency does. What exactly happens to a Canadian or Fijian male soldier's presumptions about violence, about femininity, about enemies, or about his own sexuality when he is placed in the position of maintaining peace between two warring armies? If a man can discard inclinations and presumptions with just the switch from one set of stenciled initials to another, it may mean that militarized masculinity is only shirtsleeve-deep.[39]

Any United Nations peacekeeping unit—whether in Bosnia, Cambodia, or Somalia—is in practice a compilation of soldiers enlisted in and trained by particular states. There is no direct UN recruitment. There is no UN basic training. From the UN-sanctioned action in Korea in the 1950s through the UN-sanctioned action in the Persian Gulf in 1991, U.S. presidents refused to allow U.S. soldiers to be commanded by anyone but a U.S. officer. Only in early 1993 did President Bill Clinton permit a small group of noncombat soldiers left behind as peacekeepers in Somalia to be commanded by a non-American, a Turkish general operating under UN authority. On the other hand, there are certain governments which have quite consciously viewed UN peacekeeping as a priority mission for their soldiers, and this purpose has undoubtedly filtered down through the ranks in as yet unanalyzed ways. Ireland, Fiji, India, Ghana, Finland, and Malaysia are among the countries whose governments have routinely contributed troops to UN missions. Canada's former prime minister, Brian Mulroney, announced in early 1992 that with the end of the Cold War his country's military would see UN service as its most important function after self-defense. From the south came rumblings of displeasure. Washington officials saw the Mulroney declaration as a diversion of Canadian military resources from NATO.[40] They were right.

Finland's new women volunteer soldiers serve in the Finnish contingent on loan to the UN, and Australia's military has just deployed its first women soldiers to Cambodia on UN duty. Nonetheless, United Nations peacekeeping forces remain as overwhelmingly male as most state militaries. With such a composition, it must have the same sort of policies around masculinity as other, more conventional forces do. We have yet to hear how United Nations force commanders imagine male sexuality. Are the blue-helmeted men on duty in Cambodia explicitly ordered not to patronize prostitutes? What steps are taken to prevent AIDS and other forms of sexually transmitted diseases among UN peacekeepers? Each of these policies will be informed by ideas about women, about the roles women must play if a male soldier is to be able to do his job.

United Nations male peacekeepers are as likely to have mothers, girlfriends, and wives as the male soldiers of any other military. Just as in those more orthodox forces, the contributions of these women are accepted as natural, even if policies are devised to ensure that they fill these roles. Nowhere was this clearer than in the *New York Times* discussion of the proposal that Britain's famed Gurkhas, the celebrated troops recruited from Nepal, should serve as the core of a genuinely nonstate United Nations peacekeeping force.[41] The advantage of this proposal was not only that the Gurkhas, being citizens of an impoverished Asian country, would cost less than Canadian or Finnish soldiers. Nor was it only that Gurkhas had established a record of battlefield competence and discipline. It was also an unstated plus that the Nepali men serving in the Gurkhas apparently didn't need the company of their wives while stationed abroad and didn't compensate for their wives' absence by engaging in alienating abuse of other countries' women. These Nepali men seemed to have learned a kind of militarized masculinity quite unlike that of their British, American, or French counterparts. While such different constructions may indeed exist and while they may make one set of men better at post–Cold War international peacekeeping than another, such a proposal leaves out the women. Gurkhas have earned this reputation for celibate soldiering because of what their wives absorb, are compelled to absorb, because they live under British military policies for wives. Nepali women at home in Darjeeling, India, or in

Fig. 2. The relationships of a woman in a war-torn country to UN peacekeeping soldiers and to local men are not simple. Here a Somali woman is standing between her husband and a U.S. marine on a UN peacekeeping mission, February 1993. (AP/Wide World Photos)

villages in the hills of Nepal construct their lives in ways that have made life easier for British defense planners. They have made it possible for the British to use their husbands in ways that have given the Gurkhas the image of the ideal post–Cold War peacekeepers.[42]

What is distinctive here is not the particular marriage practices of Nepali women. Rather, by making Nepali women visible we are reminded that one cannot assess which forms of masculinity are most suitable for the post–Cold War world unless one asks, Where are the women? The end of the superpower rivalry that has shaped the distribution of aid, the construction of fears, and the ferocity of hostilities has not made masculinity irrelevant in international relations. To make sense of how masculinity is being demilitarized and remilitarized today, one must pay attention to women and to ideas about femininity. The Australian woman soldier donning the UN's blue helmet to serve in Cambodia, the Vietnamese woman trying to find a client in Le Royal Hotel's disco, the international civil servant devising policies to bolster the morale of UN troops, the recently demobilized Khmer Rouge guerrilla—all are partners in a post–Cold War dance.

Chapter Two

Turning Artillery into Ambulances

SOME FEMINIST CAVEATS

What does it mean for women to "theorize" when the subject is state-sanctioned violence? Is it easier to get to the root of things when one is under extraordinary pressure or when one has the space to think? Most women lack the requisite resources—"a room of one's own"—to produce poetry, novels, and theory. But women need something more fundamental than privacy, a personal computer, and business connections to write down their ideas and get them published. They need physical security. The feminist theorizing that one might read over coffee or discuss with friends exists because some women in some countries have had the physical security necessary for devoting their energies to a project beyond day-to-day survival. Other women can't engage in sustained thinking and writing about war and militarism because they lack a sense of elementary safety. Not many books of feminist theory are coming out of Somalian refugee camps or Sarajevo cellars these days. Ironically, the more a government is preoccupied with what it calls national security, the less likely its women are to have the physical safety necessary for sharing their theorizing about the nation and their security within it.

Thus one has to start trying to make sense of militarization with the realization that those women in the world with the most urgent need to discover the underlying causes for war, militarism, and peace are precisely those with the least opportunity to write down their thoughts and to have their words published and circulated among other women, at home or abroad. Societies in the grip of foreign or civil war and those dominated by militarized regimes have not been hospitable to women's need to print their ideas. On the contrary, women who question their own subordination are often perceived as threats to national security. Millions of women—in 1940s France, in 1980s Cambodia, and in 1990s Bosnia, Angola, and Peru—have thought hard about why it is men who soldier, why rape is deemed so natural a complement to war, and why the very concept of a peaceful society is derogated as "feminine." That is, millions of women whose ideas have never sat invitingly on a bookshelf have engaged in feminist theorizing about militarization.

They don't all agree. Two feminists can employ feminist curiosity and feminist tools of investigation and yet come to quite different convictions. A lot of the disagreement—important disagreement—is going on outside academia, far from publishing houses or even Xerox machines. What appears here and elsewhere in print, therefore, is only the tip of the proverbial iceberg.

■   ■   ■   ■   ■

Militarization poses a special problem for any critic wanting to be taken seriously because it has wide-ranging effects on so many different groups that it evokes a plethora of explanations. No single explanation of why militarization occurs, why it persists, seems adequate. Furthermore, a woman who presumes to theorize about militarism is too frequently dismissed, as if she had wandered uninvited into the men's locker room. Should she go further and insist on using feminist concepts to make sense of military budgets, doctrines, and hardware, she is likely to be greeted by raised eyebrows and barely suppressed smirks, even from the politest of men. Rajini Balachadran, who teaches a national security course in New York, tells of the raw incredulity that greeted her when she walked into her university classroom on the first day of the term. Would an Asian woman, a woman in a sari, have something to teach a dozen American young men about national security doctrines? She smiles now, not without some lingering pain, as she recalls how she spent that first week pouring out esoteric doctrinal terms and weaponry jargon, figuratively bombing her incredulous male students into submission. Only then could she get their attention when she introduced critical assessments of established security concepts.[1]

The currently fashionable, competing theories of militarization throw up other obstacles, especially for anyone trying to engage in feminist analysis. There are two principal nonfeminist theories intended to explain why the military's influence and militaristic values often come to sprawl so insidiously over a social landscape. Both are persuasive. The first is that militarization is a logical consequence of capitalism. The second is that militarization derives from the inherent inclinations of any state, no matter what its economic system. Neither theory's proponents are very curious about masculinity or femininity. Neither theory requires one to investigate whether it is significant that most defense policymakers are men. Neither prompts one to ask, Where are the women?

Men and women who see capitalism as the moving force behind the military's expanding influence believe that government officials enhance the status, resources, and authority of the military in order to protect the interests of private enterprises at home and overseas.[2] Capitalists and their public representatives—including those "state capitalists" who claim to be socialists—conflate the interests of business with the interests of the nation. Thus, these theorists believe it is in the boardroom rather than the war room where we should look for the origins of wars, both hot and cold. Capitalism's critics have concluded that major business firms with overseas investments are at the root of military interventionism. The composition of the military itself is of only passing interest to these critics. Their principal concern is the political economy of arms manufacture; according to them, profits drive military doctrine, not vice versa.

If these theorists are right, then the end of communist forms of state capitalism in the former Soviet Union and Eastern Europe will not bring peace. Some observers take hope from reports that the global arms trade is on a downward path: its total value in 1991 was $22 billion worldwide, and although that figure translates into an astounding amount of killing capacity, it is actually 25 percent less than the total value of the world arms trade in 1990.[3] The greatest single factor responsible for this drop, however, was not any cutback in Western arms sales; rather, it was the dissolution of the Soviet Union. By 1992, the largest arms exporters had become, in order, the United States, the former Soviet Union, Germany, China, and Britain. If the European Community (EC) is seen as a single trading partner—which is sometimes realistic, sometimes not—then it accounted for 18 percent of the world arms exports in 1992.

And, while much of the media coverage has been aimed at arms sales to the Middle East after the Gulf War, in fact the leader in the arms trade, the United States, looked to Europe and Asia for its largest weapons customers.[4] For instance, Washington, still insisting that the Japanese compensate for their unwillingness to send troops to the Persian Gulf in 1991, persuaded Tokyo defense officials to buy expensive new AWACS radar surveillance planes from American defense manufacturers rather than build the equivalents at home. This arrangement provoked unhappiness among Japanese defense contractors but assuaged the guilt of some of their senior political elites at the same time as it cushioned the post–Cold War fall of American defense-dependent companies.[5] These kinds of complex relationships—relationships that are hard to reduce to pure economics—drive the continuation of international arms sales.

In the short term, market imperatives may indeed compel the new political leaderships to dismantle their armament factories, to send home thousands of conscripts, and to slash their inflated defense budgets. But, according to the forecasts of this first group of theorists, the current promotion of capitalist economies in Russia, Poland, and Kazakhstan and the quasi-capitalist economy in China are sowing the seeds of future remilitarization—both in these countries and among their new trading competitors. Despite a few pilot conversion projects in the local arms-producing regions of Russia and the newly independent Slovakia, this prediction already seems to be coming true.[6] A dismayed Russian arms conversion specialist described the mood: "Everybody is now eager to sell arms: foundations, cooperatives, enterprises, whole regions. . . .

Everybody is requesting permission to sell arms to remedy their position, and they are ready to sell arms at the lowest prices imaginable."[7] A capitalist economy creates a political life that feeds on militarism.

Oddly enough, it may be the institutions usually thought of as the international promoters of capitalist development, the World Bank and the International Monetary Fund, that will be the principal dampeners on the world arms trade. They are already using their lending authorities to restrain Third World clients from using scarce resources for the purchase of weaponry. The term now used for this arms-restraining policy is *conditionality*. Essentially, officials of the powerful international lending institutions belatedly have concluded that arms purchases from abroad are not good for Third World development and that they can restrict such expenditures by tying strings to their loans. But not all aid officials in all lending agencies are lining up behind conditionality. Nicole Ball, an astute observer of development aid politics, warns: ". . . Some officials may welcome reduced military expenditure by aid recipients . . . Others—especially those involved with foreign affairs and defense issues as well as with day-to-day relations with borrower governments—may want to avoid jeopardizing their favorable relationship with the borrowers by raising the sensitive issue of military reform."[8]

A corollary to this explanation of militarization is that increasing numbers of workers in all the affected countries have become dependent on military spending for their own livelihoods. While workers and owners may have conflicting needs, any military-industrial complex, either in its pure capitalist form or cloaked as state capitalist socialism, weaves a complex web of interdependency among four groups: home government officials, defense manufacturing executives, unionized labor, and foreign government authorities. Some commentators would add scientists to these groups; others would subsume scientists under labor. Still other observers would add to the web local civic boosters: those mayors and their small business allies who see weapons factories as good for their communities.[9]

The capitalism-as-cause theorists generally take for granted that it is men who are the corporate executives, government officials, and workers most involved in militarization. That is, they do not believe that it is useful to investigate or try to explain this male predominance. The chief executive officer (CEO) of General Dynamics is a man; so is the defense minister of Sweden. Yet, for the purposes of dissecting the military-industrial complex's societal consequences, both become simply capitalists or the representatives of capitalism. Similarly, the people who have built up South Africa's formidable state weaponry establishment (Armscor) and the people who put on elaborate arms fairs to sell French and British weapons are seen, not as men, but as advertisers or bureaucrats or corporate functionaries. Yet theorists Peter Hall and Ann Markusen, in describing the scientist-entrepreneurs who founded the companies which eventually became the most prominent U.S. defense contractors, do entice readers with this parenthetical note: "A particular group of (typically male) actors constitute the 'founding fathers.' "[10] Typically male? No more is said. Readers are left to wonder about the maleness of any of the actors who have created what the authors call America's "gunbelt."

Women's existence in military-industrial complexes, then, is almost invisible in this influential body of theory. Here are a few glimpses. We know that in any country's defense industry women do most of the clerical work and most of the electrical wiring that needs to be done to turn out modern weaponry. We know that a growing proportion of the South Africans employed in the country's weapons companies are women.[11] We know that white men comprise 50.9 percent of Silicon Valley's professional employees, while women of color comprise only 8.8 percent; on the other hand, white men comprise a mere 9.7 percent, and women of color 45 percent, of the assembly-line work force.[12] We know that 32 percent of all the defense workers in Los Angeles are women, and a significant proportion of them are women of color.[13] These are but a few pieces in a patchwork quilt of knowledge. We need to travel much deeper into the actual processes, the day-to-day routines of the defense industry, if we are to find out what needs to be done to convert even a single weapons factory into a producer of goods more relevant to the post–Cold War world.

In an unusual testimony, Jean Alonso, a Raytheon employee working on the company's famed Patriot missile, described the reality of gender on the factory floor of the American military industry. As a single mother in her early forties, she remembers, she was pleased to have finally landed a "real" job.[14] When the diplomatic process in the Persian Gulf was being aborted and a military confrontation seemed inevitable to Alonso and her workmates in Andover, Massachusetts, she noticed a gender gap developing: "A kind of pre-game excitement seemed to be stirring among some of the men. The only organized attempt at opposition to the war came from our informal women's group." This was a group that had initially come together to press the male leadership of the electrical workers' union to take sexual harassment seriously. The union local's membership was 47 percent women, but women's concerns were pushed far down the agenda. Sexual harassment had been as integral to missile-making as was the collusion between the Pentagon and defense companies. Yet women had found it hard to get the issue of harassment on the bargaining table, and because the New England recession was jeopardizing jobs, no one wanted to rock the corporate boat. At this juncture in the evolving political tension between men and women at Raytheon, the Gulf War broke out, and the gender gap seemed to close again. The weapons that the workers were producing made the headlines. Women as well as men around Jean Alonso became excited, forgot talk of a women's committee in the union local, and took pride instead with being "on the map" as they began to imagine that their employment future was a little more secure. Within six months, however, Raytheon began laying off workers at its missile plant. The prewar sense of insecurity and passivity seeped back into the spirits of wirers and welders. It was as hard as ever to get the nervous male union leaders to pay attention to sexual harassment.

Still, the capitalist-centered explanation is compelling. When a self-conscious feminist opened her morning paper in 1985 and read that the average operating cost for a single American aircraft carrier (e.g., food for the crew, spare parts for the ship's eight hundred daily repairs, and the fuel to keep it in motion) was $490,410 per day, not including wages, she might have been excused if her usually gender-sensitive thoughts did not turn immediately to concepts of masculinity or of cultures of misogyny. It was only natural if she wondered, Who can be profiting from such incredible expenditures? Theories about how capitalism and state capitalism foster the economic interdependencies we now call military-industrial complexes have the ring of plausibility. They make a lot of sense even though they render women—and men, as men—virtually invisible.

A second set of explanations for militarization has grown out of the conviction that once political power is organized into the formal, centralized structure of a state, those who control that state tend to expand the use of state-sanctioned force to ensure compliance within the society and to protect it from outside assaults, real or imagined. States by their very nature, these theorists argue, are inclined to coercion. When public power is hierarchically structured and is invested with vast material resources and symbolic centrality in the lives of citizens, militarization appears all but inevitable.

Headline writers urge us to look at politicians as the chief architects of Cold War and post–Cold War militarization. Russia's Boris Yeltsin, Serbia's Slobodan Milosevic, Saudi Arabia's King Fahd—these men, the nervous guardians of their own power, will determine whether weapons industries wither or thrive. Next to such men, ordinary civil servants appear gray and uninteresting. But they are far from bloodless. Bureaucrats have their own worries, their own satisfactions, and their own loyalties to their agencies' own parochial interests.

Shared water coolers, office gossip, teamwork, and even long, tedious meetings can create a small but intense world, a sense of prized community, for the people working inside any large government establishment. An innovative weapon or even a new all-weather boot not only serves the government's overall security doctrine but also may represent a bureau's own mission, its esprit de corps. This less tangible factor helps to explain why military budgets grow even in peacetime and are so hard to cut when enemies disappear.[15]

The relative lack of accountability of civil servants, however, pales in importance next to the secrecy with which most militaries operate.

Military bureaucrats have relied on the sense of global danger nurtured by the Cold War to retain their cloaks of secrecy. Even elected legislators and independent journalists have hesitated to lift this cloak for fear of being charged with jeopardizing "national security." Now, with the superpower rivalry ended and the alleged communist threat no longer looming, military bureaucrats may be tempted to conjure up new threats to feed citizens' sense of diffuse danger: militant Islam, anti-Islamic imperialism, resurgent Russian chauvinism, irrational outbursts of nationalism, Japanese rearmament, and drug warlords loyal to no state. These supposed international dangers are more than cultural constructs based on imagination as well as fact. They can also serve, as they did during the Cold War, to justify military and civilian officials' protective secrecy. It has been secrecy which has helped to fuel militarization by keeping assessments of threats and the rationale for weapons development unexamined.

The appeal of state and bureaucratic theories of militarization lies in their ability to explain parallel developments in countries with otherwise different political and economic systems. If the extreme militarization which was the hallmark of the Cold War era was fueled by the political cultures of both the Soviet Union and the United States, then maybe it is the inherent nature of states that we need to understand in order to find the cause of militarism's sprawl. Such theories also allow us to adopt a longer historical view. Using this approach, we can understand why state elites have ruled by coercion and threat and have engaged in vast military enterprises since well before the emergence of either industrialism or capitalism.

State-focused theory, like capitalism theory, generally takes the masculinization of public life for granted. The masculine character of a state elite (even when the nominal ruler might be a woman) is seen as unproblematic. It is a person's location in the hierarchy of public power that matters. Women are thus virtually invisible, except as voiceless victims. Women can symbolize the consequences of state power unleashed but presumably do not play any special role in sustaining that power. Nor are they, as victims, looked to for explanations of a state's militarizing tendencies.

．　　．　　■　　■　　■

As powerful as the capitalist-centered and state-centered explanations
of militarism have been, both focus almost exclusively on economic
relations as the most serious of all the relations sustaining militarism.
Each theory has paid too little attention to cultural politics and to the
mundane politics of military "manpower." It is in these realms that
feminist theory has discovered the seeds of militarism and the fuel that
perpetuates it. Taking seriously the politics of culture and of military
manpower has allowed feminists to reveal that ideas about masculinity
and femininity are central to the creation and reproduction of militarism.
This perspective has also exposed the surprising amount of public and
private power that states have devoted to maintaining particular constructions of manliness and womanliness.

A feminist analysis of power is particularly persuasive when it reaches
beyond an approach which looks only at consequences, not causes. For
when we ask how manipulations of masculinity and femininity shape the
causes and not just the effects of militarism, then feminist analysis will
reveal exactly how power works. It will show that militarism in its Cold
War and its post–Cold War guises requires a lot more power to sustain
than even the most cynical nonfeminist critics have imagined. If we are
satisfied with asking Where are the women? only when examining the
impacts of militarism, for instance, then we will discover that the refugees of the civil war in Bosnia are mostly women and their dependent
children, yet leave unquestioned why most of the snipers, internment
camp guards, and field commanders on all sides are men. In this way we
would not get to the heart of those gendered notions of work and danger
that went into designing the snipers' rifles or selling the artillery guns.
Paying attention to consequences alone is useful, but too timid.

Harder questions will produce more radical answers. Such questions
are being posed by British and American women working in conversion
campaigns aimed at dismantling the military-industrial structures of
mutual admiration and dependence. By the mid-1980s, there were an
estimated 232,000 women of all racial groups working for American
defense contractors. No longer were weapons companies dependent on

women merely "for the duration," as in World War II. By the later years
of the Cold War, not only had women's labor become a crucial element
in the military-industrial complex, but a hierarchical sexual division of
labor had become a pillar on which that complex rested.

Women, as low-paid workers and/or single mothers, were less likely
than working-class men to derive benefits from military spending.[16] Even
more than companies in civilian sectors of the U.S. economy, defense
contractors relied on women working in the lowest-paid assembly and
clerical jobs. Low-paid women assembled military-designed computer
chips and typed complicated defense bids; they were needed to sustain
the militarized economy and thus the Cold War. One study found that
American women working in civilian industries in the mid-1980s were
earning only 64 cents for every dollar earned by men. The same study
found that women in the defense-related industries made even less: a
mere 51 cents for every dollar earned by the men working around them.[17]

Women as well as men took part in the International Economic
Conversion Conference held in Boston in 1985. But in the course of the
three days of workshops and panels, it became clear that men outnum-
bered women as speakers and that questions about women's particular
concerns—for example, about conversion of electronics companies,
where women workers predominate, or about the impact of conversion
on families of defense workers—were being either trivialized or ghetto-
ized. So the women caucused. They insisted that their male colleagues
pay attention to these questions, that they stop imagining that, because
they were working for a progressive cause, their analysis of the industrial
side of militarism would automatically aid women. Just as Rosie the
Riveter had been sent back to the kitchen with the winding-down of
arms production at the end of World War II, so women working in arms
factories today were likely to be the most vulnerable to long-term unemployment as the end of the Cold War shrunk the number of defense
contracts—unless there was conscious thinking about how conceptions
of masculinity and femininity had shaped the defense industry.[18]

In early 1992 alone, British Aerospace and Ferranti, major British
defense contractors, cut their payrolls by two thousand workers each.

Financial observers in London estimated that, between the mid-1980s and the early 1990s, one-fifth of Britons working for defense companies had lost their jobs.[19] How many of them were women? We do not know.

Counselors in family service agencies and battered women's shelters in the U.S. report that domestic violence has increased when men have been laid off from defense companies. Such a pattern may suggest something about the masculinist cultures of defense factories. Feminists in local and national conversion campaigns are asking why it is that so many male workers in ship, tank, and aerospace factories are enamored of their jobs. Even among those male union leaders who can see the wisdom of converting an industry from arms production to socially useful production, is misogyny bred by their encouraging rank-and-file male workers to believe that women workers are insignificant to military-industrial processes?[20]

Many male employees in weapons factories may be working against their own class-based interests because they imagine that making fighter planes (or artillery guns or spy satellites) is somehow more serious, more proper work for a man, than, say, assembling buses or hospital equipment. The patriarchal assumption that military-related work is really men's work reinforces militarization and the hegemony of the military-industrial complex in ways that may be crucial for the maintenance of this militarizing alliance.

Similarly, far from the factory floor, bargaining sessions between the military professionals, the legislative overseers, and the weapons makers are gatherings of men. They are social exchanges that require certain unspoken assumptions about what men talk about and what they don't mention for fear of appearing "unmanly." These masculinized rituals restrict what can be put on the agenda.

With feminist lenses in place, one is likely to read with great interest a recent article by Nicholas Kristof, the *New York Times* reporter in Beijing, describing the seventeenth-floor offices of Poly Technologies, "the core of a remarkable Chinese military-industrial complex . . . more powerful than the Foreign Ministry itself."[21] The executive desks of Poly Technologies are staffed not simply by technocrats and party loyalists—

Fig. 3. Russian conversion: a woman whose factory recently assembled tanks now assembles steam irons. (Steven Erlanger/NYT Pictures)

ungendered cogs in China's militarized state machine—but by fathers, sons, and sons-in-law. The first head of Poly Technologies was the son of a famous general; consequently he rose quickly through the ranks himself and then moved over to the new arms manufacturing company, carrying with him his intimate ties to the army. The next company director obtained the position because he married a daughter of Chinese leader Deng Xiaoping. Daughters and marriage are significant docks from which to launch examinations of China's thriving post–Cold War arms sales to Burma, Pakistan, and Syria. "Family links between Beijing's arms dealers and its top rulers," Kristoff speculates, "appear to be one reason why China's weapons industry has rapidly become a major exporter in recent years, and why it will be difficult to curb."

. . . . .

Feminist theorizing has demonstrated that both capitalist-centered and state-centered theories may have dramatically *under*estimated the power it requires to militarize any society. Decisions about whether men and women should be trained together, policies designed to identify homosexuals, memos about men's access to prostitutes, meetings to hammer out a policy that defines the carrying of umbrellas as "unmanly" for army officers, official debates over whether to turn a blind eye toward rape during wartime or soldiers' wife battering in peacetime—all are exercises of public power intended to construct gender in such a way as to ensure that militarization stays firmly on the rails.

One of the most striking characteristics of militaries themselves is that they are almost exclusively male. While an estimated 430,000 women were serving as uniformed personnel in the world's regular military units by the end of the 1980s, they nowhere challenged state militaries' essentially masculinized culture.[22] Of the scores of state militaries that have been designed in the past fifty years, only in the U.S., Israel, Canada, and South Africa have the active-duty forces been even slightly less than 90 percent male. Thus, while we are learning more and more about the typically overlooked women who have served as soldiers, generically the military remains an overwhelmingly male institution.[23] This has been so in cultures and historical periods that otherwise share little in common. Something that existed in tenth-century China as well as in nineteenth-century Britain and in late twentieth-century Kenya has produced in their state institutions for organized violence—that is, their militaries—a profound dependency on maleness.

But maleness alone has not been deemed sufficient to guarantee the formation of militaries that states could trust. In all the societies for which we have information, ideas about what it means to be male—that is, masculinity, not mere biological maleness—have been considered by militarizers to be the sine qua non of effective and trustworthy soldiering.

Militaries are composed of men as a result of quite conscious political policies. State officials—themselves primarily male—create an explicit link between the presumed cultural and physical properties of maleness and the institutional needs of the military as an organization. The boys and men who are typically recruited or pressed into service as foot soldiers or ships' crews are drawn from the relatively powerless strata of state societies: peasants, poor urban dwellers, and members of those racial, ethnic, or religious communities held in contempt by the state elite. Yet, for a military to serve the state's interests, these boys and men must be bound to their officers—men who are usually from quite different social strata. The glue is camaraderie; the base of that glue is masculinity. In fact, nervous commanders often try to use the alleged common bonds of masculinity to reduce the all-too-obvious class and ethnic tensions among their troops.[24]

But masculinity has been so intimately connected to militarism that it is no wonder there have been questions about whether the two are analytically separable. According to one view, masculinity cannot be militarized, cannot be transformed, because it is inherently militaristic in the first place. In most cultures that we know about, to be manly means to be a potential warrior. Any man who claims that it is not and never will be in his nature to soldier is therefore taking a risk. He will more than likely be thought of by his friends, neighbors, and governors as less than masculine. We know from countless historical accounts and oral histories how widespread this risk is. Yet only if we can show that masculinity is separable from militarist values and presumptions can we imagine masculinity being demilitarized.

By contrast, other feminists believe that masculinity and militarism, although tightly interwoven at certain times and in certain cultures, can be and sometimes have been pried apart. According to this approach, these two ideological constructs—what it means to be a male and the values and beliefs that make military modes of thinking and behavior seem right and natural—have distinct histories. For instance, despite the radical demilitarization of Costa Rican society ever since the adoption of its 1948 constitution eliminated its national army, notions of masculinity are still etched sharply enough in the culture to have sustained patriarchal privileges for men and to have provoked one of Latin America's liveliest feminist movements. By remaining alert to the dynamic relationship between masculinity and militarism in any particular country or ethnic community, we are likely to assess more accurately how much public power it takes to ensure that ideas about what it means to be "manly" serve militarism. This awareness, in turn, underscores the political quality of masculinity: it is a set of ideas deserving the attention not just of militarists but of every citizen.

Those like myself who believe that militarism is separable from masculinity are especially interested in conscription. If all cultures constructed ideas about manliness such that soldiering was part and parcel of any man's proving his manliness, then governments' conscription efforts would be a lot easier. And in fact popular ideas about "becoming a man" in many societies do make it difficult for a young man to find language and imagery that will permit him to resist military call-up without jeopardizing his status as masculine, not only in the eyes of his father, mother, and male and female friends, but often in his own eyes as well. Yet, in countries as different as Turkey, Nicaragua, the United States, Guatemala, Iraq, and Israel, young men by the thousands have avoided the military draft, either by leaving the country or by resisting the law directly. Often it has been less a young man's refusal to join the military than his path of avoidance that has determined whether others considered him to have forfeited his claim to masculinity. Thus, in the 1990's in the U.S. there is still public controversy over the different paths chosen in the Vietnam War era by Muhammad Ali (conscientious objection on religious grounds), Dan Quayle (joining the National Guard), and Bill Clinton (seeking college deferment).[25] What remains constant in these American cases, as well as in less celebrated instances in many other countries, is masculinity's special salience. What varies is how masculinity can be constructed and reconstructed so as to allow for some "manly" avoidance of the state's compulsory military service for young men within the hallowed territory of manliness.

If the state's military begins to lose its legitimacy, the tension between masculinity and men's compulsory military service can become acute. This was the case in both Lithuania and South Africa by the late 1980s, when Lithuanian men came to see service in the Soviet military as violating their nationalist values and when growing numbers of South African men questioned the apartheid-upholding mission of the South African military. But the emergence of such tension doesn't just happen. It is the result of conscious politicization of masculinity by those who have a stake in prying manhood away from service in a state military.

In South Africa the organization of an anticonscription campaign by young white men became the occasion for confronting attitudes binding masculinity (especially as defined in the white community) to state military service. These attitudes are exemplified by the white serviceman who told researcher Jacklyn Cock, "I grew up during my National Service. I became a man, physically fit and independent. I'd heard it was tough but I never imagined how tough it would be. I handled it." Another young man described to her the interactions which socialize conscripts into a militarized understanding of their own masculinity: "Basics . . . is tough, you're in a situation you don't want to be in. It's very physical, you've got to fight for yourself and there's lots of group pressure too. If one guy lets the group down he feels like dirt 'cos they all get punished. This grueling 'Rambo Syndrome' takes its toll. The victims are usually 'weaklings' or those who refuse to become 'Rambos.' " By the end, another man recalled, "the army does 'make a man of you.' It brings out the best in people. I learned to relate to people better. My own personal belief in myself and my capabilities deepened . . . I learned to push myself forward, to be more aggressive, to get my own way." Even those men who as soldiers found the brutalizing of black South Africans unfair and distasteful discovered that widespread ideas about masculinity made it difficult for them to act: "The SA army cultivates this macho, tough boy image. I was wary of breaking with this."[26]

But with the organizing of an anticonscription campaign, the militaristic voices no longer could drown out the others. For the first time, there were press reports on the suicides of young white men who found their violent duties in the black townships so repugnant that they took their own lives. Men who had gone through service began to question out loud whether their killing and beating of African women and children was indeed "manly." Some men began to reconstruct their own ideas of masculinity, often drawing on their Christian beliefs. As one man explained, "The more manly thing to do is not to be a soldier. To acknowledge weakness is the greatest strength. Christ was the greatest and most manly man who ever lived. He wasn't afraid to admit weakness." By 1989, the official list of conscientious objectors stood at 1,289, not only directly confronting the South African state, but also challenging deeply ingrained white ideas about masculinity.[27]

Nudged along perhaps more by feminist critiques of conventional masculine values than by the end of the U.S.–Soviet rivalry, men in a number of countries have formed what they call the men's movement. With a far-from-coherent philosophy and no small amount of defensiveness, men who have been attracted to this movement have been reassessing the idea of the warrior. Robert Bly's book *Iron John* has become a best-seller, in part because its male readers think reassessing the meanings attached to the warrior can have immediate importance in their everyday relations with women and other men. It is far from clear, however—either in Bly's own writings or in his readers' interpretations—whether the ultimate consequence will be a reconstructed notion of manly adulthood that is immune to the old siren call of militarism.[28]

Although they do promote compliance with conscription, ideas about masculinity as they exist in civilian culture are often not by themselves sufficient for building the kind of armed force the government deems necessary. If masculinity "in the raw" were sufficient, there would be little need for the sweat, blisters, and humiliations of basic training. The role of the drill sergeant, a nineteenth-century European invention, testifies to the imperfect fit between even the notion of masculinity which encourages compliance with conscription and that required for effective soldiering. In other words, if masculinity as a social construct were inseparable from militarism, no state would risk its legitimacy with harsh conscription laws, and military institutions would not need to hire drill sergeants. Thus, any time a government fashions a male conscription policy so as to make it appear to young men—and to their girlfriends, their mothers, and their fathers—that military service is a natural step toward their culturally acceptable status of manhood, that government is using political resources to ensure that the separability of masculinity from militarism remains invisible. Nevertheless, every time a government develops a training program to turn male enlistees into soldiers, it is inadvertently acknowledging that in reality masculinity and militarism, although tightly intertwined, are indeed separable.

■   ■   ■   ■

Relatively few men who have been in the military have been in combat. Many serve when there are no battles to fight. Millions perform their duties far from actual combat, as cooks, mechanics, instructors, and accountants. Still, combat continues to have an ideological potency, in large measure because it is wielded as a criterion to divide "the men from the boys"—and, more recently, the men from the women. It is for this reason, as well as combat's status as a proving ground for upwardly mobile officers, that so much political energy has been devoted to defining combat and to defending those definitions.

Even before the introduction of so many women into U.S. and other forces, combat was salient. It was used by men to construct hierarchies of militarized masculinity among themselves. That is, the fact of being in uniform hasn't always been enough to reassure a man of his own masculinity. For instance, a woman officer in the U.S. Air Force reports that the men she knows who fly fighter planes today enjoy imagining that they are more manly than the men who pilot transports. On the American fighter pilots' pyramid of masculinity, the latter are mere "twinkie eaters."[29] That is, they don't eat quiche, but they don't eat steak, either.

If men of different ethnic or racial groups are formally relegated to noncombat roles because they are not trusted by the government with its weaponry, as African-American men were until the 1950s, then the masculinized military hierarchies take on important racial connotations as well. It would not be surprising if men whose fathers or grandfathers were barred from combat roles take pride when they are allowed to enter such positions, even if they are consequently subjected to injury and death. Being an ordinary foot soldier, an infantryman, has always had mixed meanings. On the one hand, one's claim to masculinity cannot be questioned. The soldier is doing a "man's job"; he's the epitome of the combat "grunt," likely to face the enemy in a more intimate way than even the most macho of fighter pilots. On the other hand, he is low on the status ladder; he is more likely to be covered with mud than with glory, and he enjoys only that autonomy and acknowledged adult manhood that he can manage to conjure up in his own imagination. Masculinity, therefore, is not simple in its relationship even to combat, any more than it is simple in its relationship to class stratification in the civilian world.

But it is the risking of death in the name of a larger cause, whether on the ground or in the air, that accords combat so much of its political power. Ancient Greek thinkers argued that combat offered men the hope of immortality. Human frailty could be transcended by acts of heroism that were possible only in military combat. Thus, the presumption that only masculine people can partake of combat preserves in the patriarchal state the justification of the rule of men: only they, it is mythologized, will have the requisite courage and honor.[30]

Every modern military has an official definition of combat. But the definition varies by country and by regime, according to cultural definitions of femininity, the influence and agenda of the women's movement, the official perception of contemporary weaponry and battlefield tactics, and the military's own need for and shortage of "manpower." Not even among the fifteen NATO allies is there a uniform definition of this slippery thing called combat or a standard policy regarding women soldiers' participation in it. The ideological potency of combat rests on the wobbly presumption that it is knowable and unchangeable, just as masculinity is presumably knowable and unchangeable. Once combat, like masculinity, is exposed in its artificiality, its reliance on human manipulation, it loses much of its cultural force.

On this point the American experience of the past decade is instructive. The contortions the Pentagon and Congress have gone through as each has tried to anchor down an obviously floating definition of combat not only reveal that both combat and masculinity are socially constructed, but also that much political currency has been invested in trying to construct these concepts for the sake of preserving the patriarchal order. Feminists have been at their most persuasive when they have shown that behaviors and ideas that are passed off as natural and uncontested have in reality been fought over; that there have been debates and power struggles which, if now invisible, have been swept offstage in a deliberate attempt to make the victors' stance appear more natural than it ever was. Nowhere are these principles demonstrated more clearly than in the contest over the U.S. military's definition of combat.

In 1982, U.S. Army bureaucrats revised their 1978 definition of combat. "Direct combat," an activity to which only men could be assigned, was newly defined as "engaging an enemy with individual or crew-served weapons while being exposed to direct enemy fire, a high probability of direct physical contact with the enemy's personnel, and a substantial risk of capture." "Direct combat," they continued, "takes place while closing with the enemy by fire, maneuver, or shock effect in order to destroy or capture, or while repelling assault by fire, close combat or counter-attack."[31] They then set about trying to code every job in the Army according to its likelihood of being subjected to "direct combat."

In 1983, the U.S. Army published its long-awaited list. It included all its job titles, combat and noncombat, everything from guitar player to nuclear medicine specialist to HAWK pulse radar repairer. The list set off a howl of protest from women in the military because it meant that henceforth many trade jobs would be considered to be combat positions and thus closed to women. The army spokesperson explained that technological and tactical advances in warfare had made it imperative now to include carpenters, interior electricians, and plumbers as combat positions, for men only. The issue of which, if any, jobs were exclusively male became more awkward as the military's reliance on women soldiers increased. By 1983, the deliberate recruitment of women volunteers, instituted to make up for the numbers and educational qualifications lost when Congress ended the draft in 1973, was causing strains in the army. Senior civilian and uniformed army policymakers seemed to be responding to middle-ranking field commanders' irritation at the increasing numbers of women placed in their units in jobs traditionally reserved for men. Having more women in their units meant these officers had to pay more attention to matters like sexual harassment. It meant that they had to worry more about the morale of their men, which was apparently threatened by their having to work side by side with women. The solution: keep combat as the male-only preserve, but redraw its conceptual boundaries so that it sprawled over a much wider landscape. Send the women back, if not to the nursing corps, at least to the radar room, where they belonged.[32]

But by 1983, a politically skilled women's lobby had emerged, comprising liberal feminists in Washington-based research institutes, the Defense Department, and Congress. It was well placed to monitor the army's ideological maneuvers and to blow the whistle on them. During the late summer and autumn of 1983, this alliance did battle with those in the Pentagon who wanted to expand the definition of combat so as to preserve as wide as possible a field of clearly masculinized military operations. One result was that the army had to surrender some, though not all, of its expansionist goals. For example, carpenters were taken off the list of combat jobs.[33] But, perhaps more important theoretically, this struggle also generated an impressive paper trail, which will make it impossible for anyone in the future to assert that militarized masculinity is as natural as dandelions in July.

The word battle of 1983 also encouraged the Washington alliance of liberal feminist insiders to press for further contractions of the boundaries of combat in the name of opening up more military jobs to ambitious women and allowing women into even the inner sanctum of combat. Thus, by 1990, Carolyn Becraft—one of the capital's most energetic and astute lobbyists on behalf of military women—could report with pride that Peacekeeper and Titan missile-launching positions had been opened to women in 1986, the same year that air force women flew on the mission to bomb Libya as copilots of air-to-air refueling planes; that 248 women had been among the sailors deployed to the Persian Gulf in 1987 aboard the destroyer tender *Acadia;* and that two women had commanded army companies that played combat roles in 1989 in the U.S. invasion of Panama.[34]

For those feminists and others seeking to sort out the relationship of militarism to the state, these victories may seem problematic. Do they subvert the military by depriving it of its historic claim to masculinity, thereby also demasculinizing the state which it serves? Or do these battles won by women stalking the corridors of state power have the effect of relegitimizing the military at a time when it was about to seem an anachronism?

.   .   .   .   .

Of all forms of state-organized violence, war has provided the most urgent context for feminist theorizing. Better than posing war and other forms of violence as alternative objects of attention, however, is seeing them as connected forms of state-licensed male violence. Some wars have been more fruitful than others in providing women with the impetus and resources for thinking about the connections between state violence and gendered hierarchies. For instance, because of reporting by feminists in Bosnia, Serbia, and Croatia, rape is getting more attention as a state-generated act of war, rather than merely a private, if despicable, act.

While feminist researchers such as Susan Brownmiller and war correspondents such as Daniel Lang twenty years ago documented the role of central government policies about militarized masculinity in acts of wartime rape, until recently even human rights groups have averted their eyes when the abuse took the form of sexual assaults on women by soldiers of the state.[35] In 1992, however, Amnesty International (perhaps pressured from the inside by its large number of women staffers) issued its first international report on rape as a widespread form of state denial of human rights. While it concentrated on the treatment of women in detention, its charges could be applied to the general conduct of war as well. The report confirmed reports by local women activists that the Indian, Peruvian, and Philippine governments, among others, either ignored assaults by men in its police and army forces or responded to those abuses with nothing more than taps on the offenders' wrists. Essentially, Amnesty International called on governments to risk weakening the power of masculinity for the sake of guaranteeing their political legitimacy in the eyes of a newly alert international community.[36]

If one doesn't consider the possible connections between war and other forms of violence, a focus on wars can distort our understanding of how state-organized violence reshapes relations between women and men. There is a common belief that intense militarization does not only privilege men, but can also "open doors" for women. Every day there are fresh indications of how complex the experiences of World War I and II were for American, Canadian, European, and Japanese women. As feminist scholars embark on the reconstruction of the past from below, taking seriously the diaries and oral histories of ordinary women, the patterns become more intriguing, but by no means simpler.[37]

The recent revival of interest in Rosie the Riveter, the mythical American woman factory worker of World War II, has reawakened a classic debate among feminists: does war reinforce the dominance of men and masculine conceptions of virtue and worth, or, paradoxically, does it undermine these pillars of patriarchy? To answer this important question we have to take a closer look at the state itself: is the state really so powerful that it can contain all the contradictory forces let loose by wartime mobilization?

Controversy continues to swirl around the British suffrage movement's split over support of the government's war effort in 1914 because of this larger question of whether war is more likely to strengthen or undermine patriarchy. In Kuwait in the mid-1990s a similar debate is bubbling: was the prewar Kuwaiti women's suffrage campaign advanced politically by the efforts of the many women who stayed in the country and actively resisted the Iraqi invasion, thus helping to reinstate the very regime which had denied women political rights? As horrible as the foreign occupation and the war that followed were, in the long run should Kuwaiti feminist theorists count it as an opportunity as well as a tragedy?

Those feminists who, after the fact, see wars as oppoitunities for challenging gender relationships do not believe that the ruling elite, even when equipped with all the powers of the state, is powerful enough to control the social and ideological contradictions let loose by total warfare. They do well to remind us not to inflate the patriarchal state into an omnipotent creature. Any state is only as crafty and controlling as the people who make and implement its policies. And the people inside the state are often disorganized, confused, short-sighted, and ambivalent. These feminist historians recognize, for instance, that efforts can be and have been made by an alliance of male business executives, labor leaders, and government officials to keep women war workers from mastering masculinized skills, and that emotional blackmail can be and has been used to convince women to retreat to their kitchens or to low-paid "women's jobs" when the war is over and the "boys" come home to reclaim their jobs. They also acknowledge that, in the war's aftermath, empty-headed sex symbols replace the images of strong women that filled the wartime movie screens and women's magazines. But still they contend that in societies as disparate as Britain, Zimbabwe, and Vietnam, despite all such state and private attempts to restore the status quo, expectations of women and men are irrevocably changed by their wartime experiences, and women do not suddenly lose their hard-won skills or their new sense of public place. The genie cannot be so easily stuffed back into its patriarchal bottle.

A less sanguine view of the possibilities for change derives from a close monitoring of relations between women and men, and between women and the state, decades after a war has ended. An analysis of postwar politics is critical for making sense of wartime politics. Rather than being impressed, for example, that women gain access to shipbuilding jobs during a war, these analysts note that such jobs are often deskilled at precisely the time that women are allowed to take them. Furthermore, continued race and gender stratification of war work serves to divide and thus to weaken women's collective strength. Far from liberating women, wartime experience only demonstrates the extent to which women's lives are controlled by male elites. Even though more men than women are killed in most wars, those men who survive the war continue to dominate postwar public life—not incidentally because they can claim to have been, actually or vicariously, the chief defenders of the state in wartime. It is thus only in relatively demilitarized political systems (as in Norway) that a woman who refuses to pass as a masculinized politician can hope to have a genuine chance at running the government. In other political systems postwar politics remain the politics of privileging the masculinized way of conducting public life.

.   .   .   .   .

Those who, along with many feminists, believe that it is war that demands explanation, and not the apparently diffuse processes of militarization, are understandably impatient with analyses that tend to blur war into other seemingly less life-threatening processes. Can the policies meant to make prostitution safe for soldiers on leave really be discussed in the same breath as the continuing threat of nuclear weapons? Wars also capture our attention because they appear to have recognizable beginnings and endings, making them appealingly susceptible to systematic analysis.

Yet focusing our attention on war isn't sufficient analytically. It tempts us to underestimate the kinds and amounts of political power it takes for governments to wage wars because it ignores the decisions taken and policies implemented in the prewar period that lay the cultural groundwork for waging war and that make fighting another day feasible and tolerable. Militarizing gender before the first shot is fired is necessary for governments preparing for war. Men have to be socialized from boyhood to see their masculine identities tied to protecting women while tolerating violence. Women have to be prepared from girlhood to admire men in uniforms and to see themselves as bandaging the wounds inflicted by violence rather than wielding it. Nor does militarization end with the peace treaty, the welcome-home parades, and the burying of the dead.

When war is over, women are encouraged to restore a comforting sense of normalcy by relinquishing whatever autonomy they gained while the men were away. Women are also expected to repair the emotional and physical damage done to militarized sons, husbands, and lovers. In the defeated country, women may be drawn into prostitution to service the sexual needs of occupying soldiers. The governments of both the victors and the losers are likely to see in their women citizens the reproducers of the next generation of soldiers. None of these expectations imposed on women are likely to be fulfilled unless ideas about femininity and masculinity can be successfully militarized in the postwar era. The postwar era militarized thus becomes the newest prewar era.

To chart the postwar militarization of women and of men, and individual and collective resistance to those gendered militarizing pressures, we might pay particular attention in the coming years to the relations between women and men and between women and the state in Zimbabwe, Ethiopia, Somalia, El Salvador, Nicaragua, Croatia, Cambodia, Iran, Iraq, and Kuwait. The feminist answers derived from North American and European experiences before and after World War II will become sharper and more politically reliable once they are tested in these ten countries.[38]

.   .   .   .   .

Peace is conventionally juxtaposed with war. Before war there is peace; after war there is peace. Indeed, the dichotomy has been so widely assumed to be obvious, logical, and true that peace has been on the short end of the theoretical discussion, as if all one needed to do was to determine the causes of war, eliminate them, and—voilà!—peace. In this formulation, peace is often discussed as if it were a static condition: the absence of overt, state-sponsored hostilities. In reality, peace has lacked adequate theoretical attention from patriarchal intellectuals because it has been defined in negative, often feminine, terms. When war is seen as active, heroic, and masculine, then peace becomes merely the absence of all these stirring qualities. Thus, social processes such as capital formation, building the state, and waging war have great aesthetic appeal when male scholars select topics on which to focus their energies, even in the cause of criticizing such processes.

Feminist thinking about peace is not necessarily locked into this war/ peace dichotomy. Perhaps because feminists start from the conditions of women's lives, and because they see how many forms violence and oppression can take, they are more likely to define peace as women's achievement of control over their own lives.[39]

We must nonetheless think about violence and oppression in ways that keep the distinctiveness of militarism sharply etched. It is not enough, I believe, to lump wife battering and wartime rape together as if they required identical uses of public power or involved identical relationships between masculinity and the state. Nor is it enough to conflate all wives' frustrations with their husbands' reluctance to take on child care with the problems of military wives coping with pressures from the military to perform all the tasks of motherhood as well as unpaid volunteer service on the base.

A century and a half ago, British feminists in the Owenite socialist movement were militant in challenging the oppressiveness of marriage for women. They were addressing members of a society governed by an imperial state, speaking to women and men whose political leaders were militarizing economic, ethnic, and gender relations within Britain and its colonies. Yet the Owenite feminist women did not analyze state armies or the government's claim to need to recruit and arm such globally ambitious military forces. In these women's theoretical framework, the war zone was not India, Africa, or the Caribbean; it was the British domestic household. Lack of peace, they argued, lay in the oppressive structures of patriarchal marriage. For Owenite feminists, the opposite of peace was not militarism; it was marriage.[40] Their analysis rings all too true today. This rediscovered analysis of marriage is provocative and useful insofar as it deepens our understanding of genuine peace. Yet it remains limited in its ability to help us understand the relationship between peace and militarism because it fails to trace the links between the patriarchal oppressions imposed locally and those imposed militarily overseas.

This theoretical debate over the opposite of peace and the obstacles to achieving peace is reflected in the current argument among women activists over how to maximize scarce resources in order to produce effective social change. If one believes that militarization is the chief obstacle to peace, then one would encourage a woman in a violent marriage to attend not only a rally to press for more restraints on domestic batterers, but also a rally to sharply cut post–Cold War military spending. One would also urge speakers at each rally to describe the causal links between a husband's abusive behavior and the wider militaristic culture that legitimates all forms of violence.[41] But a feminist working in an underfunded local battered woman's shelter might see militarization as a surface symptom of more basic assumptions in the culture about marriage, property, reproduction, and heterosexuality— all of which are essential to the maintenance of male privilege and the permission for interpersonal violence on which such dominance often rests. Following this line of thought, one would urge the antimilitarist activist to enlist in the struggle against wife abuse, on the grounds that stopping legitimized oppression in personal relationships is the most theoretically efficient way to end militarism.

The practical and theoretical links between heterosexist domination and the military's exploitation of women need to be clearly drawn, however complex these links may be and however many other issues claim our energies and resources. Moreover, rather than imagining war and peace as opposites, we must clarify the ways in which "peacetime" conditions such as those under which American and European women currently live actually foster wartime conditions such as those faced by women in Armenia.

■   ■   ■   ■   ■

In contrast to the apparently limited definition of war, the concept of militarization seems vague. It's harder to assign dates at its beginning or its end. But its temporal diffuseness becomes its feminist theoretical strength. Analyzing militarization casts a theoretical spotlight on a convergence of social processes—cultural, economic, and political. Seen as a process rather than an event, militarization is analytically compatible with other processes examined by feminists, such as industrialization, colonization, division of labor, reproduction, liberation, and sexual harassment.

To make sense of distorted ideas about masculinity and femininity, exploring the concept of militarization permits the investigation of ideological change. We can trace any community's or government's ideas over decades and generations to see how presumptions about masculinity are either bolstered or challenged by other ideological constructs such as authority, nationhood, the enemy, sexual pleasure, and the state.

This is not to say that all analysts of militarization give sufficient attention to its ideological dimensions; some treat it as merely a technological process, some as simply a diplomatic process, and still others as an economic process. But since militarization can be explained only by naming its causes, its analysis does have the inherent potential for pushing us to watch for any changes in a particular culture. What is happening, for example, to Armenians' collective notion of masculinity? Has it undergone a radical militarization since the mid-1980s? If so, this has profound implications, not only for the nascent Armenian state, but also for Armenian women, in their relations with their husbands, sons, and compatriots and in their relationship to this new state.

Finally, the concept of militarization is especially valuable for anyone embarking on theorizing because it encourages rather than dampens cross-cultural dialogue. North American and Western European women have drawn their questions and hunches mainly from wars, especially those experienced firsthand. American women, for instance, have used the Rosie the Riveter myth to explore the state's ideological manipulations of women's family and work expectations, but remain relatively ignorant of how the Iraqi Baathist regime promoted women into civil service posts in a strategy for fighting its prolonged war against Iran during the 1980s. What did this policy mean for Iraqi men's expectations of marriage and employment when they returned home after Baghdad and Teheran signed their cease-fire agreement?[42]

Third World women theorizing about war and peace and militarism have been, perhaps, the most convinced that militarization is the concept that best shows how power is used to distort relations between women and men. They have deemed all sites to be useful for their investigations into how men learn to behave toward women and toward other men in ways that mire them in militarism. Feminists from Chile to Korea, from India to South Africa, and from Thailand to Guatemala have turned their observations toward men's behavior in police stations, in peace movements, in torture chambers, in base town discos, in guerrilla camps, in legislatures, in political parties, in factories, and in bedrooms. They have discovered how militarization can be and has been promoted in each of these settings, with disastrous consequences for women.[43]

. . . . .

Our own historical period may rank as the most thoroughly militarized in history; more people in more societies have been dependent on or controlled by the military and military priorities—that is, have become militarized—than perhaps at any previous time. Military expenditures, military authority, and militaristic values and ways of thinking have influenced the flow of foreign trade and have determined which countries receive agricultural assistance. Militarism has shaped the design and marketing of children's toys and of adult fashions and entertainments. It has influenced fathers' hopes for their sons and voters' presumptions about electable candidates. Militarized mythologies of valor and safety have influenced the self-esteem and security of millions of people. Yet the very breadth and depth of militarization in so many countries makes it difficult to develop unambiguously feminist theories of militarization.

Feminist theorizing is distinctive insofar as it reveals how much of social practice depends on deliberate manipulations of gender. It takes culture seriously; it is on the lookout for even the most seemingly trivial efforts of state officials to shape ideas about what it means to be womanly or manly. Still, the very darkness of our times—whether measured in megatonnage of nuclear explosives or in numbers of refugees—has tempted many to dilute their distinctly feminist approach. Although the spread of military beliefs and influence cannot be sustained unless fueled by the hierarchical arrangements of gender, some may have hesitated to press the issue in a group that has come together out of quite different concerns about militarization.

The composition of an antimilitarism campaign is often diverse: men and women who see a threat to democracy in the government's use of force to quell popular protest, aboriginal people who fear the escalating demand for uranium deposits under their already scarce lands, mothers alarmed over the conscription of their sons, parents desperate to locate "disappeared" children, workers opposed to their employers' stubborn dependence on military contracts, citizens alarmed over the government's willingness to lease land for foreign bases, and men who feel that their own male honor is violated by soldiers who rape their wives and daughters.

Militarization, in contrast to other forms of gender oppression, really does injure men, literally as well as figuratively—on the battlefield, in jail cells, and as objects of forced conscription. Thus, despite the best efforts of a militarizing state to manipulate ever-potent notions of masculinity, men can be mobilized as allies in antimilitarist campaigns. At the same time, however, they are hard to convince of the need for a feminist analysis of what causes and perpetuates militarization. A man may feel so threatened in his masculine identity that he may refuse to admit that the meanings assigned to femininity and masculinity—not just as abstractions, but as part of his everyday guide to behavior—might shape his idea of what is a trivial issue as opposed to what is politically significant, demanding his public attention. To overcome these very real theory-in-action dilemmas, a feminist must demonstrate exactly what is lost, analytically and strategically, when gender considerations are left out of the explanation. At the very least, a proponent of feminist theorizing must show convincingly that if the social constructions of femininity and masculinity are ignored or trivialized, we all will fail to grasp why people's lives have become increasingly dominated by military values and agendas, and our actions will fail to reverse these trends.

Most radically, a feminist analysis implicates patriarchy—not just the capitalist military-industrial complex, and not just the hierarchical state—in the causation of militarism. It is the entire patriarchal structure of privilege and control that must be dismantled if societies are to be rid, once and for all, of militarism. This message may be difficult for many women and men to hear in the wake of the collapse of the second superpower and the consequent reduction in tensions between nuclear-armed alliances. Isn't the Cold War's final curtain enough to warrant a sense of relief and accomplishment?

No, unfortunately. As long as patriarchal assumptions about masculinity and femininity shape people's beliefs and identities and their relationships with one another, militarization, however temporarily stanched, lies dormant, capable of rising again, and yet again.

Chapter Three

Beyond Steve Canyon and Rambo

HISTORIES OF MILITARIZED MASCULINITY

I grew up with a blue-haired Superman fighting Nazi spies. But it was a golden-haired Steve Canyon who was my comic strip passport to wartime Asia. My father, serving as a flight surgeon with Allied commandos in Burma, was part of that group of British, U.S., and Australian soldiers who inspired Milton Caniff to draw his famed "Steve Canyon" strip. Much like novelist Bobbie Ann Mason's character in *In Country*, the teenage Kentucky girl, who made sense of her father's death in the Vietnam War by watching TV reruns of *M*A*S*H*, I began to formulate ideas about what it was like to be my father in World War II Burma by reading "Steve Canyon" comics.[1] Perhaps even the men who actually served in those unconventional commando units today mingle their memories with images from "Steve Canyon" and "Terry and the Pirates."

My mother, on the other hand, didn't inspire wartime comic book creators. She was neither the Dragon Lady nor Cheetah. And I don't remember her ever reading these strips. She took care of my brother David and me, essentially as a single parent, for months at a time. She cooked meals and provided a home-away-from-home for my father's army air corps friends when they and he were back in the United States between overseas duties.

Each of us in our own way took for granted a symmetry between masculinity and militarism, whether it was presented in popular culture or in the lives of family members. I didn't give any thought to whether the link between masculinity and militarism had to be forged. I didn't wonder about how that forging was accomplished. I didn't imagine debates, obstacles, strategies, setbacks, or costs. It is only now, forty-five years later, as I read my mother's enticingly cryptic diaries from those years, share remembrances with my brother who is a veteran of a militarized peace, listen to my father describe plans for commando reunions in London and California, and compare "Steve Canyon" reprints with the latest "Rambo" cartoon narratives, that I have begun to ask questions.[2]

How have men from different cultures had their notions of manhood—and womanhood—shaped and reshaped by officials so as to permit governments to wage the sorts of wars they have imagined to be necessary? What contradictions or failures have had to be camouflaged in order for the ideological symmetry between masculinity and militarism to appear unproblematic, "natural"?

In the late 1980s, *Rambo* caught the imaginations of millions of people. For a time it was the top film in both the United States and Great Britain. In 1986, Moscow viewers of smuggled *Rambo* videos had the chance to see a Russian counterpart on the big screen. Mikhail Nozhkin, star of *Solo Voyage,* a film shot in Cuba and the Crimea about an independent, rough-and-tumble Russian commando, was nicknamed "Rambo" by local movie fans.[3] At the same time, *Rambo* videos were being viewed on VCRs around the world, by people as different as Filipino guerrillas and anti–Cold War Finns. Sylvester Stallone's character inspired fashions, dolls, and television series. "Rambo" slipped quickly into the global lingo. For many of us, "Rambo" became a convenient shorthand for a complex package of ideas and processes. Rambo's brand of militarized masculinity was compared with those of World War II movie idol deck officer John Wayne, of Reaganesque National Security Council bureaucratic entrepreneur Lt. Col. Oliver North, and of the tough commander who could cry, General Norman Schwarzkopf.[4]

One of the most important contributions feminists have made to the analysis of war and peace—and of militarized peace—is an understanding of how notions about masculinity and femininity have promoted and sustained the military. While other critical analysts have placed economic, racial and bureaucratic patterns stage front, feminists have concentrated on the social constructions of gender. The accumulation of more and more evidence from more and more societies has made feminists increasingly confident in asserting that the omission of gender—of femininity and masculinity—from any explanation of how militarization occurs risks not only a flawed political analysis but also perpetually unsuccessful efforts to roll back militarization.[5] In the 1990s, when there is such hope for a genuine rollback of earlier decades' militarization, this feminist assertion needs to be taken very seriously.

Rambo first appeared at a time when feminists were asking more questions about militarism than they had since the 1920s. Its remarkable cross-cultural popular appeal—an appeal fueled by immense infusions of corporate capital—seemed to confirm a three-part feminist analysis: first, social constructions of masculinity, not just elite interests or state bureaucracies and their cosmologies, entrench and extend the grip of militarism. Second, militarism's reliance on particular forms of masculinity is apparent in societies with otherwise dissimilar cultures and uneven levels of industrialization. Third, militarizing masculinity cannot succeed without making women also play specifically feminine parts in the militarizing process; these feminine parts, although vital, must be kept ideologically marginal.[6]

These arguments were persuasive. And Rambo's evolution confirmed them. But now I wonder if they are enough. The varieties of militarized masculinity may deserve more of our attention. Particular variations do not only spring from diverse cultural groundings; they may also be dictated by historically specific militarisms.

Rambo is not Steve Canyon; nor is he Oliver North or Norman Schwarzkopf. Steve Canyon may get a bit confused when he moves from comic-strip World War II to a comic-strip Indochina war. But he remains a warrior on a winning side. While something of a maverick with his blond persona, he doesn't feel as though he's at war with his superiors. World War II, according to this simplistic portrayal, called for a brand of militarized masculinity that served the state without depriving the low-ranking white American male of his sense of individuality and his emotional attachment to women.[7] Today's Rambo is a no less masculinized or militarized cultural icon. But he belongs to a different era in the evolution of American militarism. Perhaps his dark complexion is meant to signal to his cartoon-dependent audience that he is out of the political mainstream, politically disaffected. He openly defies his superiors. He tries to reopen a war that his own state's officials want to be over, if not won. He is so unconnected to his fellow men and women that he rarely speaks in whole sentences. Rambo is a peculiarly post-Vietnam, pre–Gulf War type of American militarized male. His message is for those American men who are pained by national humiliation and elite betrayal: don't go to veterans' therapy groups or march in peace parades; instead, engage in individualistic military adventurism that defies official hierarchies but restores a nation's "pride" in its military, and keep your emotional distance from women.

Do men from other societies have the same responses to militarized national humiliation? Americans preoccupied with veterans have been curiously uninterested in the soldiers of other countries—even their own former allies. Thus, there have been few investigations into the postwar lives of our Vietnamese comrades-in-arms: the soldiers of the Army of Vietnam (ARVN), Saigon's forces. What little information is available about Vietnamese ARVN veterans who have made it to the United States suggests that some of them, having survived postwar reeducation camps and refugee camps, have turned their masculinized, militarized humiliation toward intimidation of their fellow Vietnamese Americans. Other ARVN veterans have become dysfunctionally dependent on the women in their families.[8]

How have Kuwaiti, Iraqi, Russian, Croatian, Belgian, Dutch, German, Chinese, Polish, Egyptian, Italian, Japanese, or French constructions of masculinity been affected by their own twentieth-century military losses? Humiliation is both a gendered and an enculturated emotion.

Fig. 4. Rambo comes to post–Cold War Russia, 1992. (© Chris Stowers/Panos Pictures)

So we might expect it to be militarized in quite dissimilar ways in different countries, with the consequence that *Rambo* will be absorbed (or rejected) in quite dissimilar ways.[9]

The very definition of a war that is "lost" is problematic. The Finnish feminist Eva Isaksson has asked, "Did you ever consider whether men in countries that lost their wars really think that they actually lost?"[10] It may be that men and women in the same country (on "the same side") carry into contemporary political action quite contrary presumptions about whether there is anything to feel humiliated, repentant, or defiant about. Moreover, men of different social classes may conceive of a war's outcome in ways so disparate as to produce quite dissimilar relationships between their senses of masculinity and the state military.

So it is always useful to examine the current trend in militarizing masculinity in the context of what particular men think of as the *last* war. For example, Klaus Theweleit, the German historian, has delved into the most intimate fantasies of men in the Freikorps. What he has discovered is that this particular group of men were militarized in large part by their desperate flight from femininity. But this flight and the hatred for women it produced, which was so effectively manipulated by authorities from 1918 through World War II, wasn't fueled by an ahistorical misogyny. According to Theweleit, it was rooted in these men's particular experience of a war lost, the First World War.[11] In other words, to understand how the men in particular classes, ethnic groups, and nations embrace or discard notions of military humiliation and redemption, we need to take seriously the militarizing dynamics of "postwar" eras.

Let us take another example, one that is not idle speculation in the post–Cold War 1990s. How are the Russian and Ukrainian men who felt the sting of a lost war in Afghanistan converting that memory into hopes for their new, post-Soviet armies? According to recent reports, many of the lower- and middle-ranking male officers of both countries are marrying that defeat to lessons they have drawn from their sideline observations of the Gulf War. These Russian and Ukrainian men want to professionalize their militaries. They want to shed the amateurist masculinity of a conscript-dependent army. They want to project a newly confident militarized masculinity through the wielding of the kind of high-tech weaponry that they believe allowed American soldiers to shake their own emasculating memories of past defeats.[12]

In this post–Cold War world, however, these are not the only lessons being drawn. How does military humiliation resonate a generation later among women and men in contemporary Japan? U.S. presidents and their men have been pressuring their Japanese counterparts to remilitarize and became particularly insistent during the Gulf War, when Washington spokesmen suggested that the men who are the leaders of Japan could not be "mature" international actors unless they deployed troops abroad. A recent succession of Liberal Democrat prime ministers, starting with Prime Minister Yasuhiro Nakasone, have resisted acknowledging Japan's World War II errors and at the same time have pressed their colleagues to enhance the nation's military strength. By the time the Berlin Wall fell, Japan indeed had the world's third largest military budget (much of which goes to maintaining U.S. bases on its territory).

Yet Japanese popular notions of masculinity have not seemed easily remilitarized to date. Memories of wartime defeat do not appear to have generated a Japanese Rambo syndrome. Nor have they yet translated into popular hopes for a military force filled with professionalized "top guns." Nowhere was this clearer than in the country's 1991 public and parliamentary debate over the reinterpretation of Article 9 of its constitution. This change, pushed through the parliament in 1992, permits the government to send units of the Japanese Self-Defense Force (SDF) overseas to serve in noncombat roles with United Nations peacekeeping troops. Despite the government's legislative victory, some otherwise patriarchal politicians in both the ruling Liberal Democratic party and its leftist opposition remained unconvinced that wielding military power abroad, even under the blue and white banner of the UN, would reconfirm Japanese national influence or bolster its male citizens' collective sense of postwar manliness.

The first six hundred Japanese soldiers shipped overseas under this act, who were members of an engineering corps, were sent to keep Cambodia's fragile peace by rebuilding roads and bridges. In the United States there is enough post–Cold War economic anxiety for many Americans to ignore the two decades of Washington pressure on the Japanese to remilitarize and instead to imagine Japanese peacekeeping engineers as the direct descendants of the Imperial Army. Carrying briefcases instead of rifles and wearing berets instead of helmets, these Japanese engineers scarcely appeared to be models of military imperialism. Yet the *New York Times* chose to headline its report of the men's arrival as "Japanese Sun Again Rises Overseas."[13]

In 1989, Japanese soldiers in fact were so poorly paid and held in such low repute that the military fell 14 percent short of its recruitment targets. Corporatized and commercialized masculinity evidently is not as easily translated into militarized masculinity as it was in Britain in the 1930s, when Virginia Woolf charted that conversion in her landmark essay *Three Guineas*.[14] Japanese feminists, however, are not quite ready to shelve Woolf. Some of them are closely monitoring what they believe

Fig. 5. What is the meaning assigned to the Japanese parliament's 1992 approval of troops being sent to take part in the UN's Cambodia peacekeeping operation? This photo accompanying a U.S. newspaper story seems designed to provoke in Americans memories of an aggressive past. (© Robin Morgan/Gamma Liaison)

are important, if subtle, efforts by the government to transform postwar economic models of Japanese masculinity and femininity to make them more amenable to a U.S.–backed military buildup.[15]

Thus, men in various societies do not sift alleged national humiliations through the same militarized sieves; men in other countries did not respond to Rambo's individualistic defiance as many American men did in the 1980s. In every country where Rambo has become a cultural hero, students of militarization need to describe exactly what qualities of both the character and the narrative are attractive to that society's men. What do these qualities, in turn, tell us about how men in that society might be drawn to support militarism or to reject it?

.   .   .   .   .

Fig. 6. September 1992. Japanese male soldiers arriving for UN duty in Cambodia look more bureaucratic than militaristic. (AP/Wide World Photos)

A drill sergeant is a drill sergeant is a drill sergeant. Are we certain about that? Another territory whose exploration might provide us with a clearer understanding of the varieties of militarized masculinity is that of military recruitment and training programs.

The British government is an old hand at militarization. One of its successful imperial strategies was to build armies out of local colonized labor. To do that, British officials had to find ways to persuade local male rulers that their personal authority and status would be enhanced if they allowed the British to build them "proper" armies filled with "proper" soldiers. Then the officials had to persuade thousands of male peasants and nomadic herdsmen that their manhood would be enhanced within their own families and communities if they would enlist in the newly created, British-controlled armies. Finally, the officials had to devise complex formulas for marriage and child-rearing to permit the soldiers to feel respectable as husbands and fathers, yet not burden the

British military with too many noncombatants. Nothing was automatic about any of these processes. Creating modern armies out of traditionally gendered materials was never an easy task. It involved a subtle mix of persuasion and coercion, always shaped by the peculiarities of time and place.[16]

This complex historical process was more than a matter of exporting British notions of militarized manhood to different ethnic communities in India, Nigeria, and Malaysia. From reading old training manuals and eavesdropping on British colonial officials' reminiscences, it appears that considerable adaptation was required to make this imperial strategy work.[17] That is, masculinity could not be militarized in India or Nigeria in exactly the same ways as it was militarized in Scotland. Furthermore, women in these countries were thought of by the empire's security architects as playing slightly different roles in order to sustain the "manly soldier" needed by the empire. This subject was rarely talked about in formal reports and is typically ignored entirely by military historians. But it was analyzed at length by British feminist reformers in the 1880s, when, having won the repeal of the patriarchal Contagious Diseases Acts, they launched an international campaign to expose the British government's policies toward military prostitution in India. Campaigners writing in their journal *The Dawn* noted that British male officials believed that, for some reason, Indian male soldiers did not use Indian women as prostitutes in the same ways as British male soldiers posted in India did. The bureaucratic debates over how to reduce venereal disease (VD) among British soldiers stationed abroad became a discussion of differences in the militarized sexuality of British soldiers and that of the empire's foreign soldiers.[18]

World War I and World War II were both fought by major powers with men (and, less visibly, women) from their respective colonies. The British government used Indian and Caribbean men as soldiers; however, there was a heated intraministerial battle over whether it should recruit West Indian women and whether those women enlistees should be permitted to serve in Washington or London or be kept in the colonies.[19] The Japanese government used Korean men, but only in 1992 did its successors admit that the military itself had also had a formal policy of forcing Korean women to work for it as prostitutes.[20] The French military used Vietnamese, sub-Saharan, and North African men; the Germans used East African men; the Americans used Native American, Hawaiian, Puerto Rican, and Filipino men. Out of these wars male officials drew lessons about what sorts of masculinity "worked" in combined military operations. But, with few exceptions, we know little about how the men from the colonized societies experienced the militarized standards of manhood or how their experiences shaped postwar nationalist movements and the relations between local men and women and between imperial and colonized men.

Nor have we been curious enough about how postcolonial military policies concerning training, leadership, sexuality, marriage, and weaponry have been influenced by these World War I or World War II interactions between colonizing and colonized military men. Studies of the career patterns and military curricula of Morocco, South Korea, the Philippines, and Jamaica might be good places to start in understanding the varieties of masculinized military cultures around the world.

The British government, despite its shrunken empire, continues to export its military training expertise energetically. The export of training is often an instrument for promoting the sale of military equipment, but it is also more. In November 1986, the British government signed an agreement to start training Mozambican soldiers. Reports suggested that it was the Zimbabwean regime of Robert Mugabe, a supporter of the besieged Mozambican government, which smoothed the way for this military training agreement. Evidently, Zimbabwean officials have been pleased with the impact of the British military program on its own army, a force that had to be rebuilt—and remasculinized, with the demobilization of most of the women guerrilla fighters—at the end of the Zimbabwean revolutionary war. Can contemporary British military strategies for turning 1980s British middle-class men into officers and working-class (often, in fact, unemployed) urban men into useful soldiers be applied to rural Zimbabwean and Mozambican men of different ethnic groups with no adjustments?

What do officials of the importing governments hope to gain by subjecting their military men to foreign training? Perhaps such a policy choice implies the disappointment of the elite with their society's current constructions of masculinity. Perhaps it suggests that the country's male officials imagine their own male citizens to be "undisciplined": that is, they worry that the traditional constructions of masculinity in their own societies (or at least in the ethnic communities from which they choose to recruit most of their soldiery) are too "wild" or disorderly to serve the regime's goals of national unification, social order, and state security. Alternatively, or perhaps simultaneously, the current elite might imagine that the conventions of manhood among the male population are too dismissive of the sort of modern weapons technology that requires literacy and patience. Thus, they might conclude that U.S., French, British, Israeli, or, until recently, East German or Argentinian approaches to militarizing masculinity will produce the kinds of soldiers they think they need. And the exporting officials are more than eager to comply.

Elite officials who invite foreign soldiers to train their men may go so far as to imagine that their own men, subjected to such manipulation, will return to civilian society after military service as more productive farmers, more loyal government supporters, and more responsible fathers. Certainly all of these assumptions are encouraged in the exporting governments' own recruiting promotions. What do the importing officials assume about the reactions of their women citizens to their fathers', husbands', and brothers' new attitudes?

Some regimes have had rather ambivalent feelings about employing foreign trainers to improve the forms of masculinity propping up their state militaries. For the line may be quite fine between a form of masculinity that is enhanced in its combativeness and discipline and one that is impatient with perceived inadequacies in the manliness of civilian superiors. Thus, in the wake of Kuwait's embarrassing military occupation by Iraq, the ruling Sabah family, autocratic and patriarchal but not known for the militarism of its male members, appeared to waffle on the question of reshaping its soldiers' masculine identities. On the one hand, the government contracted the U.S. Army Rangers, an especially masculinized force, to conduct desert training exercises with Kuwaiti soldiers. And a Kuwaiti lieutenant colonel recalled that "the best moments of my life were working with the [U.S.] Marines." On the other hand, the Sabah regime has continued to use a political patronage system to promote military officers, a system which relies less on the criterion of militarized manhood than on masculinized personal loyalty.[21] Simultaneously, the Sabah regime has ignored the military competence of numbers of Kuwaiti women who took part in the anti-Iraqi resistance. It would seem that neither promotion of militarized masculinity nor acknowledgment of women's capacities to confront violence serves to secure the current regime.

The flow of consequences from the internalization of military training has never been one-way, however. The men who have acted as colonial officers, international liaisons, or foreign advisors have returned from their assignments with lasting notions about the masculine traits in their own societies that make them, as men, "naturally" braver, more inventive, more professional, more disciplined, and better soldiers than the men from the cultures they have been sent to train. Usually there is a strong element of ethnocentrism and even outright racism blended into these paternalistic, militarized, masculinized memories.

In the January 1987 issue of an American magazine called *Vietnam Combat,* a publication devoted to recalling the brave deeds of rank-and-file American men (not women) who served in Vietnam, there was a full-page photo showing a tall, white American soldier wading through a Vietnamese rice paddy carrying an almost toylike M16 rifle. Next to him walks a shorter Vietnamese man in battle fatigues; he is carrying a much more potent and heavier piece of weaponry. What ideas did the militarized Big Brother bring back to the United States about his militarized little brother's bravery, loyalty, intelligence, and sexuality?[22] We won't have a true picture of the complex political experience we so glibly call the Vietnam War until we have a feminist history of Saigon's army, the ARVN. And whatever the masculinized, militarized memories American military advisors brought back with them, they are likely to have their institutional roots in the 1950s training programs in the Philippines and Panama, with tentacles reaching forward to 1980s training programs in El Salvador and Honduras and from there into 1990s training programs in Peru and Kuwait.

For several centuries, then, the militarization of masculinity has been driven by both domestic and international processes. These are not simply amorphous cultural ebbs and flows; they are specific historical and contemporary processes that can be researched and documented. There are also institutions to be studied: their routines, their policies, their debates, their language. The U.S. Army's Fort Bragg, Britain's Sandhurst, the government-run jungle combat schools in Malaysia and Nigeria, the Philippine Military Academy, the U.S. military's international training school in Panama—all are potential sites for researching the international processes of militarizing varieties of masculinity.

．　　．　　．　　．　　．

A third arena in which possibly diverse forms of masculinity have to be harmonized for the sake of effective military operations is in the joint military maneuvers of international alliances. These institutions are post–World War II phenomena, based largely on elite male officials' presumptions about what worked and what didn't work during World War II military operations. Milton Caniff's wartime comics hint at the dynamics between men from different cultures who have been thrown together by their governments in joint operations. The Australian, Scottish, and American characters in "Steve Canyon" regularly joke with each other about their respective manliness. There is friendly competition among them for local Asian women.

As the major powers during the Cold War grew determined to create separate and competing networks of military alliances around the world, more women and men were pressed to harmonize their resources, skills, and fears with coordinated military actions. Most critics of these sprawling global alliances have focused on the friction generated between the supposed allies by trying to synchronize dissimilar legal and industrial institutions. For instance, in recent years there have been rumbles of discontent throughout NATO because its American partner's call for the "standardization" of NATO tanks, rifles, and computers has seemed to be one more attempt by Washington to compel everyone else to "buy American," to the disadvantage of each country's own needy defense contractors. Before its demise—and hastening its unraveling—the Warsaw Pact suffered its own simmering internal discontent; the Soviet Union's East European partners resented Moscow's imposed unequal division of labor, which it rationalized as necessary for the cohesiveness of the military alliance.

Although much less talked about, incompatible forms of militarized femininity and masculinity have also been reconciled within military alliances. The Warsaw Pact had little problem here, since across the alliance there was official agreement that male conscription could guarantee the virtual exclusion of women from its militaries.[23] The principal obligations of women in the Warsaw Pact countries were to produce sons who could be enlisted in their adolescence and to be compliant mothers of soldier sons. But, with the exception of the Soviet Union's Muslim women, few women seemed eager to meet the alliance's needs. The Cold War was marked by falling birth rates throughout the European regions of the Warsaw Pact. If the women of Russia, Estonia, Poland, and Czechoslovakia couldn't influence their regimes' military doctrine, they could at least respond to the double burden placed on women in their societies by having fewer children. As the alliance came undone after 1989, many women went on to the next step: they began refusing the role of compliantly militarized mothers. Suddenly, as the alliance disintegrated, sons' relationships with their mothers took on strategic salience for the Warsaw Pact.

The differences between countries' official attitudes toward women serving in the uniformed services have been far more blatant inside NATO. The alliance's legislators and military bureaucrats have shaped and reshaped their respective personnel policies with one eye on the personnel needs dictated by military doctrine and the other eye on the preservation of the ideological bond between masculinity and military service. But the member countries' solutions have been strikingly different, so that by 1990 NATO revealed a somewhat awkward disparity. On the one hand, the forces of the U.S. and Canada, both dependent on volunteers, had enlisted enough women to make up over 10 percent of all active-duty personnel. American representatives—even those who had initially been skeptical of and even hostile to the idea of taking in large numbers of women and training them to be more than secretaries, nurses, and radar specialists—now tended to hold up these figures as proof of their military's social enlightenment. Because of the U.S. government's disproportionate influence in NATO, U.S. officials naturally began to measure their alliance partners' social sophistication partly by their ability to incorporate at least token numbers of women without jeopardizing the military's still-crucial identification with masculinized patriotism.

Defense policymakers in Portugal, Spain, and Turkey did make begrudging, token gestures, accepting a handful of women volunteers into their forces (9, 96, and 152, respectively). Officials of what was then West Germany used women for military purposes but kept them in civilian roles so as not to call up dark memories of Nazi wartime exploitation of women. Thus, by 1990, a mere 459 women were listed as serving in the uniformed ranks of the West German forces. The Italian government, like the West German, relied on male conscripts to fulfill its NATO quotas. Italy's conservative Christian Democratic policymakers, however, wouldn't even salve NATO headquarters' tender feelings by engaging in tokenism: they persisted in excluding women from their military altogether.[24]

Today NATO is struggling to define for itself a new raison d'être in the wake of the disappearance of the Soviet threat. There is more talk of redefining "security," of NATO's spreading its wings and taking on broader social issues. As these changes take place, the disparate gender politics among its member governments take on even more importance. For instance, there is no consensus within NATO about whether masculinity should enjoy an exclusive hold on combat. The Dutch were among the pioneers in allowing women to enter combat jobs. There was a flurry of nervous speculation along NATO corridors in Brussels when, in the mid-1980s, the first Dutch women boarded combat ships. The Norwe-

gian government soon followed the Dutch. By 1990, the governments of
Belgium, Canada, Luxembourg, Portugal, Spain, and Denmark had
lifted their bans on women in combat, often because women's advocates
had insisted that the military be made to abide by laws against sex
discrimination, and often with little change in the virtually all-male
composition of infantry, armored, or pilot corps.[25] The alliance survived.

Yet, as each male elite within NATO has, often clumsily, navigated its
way between gender conventions and military "manpower" needs, each
has sculpted its own idiosyncratic definition of combat—and thus of what
is, allegedly, irreducibly masculine. Is combat killing other human beings?
No. American policymakers (reluctantly) allowed women in the underground bunkers to serve on crews trained to launch deadly intercontinen-
tal nuclear missiles before they would allow women to serve on board
"real" combat vehicles such as submarines or jet fighters. Is combat being
killed—in uniform—by the enemy? No. Women who have served in
noncombat nursing corps have been among the casualties of war for
several generations. All of the American women soldiers killed during the
Gulf War were assigned to "noncombat" roles.

As the British, French, U.S., and now-unified German NATO member
states have stubbornly resisted attempts by some women's rights activists
to open combat jobs to women soldiers, it has become ever more clear
that combat is a delicate ideological instrument. It has to be defined
narrowly enough to allow military planners to recruit and deploy women
to fill the perceived gaps in manpower, yet it must be defined broadly
enough to preserve what are imagined to be the militarily useful distinc-
tions between men and women. Defining combat has been a political
high-wire act.

There are also growing differences within NATO over the supposed
relationship between homosexuality and "national security." By early
1993, only four of the alliance's fifteen members—Britain, the United
States, Greece, and Portugal—still clung to explicit bans on gay men and
lesbians in their armed forces. Among other governments closely allied
to the United States, Australia had just recently lifted its ban, and Israel's
policy of imposing no ban but blocking the promotions of known homo-

sexuals was being challenged. The Canadian parliament was pressed by feminists and gay activists in 1986 to end the exclusion of lesbians and gay men from the Canadian armed forces. In 1989 Michelle Douglas, a Canadian lesbian who had been forced to resign from the air force, challenged the ban of the Department of National Defense, claiming it violated the 1981 Charter of Rights and Freedoms. Faced with defense officials who no longer seemed to believe their own, old arguments, the Canadian federal court judge Andrew MacKay ruled in favor of Douglas, concluding that her constitutional rights had been violated and that any prohibition of homosexuals from the country's armed forces was "contrary to the Charter."[26] The court ordered the government to pay Douglas $100,000 in compensation. By 1991, Canadian defense officials were taking concrete steps to dismantle their military's institutionalized homophobia.[27] But it wasn't until a year later that the Canadian Department of National Defense formally announced that it would no longer prohibit gay men and lesbians from serving, being promoted, having access to career courses, or gaining security clearances in the armed forces.[28] As the debate over gays and lesbians in the military raged to the south of them, Canadian defense officials told reporters that dropping their own ban had scarcely caused a stir in Canada. The local press was far more interested in Canadian soldiers' peacekeeping operations in Bosnia.

Britain's military, on the other hand, continued its exclusion of gay and lesbian soldiers. It was the only arm of the British government which parliament had exempted from the Sexual Offences Act of 1987, which decriminalized homosexuality. In 1991, however, a House of Commons committee reviewing military manpower policies, having been intensely lobbied by gay rights groups, hinted that the time had come when the military's antihomosexual policy would lose parliamentary support.[29] Months later the parliament as a whole moved to drop homosexuality as a criminal offense in the military code. Begrudgingly, the Conservative government agreed: "It is now the view of the government . . . [that] this is a sensible measure of decriminalization whose purpose is to tidy up the difference between military and civil law."[30] But lesbians and gay men would continue to be discharged if discovered.

Debates in Canada and Britain became grist for the Australian political mill. Australia is not a member of NATO, but has been counted on by Washington strategic planners as a partner in Pacific joint maneuvers and in the conduct of war in the Persian Gulf. The ruling Labour Party refused to get ahead of its American military partner on the issue of homosexuals in the military. Defense officials—often to the dismay of colleagues in the health ministry worried about such a ban deterring gay men from participating in AIDS prevention programs—insisted in early 1992 that the Canadian and British reforms were not pertinent to Australia. But when the attorney general took the side of a lesbian who challenged her dismissal from the military, the Labour cabinet, as well as members of parliament and the general public, became involved in the debate. Finally, in late 1992, following the recommendation of a Labour party committee, the prime minister ordered the Australian defense ministry to drop its ban on homosexuals.[31]

In the United States, political mobilization among lesbians and gay men is light-years ahead of where it stood in the 1940s, when gay and lesbian soldiers fought at least two wars: one against the Axis powers and a second against officers and psychologists devising ever-more-subtle tests to weed out homosexuals. One consequence of the American gay political mobilization was that the U.S. government faced multiple court actions brought by women's, gay, and civil liberties groups challenging the legality and the logic of discharging women and men accused of homosexuality.[32] As the gay vote became strategically visible during the 1992 presidential campaign, the question of the political significance of the ban on homosexuals in the military became a national issue. Within the Republican Party a chasm was opening between Christian conservative activists who campaigned against homosexual rights and establishment party regulars, many of them in elected office, who believed that a platform of intolerance would lose Republican candidates more votes than it would attract. In the wake of George Bush's loss, the battle for control of the party became even more intense.[33] AIDS activists and gay and lesbian rights activists had been visible participants in the Democratic Party's 1992 national convention. Clinton's campaign managers, who had become conscious of the potential support to be garnered from gay and lesbian voters, came out in favor of ending the ban. It seemed that if their candidate won, Democratic leaders would treat the new president's lifting of the ban as a non-issue.

Polls taken during the campaign showed that 80 percent of American voters believed that homosexuals deserved equal job opportunities and equal rights before the law. A gender gap emerged, however, when people were asked whether they accepted homosexuality as a lifestyle. Almost 50 percent of American women polled said they believed homosexuality was an acceptable lifestyle; only a third of their male counterparts agreed.[34] If many of the two-thirds of American men disapproving also perceive the military as a public institution in which they have a special stake, then they would likely feel personally threatened should homosexual men be accepted as able to soldier.

Before his inauguration, Bill Clinton announced that he remained committed to lifting the ban on homosexuals in the military. He made the announcement on Veteran's Day, speaking in Little Rock to a mostly male audience of veterans from several wars, all of whom had served in U.S. armed forces whose institutional culture had been informed by the 1944 antihomosexual ban and its rationales.[35] In the decade between 1982 and 1992 alone—a decade in which the proportion of women soldiers had grown rapidly—more than seventeen thousand soldiers had been dismissed on grounds of homosexuality.[36] Clinton tried to reassure current military commanders that he would seek their advice when devising the implementation of the policy reversal. He sought to soften the blow to those senior officers who believed that lifting the ban would undermine the institutional culture—usually discussed in terms of "morale" and "discipline"—which brings young men and women into the military's recruiting offices, persuades mid-career and noncommissioned officers to reenlist, and gives senior officers a sense that they can bond with subordinates over whom they wield authority.

A significant number of these senior officers remained unconvinced. Through retired Admiral William Crowe, a former Chairman of the Joint Chiefs of Staff and adviser to Clinton, a number of admirals and generals informed Clinton that he would face resistance if he tried to upset what they deemed an armed forces tradition. One marine corps general explained his own opposition to the lifting of the ban this way: "We were standing in this shower tent, naked, waiting in line for 35 minutes for a five minute shower . . . Would I be comfortable knowing gays were there standing in line with us? No. It just introduces a tension you don't need."[37] It seems to be the *knowing* that matters. In the wake of Clinton's announcement that he intended to keep his campaign pledge, some of these same senior officers told a *New York Times* reporter they realized that there were probably gay men in the shower line, that gay men and lesbians served in virtually all branches of the U.S. military. But under the ban, they had had to keep their sexuality secret. It was this secrecy, this denial of identity, that these officers believed was essential for military morale and discipline.[38] On the other hand, according to National Public Radio reporter Scott Simon, while he was covering the Gulf War many American gay men and lesbians serving in Saudi Arabia told him they felt less anxious about their peers than about their commanders. They told Simon that it felt possible to reveal their sexual orientation to their heterosexual comrades in the sand-swept trenches precisely because the heterosexual and homosexual troops had so many more important worries in common.[39]

On bases back in the United States, however, the implementation of the ban on gay men and lesbians also was erratic, often dependent on the attitudes of particular local commanders. In this sense, the U.S. military policy on gays and lesbians resembled the institution's policy on prostitution: as long as it was not allowed to become an issue among the wider electorate, implementation was left largely to the discretion of officers down the chain of command. The commanders of Camp Lejeune, the largest Marines base on the East Coast, for instance, had adopted a policy of lax enforcement. The owner of Friends Lounge, a gay bar close to the base, told Eric Schmitt of the *New York Times* that approximately 70 percent of his patrons on weekends were military personnel, and yet for the last four years neither the local police nor the Marines authorities had bothered him. Gay marines "can be themselves here and then go back to the base and do their jobs," he explained. On the other hand, precisely because the implementation of the ban was so apparently fluid while the ban itself, especially since being explicitly codified in 1982, was rigid, many gay men and lesbians in the armed forces adopted a strategy of considerable caution. Michael Gary, now out of the army and the founder of an association of gay and lesbian alumni of West Point, recalled, "When I was at Fort Bliss in El Paso, I drove six hours to a gay bar in Tuscon because I was so paranoid of being seen in town."[40]

The ban itself takes the form of a Defense Department directive which covers not only homosexual behavior but "a propensity to engage in homosexual conduct." That is, the U.S. policy has been based on the claim that not only particular acts but even an identity that might dispose one to participate in such acts "seriously impairs the accomplishment of the military mission."[41] The very vagueness of the 1982 directive allowed implementation to vary widely. In 1982 the Defense Department reported that 1,800 military personnel were discharged from active duty on grounds of homosexuality; by 1992, that figure had dropped to less than 800.[42] In that year, when the ban on gays became an electoral issue for the first time, the Navy discharged 7.3 people for every 10,000 under its command on charges of homosexuality; while the Marines discharged only 3.1 for every 10,000, the Air Force 2.4, and the Army 2.3.[43] Either gay men and lesbians were far more likely to seek out naval careers, or homophobia was not uniform across the services. Moreover, during the same year enlisted personnel were four times more subject to discharges based on homosexuality than were officers, suggesting that those members of the services with the least access to the sorts of privileges that insulate one from investigators' instrusion were those most vulnerable to punitive action.[44]

Commanders and investigatory officials in the several branches also seemed much more alarmed at the presence of lesbians in their ranks than that of gay men. Defense Department figures revealed that during 1992 women were more than twice as likely to be dismissed from active military duty on charges of homosexuality than were men: 8.1 women for every 10,000 troops, as opposed to just 3.4 men for every 10,000 troops.[45] This discrepancy took on particular meaning when, following

President Clinton's announcement that he intended to go ahead with his decision to lift the ban, a full-scale national debate broke out.[46] All the major participants in that debate—the Joint Chiefs of Staff, ordinary soldiers, members of both parties in the Senate and House of Representatives, gay and lesbian rights activists, conservative activists inside and outside the Republican party, individual voters calling the White House and radio talk shows—appeared to focus their attention not on lesbians but on gay men.[47] At first glance, this seems a contradiction: the military *acts* as if lesbians are the chief threat to its culture, whereas military and civilian policymakers *talk* as if lesbians aren't an issue and gay men are the threat.

The discrepancy becomes less puzzling if one sees the persecution of lesbians as the persecution of women in an institutional culture long dependent on masculinity, heterosexualized masculinity. Women have been subjected to a variety of pressures intended to make them aware that they are not wanted in the military. Sometimes it has taken the form of exclusion from combat roles, those most likely to lead to promotion; sometimes it has taken the form of sexual harassment; and sometimes it has taken the form of accusations of lesbianism.

Still it is possible to unravel this paradox fully only if one recognizes that the gays-in-the-military debate is part of a much larger American post–Cold War debate about the kind of gender order that guarantees this society's national security. In this context, Hillary Rodham Clinton's role in the Clinton presidency, the lack of affordable childcare, new challenges to the masculinized congressional culture, the prevention of AIDS, prospective women cabinet officers' access to legal household employees, the Navy's failure to prosecute Tailhook sexual harassers, and the proposed tolerance of gay men and lesbians in the country's military are all tied in a knotty bundle. Together they pose the question of what sort of relationships between women and men will provide the basis for a unified, confident, legitimized society now that comparison with a demonized Soviet Union no longer provides that sense of confident, legitimate unity.

How each regime in an alliance goes about resolving its military's

gendered "manpower" dilemmas depends on (a) how potent each country's women's movement and lesbian/gay movement are and how willing
they are to work together; (b) how committed those movements are to
asserting the right to serve in the state's military as a form of liberation;
(c) how tightly woven the image of civilian manhood is in the fabric of
patriotic citizenship; (d) how militarized the elite's definition of national
security is; and (e) how available for military service young men are who
come from the classes and ethnic groups trusted by the present regime.

The "manpower" politics of a multinational military alliance such as
NATO, consequently, will be the product of the dynamic between these
domestic conditions as they continue to be worked out through the once
unequal and currently transitional structure of NATO itself. The dismantling of the Warsaw Pact has not brought these gendered politics to
a halt. If German and French defense planners begin to wield more
influence within NATO and U.S. influence wanes, blatant homophobia
within the alliance might decline; but the last decade's tilt toward expanding the roles of women in the alliance could come to an unheralded
end and, with it, the temptation for younger American and Canadian
women to imagine first-class citizenship as resting on military service. If,
on the other hand, a political shift inside NATO is accompanied by a
joint decision to save the alliance by transforming it into a broader social
policy instrument—thus redefining "security"—then perhaps even
those member regimes currently unenthusiastic about modest moves to
demasculinize their forces will find it strategically useful to continue the
expansion of women's roles in NATO.

.   .   .   .   .

Ever since the machine gun and aerial bombing revolutionized warfare, defense establishments in the most advanced industrialized societies
have needed more than foot soldiers and generals. They have also needed
psychologists, cartographers, factory managers, engineers, and physi-
cists. Are the forms of prescribed masculinity identical for an aerody-
namics engineer and a bomber pilot? Has our fascination with the social
construction of a Rambo or a "top gun" blinded us to the sorts of gender

pressures experienced by those men and women employed in the industrial and scientific establishments on which militaries now depend?

Most of our descriptions of civilian workers, business managers, scientists, and intellectuals in military contract work are of American men. The most deservedly celebrated feminist ethnography—a "village study" very close to home—is Carol Cohn's study of American defense intellectuals, which describes how a particular group of civilian men have created a masculinized subculture to sustain their military work. Cohn found a group of men who, though they spent their days talking with each other about the finer points of nuclear war, were "unusually well endowed with charm, humor, intelligence, concern, and decency. I liked many of them." As she spent more time with these men, going along with them on field trips to laboratories, submarine bases, and war games, she began to piece together their masculinized culture: a set of facades, etiquettes, fears, and hopes which seemed to permit them to sustain their individual sense of legitimacy and to bond together around a denial of death. They relied on a distinctively sexualized language.

After a trip with a group of defense intellectuals to the General Dynamics Electric Boat facility in Groton, Connecticut, to get a close look at the nuclear-armed Trident submarine, Cohn tried to understand why her male companions wanted to "pat the missile." She wondered, "What is all this 'patting'? What are men doing when they 'pat' these high-tech phalluses?" Then she began finding an answer to her own question: "Patting is an assertion of intimacy, sexual possession, affectionate domination." But patting had a more ambiguous meaning for these male defense intellectuals, for they constantly seemed to want to deny the actual function of the weapons whose uses they were hired to devise. Such a denial was a crucial thread in the bond that held them together in their peculiar, militarized "village." As Cohn explains, "Patting is not just an act of sexual intimacy. It is also what one does to babies, small children, the pet dog. The creatures one pats are small, cute, harmless—not terrifyingly destructive. Patting removes the object's lethal purpose." Thus, a man who refused to pat the missile might have his manhood called into question and at the same time might crack open the delicate shell inside of which his male companions lived their militarized lives. A woman who openly refused to pat the missile would most likely be dismissed as "hysterical."[48]

William Broad has reported on another civilian subculture of the masculinized military, the Lawrence Livermore National Laboratories in California. Livermore is the site of the most esoteric research for the Strategic Defense Initiative (SDI, or "Star Wars"), research which is scheduled to continue into the mid-1990s. Broad is not a feminist. He is barely curious about varieties of masculinity; the women whose less dramatic labors or emotional validation sustain SDI research and political lobbying are left off his canvas. Yet he does provide us with an inside look at how these male scientists talk, dream, and joke.[49] Few of them are married or have girlfriends. Most of them seem to live at their computer terminals, except when they take breaks to drink cokes or consume great quantities of ice cream. They don't appear to be particularly violent; they don't wear army surplus fatigues; they don't have rifles mounted on the backs of their pickup trucks. They have a penchant for boyish pranks. And they seem to thrive on competition and to see both the scientific world and the larger world as places where rivalry is the norm.

Their cherishing of competition is the ideological trait that makes them likely candidates for militarization. The older men who recruited these young scientists in the 1980s deliberately played upon their competitiveness to attract them to SDI weapons research. Still, they appear unlikely candidates for military basic training: they are too contemptuous of collective discipline, and their notions of action seem more cerebral than physical. However, they clearly find deep reassurances of their own manhood in the militarized science they do. And federal decision-makers who have imagined militarization to be the bedrock of American security need for those ice cream–consuming pranksters to feel those reassurances. Their need for them, as much as grant money, is what makes this generation of male scientists militarizable. Admirers of Sylvester Stallone might disparage the Livermore men as "nerds," but their notions of masculinity have been no less essential for militarizing American society than those of jet bomber pilots or M16-wielding "grunts."

The men who lure scientists into militarized laboratory communities appear to have notions about their recruits' sexual needs not shared by their army or navy counterparts. For instance, institutionalized homophobia doesn't seem to send off warning sirens when a young male engineer eschews girls. Nor do the men responsible for the morale of the Livermore scientists seem to think they require brothels and massage parlors just outside the laboratory's gates. Why hasn't anyone in the Defense Department suggested that these "Star Warriors" be sent to VD classes as their soldier counterparts are?

Richard Rhodes's new history of the making of the U.S. atomic bomb has been glowingly described as exhaustive and comprehensive.[50] But when it comes to the gendered dynamics of this militarized scientific enterprise and the peculiar community it fostered in the New Mexican desert, Rhodes's curiosity suddenly wanes. Not only are the roles that women played outside his realm of historical curiosity, but so too are the principal male actors' notions about themselves as men interacting with women and with other men. For instance, Rhodes slips into a light-hearted section on the ways members of the Los Alamos community entertained themselves with a tantalizingly brief account of an official debate over prostitution and "loose women." The discovery that regular visits were being made by men to the single women's barracks had set off an official discussion about the dangers of venereal disease, the needs of men, and the authority of the army and of civilian officials. Referring to the visiting routine, "We did decide to continue it," one official tells Rhodes. But we learn nothing more. Rhodes and his interviewee seem to share some unspoken, cross-generational, masculinized understanding that, even in the Manhattan Project, "men would be men." That understanding shuts the door on what might have been a revealing exploration into the ways in which militarized male scientists match or diverge from their infantry counterparts. Rhodes's failure of curiosity rests on assumptions about the sexual needs of male scientists. It may be that militarized masculinity takes one form when men are socialized into the world of nuclear warfare planning and quite a different form when men are socialized into the world of what is euphemistically called conventional warfare.

Still to be written are feminist descriptions of how masculinity—and thus femininity—are constructed within companies and factories reliant on defense contracts. From Hilary Wainwright we do have a sense that at least some British women working today in the usually feminized electrical units of defense factories do not seem to receive the ideological or monetary rewards that their male counterparts do from working on weapons. However, they may be encouraged to see themselves as supporting "our boys," like some sort of surrogate militarized mothers.[51] But what of white-collar middle managers and senior executives—the largely masculinized management strata of aerospace, armaments, and electronics companies who have made conscious decisions to pursue local and foreign defense contracts? Perhaps their sense of manhood is boosted by their involvement with such products and by regular contact with military officers.

The wives and lovers of these men have to make adjustments in order to support and validate these choices. Marriages can be strained when husbands become more and more involved in secret work, when their business days are shaped by state security concepts, or when their professional colleagues are military professionals. When a corporate contractor's wife refuses to make adjustments in her marriage to accommodate such steps toward deeper militarization, she may send small tremors through her country's military-industrial complex.

It would be a mistake, I think, to imagine that because each one of these cogs in the increasingly complex military machine seems to be shaped by notions of masculinity, all the parts automatically work together in smooth precision. "Grunts," "nerds," "defense intellectuals," "captains of industry," "the brass"—each role may be masculinized and militarized. But common transformations may not create bonds of trust or respect. William Broad's SDI scientists and Carol Cohn's defense intellectuals both talk quite contemptuously of the military officers and the civilian politicians they deal with. Conversely, uniformed military men of various ranks often dismiss scientists and intellectuals as too removed from reality (as they see it). To a soldier, patting a missile is a far cry from firing it. It would not be surprising if some of this mutual derision were translated into comments about the other group's tenuous hold on manliness and failed relations with women.

.   .   .   .   .

Putting Rambo in his place and acknowledging varieties of masculinity bound by time, culture, and subculture need not induce intellectual paralysis. Such an effort could show us what any government serious about demilitarization needs to do. Looking closely at the varieties of ways in which masculinity can be militarized may shed light on tensions and contradictions within those military systems, exposing them as less impermeable, more fragile.

Moreover, militarizing societies do not all construct the same divisions of labor or the same varietes of masculinity to sustain their military systems. The former Soviet Union, France, Britain, Israel, and South Africa may come closest to replicating the current American masculinized and militarized division of labor. Each of these states has been trying to build its own scientific and industrial military infrastructure. Each prides itself on its capacity to absorb information and make plans.

But are Russian weapons engineers afraid that other men will call them nerds if they carry calculators clipped to their belts? Are Israeli defense intellectuals as prone as their American counterparts are to looking down upon uniformed military men? Israeli men working as engineers in the country's large weapons industry are said to sympathize with their male counterparts in uniform because the engineers, too, serve as military reservists until the age of fifty-five. Not many societies, however, have a conscription system that promotes this empathy between men socialized into different forms of militarized masculinity.

Each country may be distinguished by its own brand of tension between militarized masculinities. Consequently, different groups of

women may be pressured to play somewhat different roles to reduce or
mask those tensions and keep the military machine running smoothly.
We scarcely know yet how to describe the marriage politics that help to
sustain the military-industrial complex of the United States, much less
those of Italy, South Africa, or Brazil.

.   .   .   .   .

Militarization is a tricky process. It occurs both during those periods
of intense militarization that we call "war" and during the periods that
we refer to as "peace"—or as "prewar" or "postwar" or "interwar."
Militarization is occurring when any part of a society becomes controlled by or dependent on the military or on military values. Virtually
anything can be militarized. Toys, marriage, scientific research, university curricula, motherhood—each can be militarized. Fatherhood, AIDS,
immigration, racism, fashion, journalism, and comic strips can be militarized. Even gay rights can be militarized. Each one of these processes
involves the transformation of meanings and relationships. Rarely does
the transformation happen without the use of public power and authority. Occasionally the process is reversed. American children seemed to
demilitarize their play in the early 1970s, as evidenced by the sharp fall
in sales of G.I. Joe dolls. Chilean women are consciously working to
demilitarize their children's play in the 1990s, turning children away
from the games of hiding and torturing they learned during the Pinochet
years.[52]

Those American, Canadian, European, and Japanese scientists who
are refusing in the 1990s to take part in SDI research are trying to
demilitarize their professions. Women in any country who refuse to see
their sons accept conscription or voluntarily enlist in the military as a
valid way to cope with civilian unemployment are taking steps to
demilitarize motherhood. University teachers who encourage their students to assign as much analytical "seriousness" to pacifist movements
as to national security policymaking are demilitarizing at least a small
part of their curriculum.

Whether one is tracing militarizing or demilitarizing social processes, one must chart how women and men in any particular historical setting comprehend what it means to be "manly" and what it means to be "feminine." Not only have government and military officials been affected by their own perceptions of manliness and femininity, but many of them have also attempted to design policies to ensure that civilians and soldiers relate to one another in those gendered ways that ease the complicated process of militarization.

Chapter Four

Bananas Militarized
and Demilitarized

When I decided the time had come to try to make feminist sense of U.S. foreign policy's penchant for militarization, Central America was the first region I turned to. It was the mid-1980s. Many women active in feminist and nonfeminist peace groups were becoming alarmed as they learned from Central Americans just how completely their communities' social fabrics were being unraveled by the destructive alliances formed between local elites and Washington policymakers in the name of Cold War anti-Communism. Yet both the scale of the violence and the potency of the militarizing alliances loomed so large that feminist questioning seemed beside the point. Not that feminists didn't suspect that the politics of masculinity and femininity were indeed at work. Rather, the mid-1980s political environment was such that it was hard—risky even—to insist that those feminist hunches get a hearing at Central America peace meetings and rallies.

Now, almost ten years later, when Americans' memories of the Grenada invasion are fading, Panama has disappeared from the television screen, and cease-fire agreements are altering the political landscapes of Nicaragua and El Salvador, and potentially Guatemala as well, there is the danger that, once again, feminist questioning will not be taken seriously. This time it will be the rush of demilitarization rather than the momentum of militarization that may dull feminist curiosity. Demilitarization may tempt people concerned with Washington's Central America policy to disregard the reliance of that policy on peculiar relationships between women and men and the relation of each to the post–Cold War international system.

Is there a feminist analysis of the 1992 Salvadoran cease-fire agreement? Does the new, autonomous organizing of Nicaraguan women reveal something important about political life in that postrevolutionary, post–civil war society? Is the American government's current drive to construct a "continental" market a post–Cold War strategy that depends on the continued feminization of cheap labor?

Yes. The answer to all three questions is Yes. During the height of the militarization of the 1980s, the reward for paying attention to women's lives was a clearer vision of how that devastating process really worked. So, too, today: if one takes women's experiences seriously, one has a much better chance of understanding the consequences of the peculiar politics of Central America's demilitarization. That clearer understanding, in turn, will throw light on the new power relationships between the United States and each of the countries in the region. Demilitarization as it is currently progressing in the 1990s may not be putting much of a dent in the patriarchal quality of either Central American political life or U.S. foreign policy.

Before looking more closely at the gendered politics of Central American demilitarization, however, we need to recall the ways in which feminist curiosity provided a launchpad for making new sense of the 1980s militarization. For that militarized era wasn't just the best-forgotten "bad old days." It was also a time that compelled Central American women and men to relate to one another in ways that shape the sexual politics of today's demilitarization.

ANTI-IMPERIALISM WITH BLINDERS ON

When one finishes writing a book, one inevitably feels a curious mix of elation and uneasiness—elation from managing to come full circle in one's thinking, and uneasiness because it's almost certain that important puzzles have been left glaringly unresolved. Thus, in 1983, when I completed *Does Khaki Become You?*—an exploration into how and why militaries attempt to control women—I had a sense that it might be more than just military operations that were gendered; perhaps it was the whole network of power and dependence we call "the international political economy." But at the time I had neither the insight nor the nerve to pursue that hunch. For the moment, I left explaining the patterns of global power and profit to those historians and social theorists who continued to deem gender (including their own) irrelevant.

The well-known commentators who then occupied the center stage of almost any critical discussion of imperialism or foreign interventionism apparently believed that there was little to be gained by looking at women's lives. Emmanuel Walterstein, Walter Rodney, Samir Amin, Perry Anderson, Noam Chomsky—some of these men were from what then was called the First World, and others were from the Third. Together, they had helped fashion the intellectual tools many of us still use to explain how Exxon, NATO, the International Monetary Fund (IMF), and Hollywood have come to distort relations between the world's rich and poor. But these men almost never asked whether it mattered that the Third World's investment-attracting cheap labor was made cheap by being feminized. They scarcely ever wondered whether the IMF's standard package of austerity measures, imposed on Third World governments, changed the power relations between women and men in these countries. Moreover, they did not seem to believe that the expansion of Third World militaries through foreign arms sales and the influx of military aid depended at all on changing notions of what constitutes "masculine" behavior, either in those countries or in the donor countries. As these writers' eager audience, we virtually never were prompted to figure out what the connections might be between international debt, foreign investment, and militarism on the one hand and rape, prostitution, housework, and wife battering on the other hand. The message one came away with from these books was: the former are inherently "serious" and "political"; the latter are "private" and probably trivial.

Yet surely everything we have revealed in the last three decades of the women's movement suggests that we should be wary of any analysis or any organizing strategy that presumes that economic and emotional relations between women and men are outside the pale of serious politics. By the mid-1980s, in fact, many women in left-wing and social justice movements dealing with domestic issues were challenging male activists who were most comfortable leaving it to the women to take up "women's issues," as if those questions were peripheral to such a movement's central thesis. They had become convinced that if one asked "Where are the women, and what are they doing?" entire campaigns would be more firmly grounded in political reality and would have a much better chance of achieving their public goals. Only belatedly, however, were many of these same women starting to imagine what a distinctly feminist analysis of international politics would look like.

GENDERING A BANANA REPUBLIC

Bananas. Sugar. Coffee. Cotton. Limes. Cocoa. Rice. These are the raw products for which the countries of Central America and the Caribbean have been famous. Each product has its own history. Most have been nurtured not just by the region's warm climate and rich soil but also by foreign capital and by hierarchies of class and skin color—and gender. When militaries have been sent into these countries it has usually been to protect those hierarchies and the rewards those at the top have garnered from their control of sugar, coffee, bananas, and other products for export. In the last two decades other, less traditional industries have been added: tourism, cattle raising, melons and broccoli farming, garment-making, electronics assembly, oil refining, and most recently, office work.

Both the more traditional and the recently introduced products have been enmeshed in global struggles from the outset. The colonizing governments (Spain, Britain, the Netherlands, the United States, France) and the internationally competitive companies (Gulf and Western, Tate and Lyle, Bookers, United Fruit, Geest, Alcan, Kaiser, Coca Cola, Del

Monte, and Dole) have waxed and waned in their fortunes, have bar-
gained and fought each other, and have withdrawn from some places in
order to intervene in others. The constant has been the extreme vulnerability of the region's local peoples to decisions made outside their own
societies, though often with the collaboration of members of their own
national elites.

Where are the women? Most historical accounts we have of these
external decisions and of how Caribbean and Central American people
have tried to cope with—or at times resist—them are written as though
the principals concerned never had gender on their minds. But is this
true? For instance, new work being done in this country by African-
American women historians suggests that sexist strategies shaped the
ways in which racism was developed to rationalize and organize slave
labor. European plantation managers constructed gendered labor divisions in ways that guaranteed that the cultivation of sugar and cotton,
for instance, would generate profits for the overseas companies and their
local allies. In those Central American societies where colonists' use of
African slaves was less prevalent, racism nonetheless was wielded in
order to create domestic stratifications of color that served to coopt the
Hispanicized peasant and exploit the Indian. The formulation and—
even more interesting for us today—the replication of these divisions of
Central American labor were accomplished with the help of sexism.
Laws governing marriage and child custody, policies to guarantee men's
waged labor, rationalizations for missionary work—all were crucial
tools for economic exploitation and colonial order, and all leaned heavily on conscious presumptions about masculinity and femininity.

These early uses of sexist strategies have had lasting effects. They have
helped to sustain patriarchal notions within the black, Latino, and Indian communities, notions which present obstacles to effective political
action even a century or more after slavery's abolition. The present-day
politics of Jamaica, Trinidad, Dominica, and Guyana demonstrate the
legacy of gendered racist divisions of plantation labor. Thus, theorizing
about late twentieth-century Caribbean or Central American "plantation societies" will be shaky at best if it is carried on as if women and

men experienced slavery in identical ways or as if the politics of postslavery communities were free of the legacy of the colonists' patriarchal strategizing.

We have heard a lot about the potency of machismo ideology, about how women in the insurgent movements of El Salvador, Guatemala, and Nicaragua have struggled against the presumption of male privilege inside their own organizations. We need to go further, however, and ask how machismo has supported the racist stratifications on which most of the coffee, sugar, and banana companies have depended for their own operations. We often proceed as if ideologies of male dominance and ideologies of Indian inferiority each have a place in Central American history, yet never the twain shall meet. Of course, they do meet. Moreover, in most of our political organizing it is racism that gets treated with more seriousness, as if Hispanicization and its complementary exploitation of Indians is what "really" explains how profits are squeezed out of sugar cane, banana trees, and coffee beans. Machismo's role in the process is hardly considered by the analysts of international economy. Or, if it is, it is not discussed in ways that could tell us how sexual divisions of labor have been used to support racial and class divisions of labor.

Take the banana. The banana's history is embedded in the history of European colonial expansion and, later, of North American neocolonial intervention. It is also tied integrally to the ways in which women's relations to men have been shaped by local governments and foreign companies, bolstered from time to time by U.S. military intervention. So the banana may be a good place to start in our fashioning of a feminist analysis of American militarization of Central America in the 1980s.[1]

The banana is not native to Central America. Its original home was Southeast Asia. By the 1400s the banana had spread westward to become a basic food on the Guinean coast of Africa. When Spanish slavers began raiding the coast, capturing Africans, and shipping them to the West Indies and South America, they started shipping bananas as well. The banana, then, entered this hemisphere as the slavers' choice of a cheap and popular African staple to feed enslaved women and men.

The yellow bananas familiar to North American consumers were not developed as a distinct variety until the nineteenth century. They were first served at the homes of wealthy Bostonians in 1875. The United Fruit Company, which over the next century came to behave like a surrogate state in much of Central America, grew out of the American popularization of this humble globe-trotting fruit. Its marketing success wove an invisible but crucial political link of interdependence between the women of North America and the women of Central America.

In the 1940s United Fruit took the lead in launching a brand name for its own bananas: Chiquita. Standard Fruit, its chief competitor, followed quickly on its heels with its own brand name: Cabana. Thus began a marketing competition to win the allegiance of American and European housewives and their local grocers. Today the marketing director's dream remains persuading predominantly female consumers that bananas from one company are better than bananas from another company.

The conventional way of thinking about how and why it was "banana republics" that American officials wanted to preserve—by force, if necessary—in Central America focuses on the class alliances made by United Fruit and Del Monte executives with the local political and economic elite, on the one hand, and with Washington policymakers on the other. All of these players have had a common stake in keeping banana workers' wages low and their political consciousness undeveloped. The North American or European consumer-housewife is scarcely imagined.

And who, exactly, *are* the workers whose political mobilization has struck such fear into the hearts of banana plantation executives and their local allies? Photographs of Honduran banana worker union members always show lots of men. Do only men work on the major banana plantations, or is it only the male workers who are employed in the banana industry in situations that allow them to unionize? Where are the women? Women do work in sectors that make bananas profitable for this triple alliance of elites, but the waged work they do—cleaning and packing—is so marginalized that they develop a different sort of political consciousness and are excluded from the unions by their fathers and brothers, who imagine their own conflicts with management to be more "political," more "serious," than those of the women. Other Central American women do not receive any wages for the work they do to sustain the plantations of United Fruit or Del Monte. Instead, they are at home doing unpaid subsistence farming, child care, and cooking so that the men in their families can take seasonal plantation jobs.

By the 1980s, feminists in scores of industrialized and Third World countries had begun to reveal how even those mining and agricultural operations that recruit only male workers nonetheless depend on women's work. For if women were not relegated to doing the hard but unpaid work of subsistence farming and household maintenance, the companies would not be able to pay their male workers such low wages. The unpaid work that women do—and the patriarchal assumptions on which that work depends—allows for the survival and reproduction of those paid workers.

Thus, the banana republics that U.S. militarization was intended to sustain have relied on patriarchal political arrangements in at least two ways. First, the colonially seeded culture of machismo serves to legitimize local class and racial stratifications; that is, the subjugation of all women helps perpetuate the inequalities among the country's men. Many men who are denied access to decent jobs or to public decision-making continue to feel powerful as long as they can control the women in their daily lives. Second, the gender, class, and ethnic strategies of labor and profit that foreign companies have used serve to perpetuate low wages and attenuate union organizing. These propositions operate together to sustain the kind of internationally dependent, economically lopsided, militarized society we have come to call a "banana republic."

Economic changes in the region during the 1970s and 1980s were initiated by foreign corporations and governments and were designed to resecure their hold on the region. In part because of growing militarization and its resultant social unrest, and in part as a global, in-house strategy, some of the largest banana companies have threatened to cut back their Central American operations. Hondurans and Costa Ricans have been told that countries such as Ecuador and the Philippines now look greener for banana operations. These corporate decisions have been reported in terms of their effects on unemployment in already-fragile Central American economies. Scarcely anything has been said about what they have meant for relations between women and men.

In response to the last decade's global corporate reorganization, some Honduran peasant women have tried to develop cash-generating projects such as making straw hats and processing cashew nuts. This local innovation needs to be seen as a strategy to redistribute power within an internationalized political economy. The women who have begun these small cooperatives, if successful, could make the banana republic system of dependent politics a bit less tenable. The Honduran women starting to make straw hats and process cashews through their cooperatives intend to reduce their earlier dependence on exploitative middlemen— the *coyotes*—and to gain some social autonomy as women. The men in these women's families are mostly unemployed banana workers. Women, as mothers and wives, joined women's straw hat and cashew nut cooperatives in part to offset the resultant decline in household income. In the long run, the banana companies' layoffs and the women's cooperatives' income production could alter more than simply the household distribution of influence. Together, these changes could diminish the political prominence of the Honduran banana workers' union. If so, will Honduran women thereafter demand a larger say in leftist political organizations?

It is reasonable to predict that whatever change or resistance to change flows from these twin economic changes will be played out not in the public plaza but in thousands of peasant homes. Any commentator who treats a "workers' family" or a "rural household" as monolithic, who hesitates to step over the threshold out of some naive notion of where the international system ends, risks missing real political transformation.

Central American women fashioned their own critiques during the last decade to challenge the conventional masculinist notions that gender was politically irrelevant and that women were politically valuable only as auxiliaries. Jamaica's populist women's theater collective, Sistren, created a play about women sugar workers.[2] They used both the script and the very act of putting on the drama to remind the country's poor women (and foreigners as well) that, although Jamaican postindependence politics were dominated by men, in part because it was men who had led and filled the ranks of the preindependence militant sugar workers' union, even the sugar industry, had not been an all-male affair. Women, too, had worked to generate profits for Tate & Lyle, the giant British company. But they and their labor were made politically invisible in ways that continue to obstruct Jamaican women's entry into the nation's political life.

Similarly, before the U.S. military invasion, Grenadan women had been organizing to make their work in the cocoa industry (a principal export sector) more visible. Grenadan women in the revolutionary movement began to insist that the men take their work seriously and to develop government policies which would dismantle the sexual divisions of labor on which the island's cocoa business has relied. These important developments in sexual politics were cut short by the landing of the U.S. Marines. The postinvasion Grenadan society of the late 1980s thereafter was "developed" on a stark sexual division of labor, with the expansion of the tourist industry and the (not terribly successful) attempt by Washington officials to "secure" Grenada by inviting American light industries to establish cost-cutting assembly plants there. Both tourism and light assembly are notoriously feminized industries. The chief political difference between them and the older cocoa industry has been that in the former industries it has been a lot harder to make women's cheap labor contribution invisible.

CHAMBERMAIDS CLEANING AMERICA'S "BACKYARD"

As landlessness increases in Central America, women and men have been driven to make quite different choices about how to survive. There is no reason to believe a priori that landlessness is any less gendered than plantation labor is. One indication that it is not is the rising numbers of women migrating from the countryside to the towns to seek jobs as low-paid seamstresses and, if they are less lucky, as domestic workers. According to one estimate, 64 percent of all women working for wages in Guatemala City today are employed as domestic workers. Many of these women are Indian women working for Latino families. Many are also the sole caretakers of children.[3]

Among them was the young Rigoberta Menchú. This Guatemalan Indian woman, who was awarded the 1992 Nobel Peace Prize for leading a movement for Latin American indigenous people's human rights, learned some of her lessons about how a military-backed regime could serve white landowning class interests not only from watching her peasant father's struggles to organize fellow landless Indians, but also from her experience working as a maid for a wealthy white family in Guatemala City. The awarding of the Nobel Peace Prize to Rigoberta Menchú provided an excellent chance for mainstream journalists to ask "Where are the women?" Few of them took advantage of that opportunity. Most of the journalists covering the Swedish Academy's announcement seemed to feel most comfortable treating Menchú as an ungendered Indian rights advocate. That she had worked as a maid, that she had witnessed her mother's rape, that before she became well-known she had received support from women's groups in other countries—all of these realities which helped explain Rigoberta Menchú's own politicization and political analysis appeared to make many people in the media uncomfortable. And so an opportunity for serious understanding of the workings of militarization was lost.[4]

The fact that more Latin American women were working in domestic servant jobs than in any other type of waged employment in the 1980s was an important clue to what kinds of class transformations were occurring in the wake of changes in the international economy. Having household servants became one of the most visible signs of having joined the region's middle class. The exodus of more and more peasant women from the countryside, where they could no longer support themselves and their children, to the towns, where they had to accept low-paid jobs with minimal workers' rights, allowed more and more Central Americans with relatively secure incomes to imagine that they had arrived in the middle class. For the man of this class, it was an arrival that was potentially accompanied by a peculiarly masculine privilege: sexual access to a young rural woman under his own roof who had only minimal resources with which to resist his demands. For the woman of this growing middle class, the role of employer may have subverted any sense of shared destiny with the poor women in her own country.

Simultaneously, prostitution was being integrated into this gendered and globalized political economy. A woman working as a domestic servant was frequently fired by her employers if she became pregnant. If the male employer got her pregnant, he might fire her to cover up his own actions. The women of the house, on the other hand, might fire her as a way to deal with her husband's "indiscretions," turning her anger on the victim. Those women, as well as women from the countryside who were never lucky enough to find jobs (or who found jobs in a factory assembling bras or transistor radios only to be laid off soon afterwards), still had children or parents to support. Thus, they often turned to the income generator of last resort, prostitution.

To understand what changes were occurring in Central America during the era of Cold War militarization, therefore, we need to go beyond simply talk of "landless peasants" or "peasant mobilization." What kind of politics did a woman learn from being the sole caretaker of someone else's child? What understandings about power came out of working as an Indian maid in a Latino home? At what point did sexual harassment by the father or son of that household begin to inspire resistance—resistance supported by whom?

In the Caribbean, as well, more women resorted to domestic work during this era. Some island women sought jobs as domestic servants in their own countries. Thousands of women from the 1970s onward migrated to Canada, the U.S., and Europe in search of ways to support themselves and their children. Some of them started to overcome the isolating effects of such work to speak out and to organize politically. In the United States one such organization includes both Caribbean and Central American women, as well as U.S.–born Latina and black women.[5] What would our political analysis look like if we took these domestic workers' political messages and organizing efforts as seriously as we did those of male activists and social theorists? Militarization occurs in large part because governing regimes cannot keep the lid on social unrest stemming from maldevelopment. The growth in domestic service represents women's private coping with the maldevelopment which gave the elite in several of the region's countries undeserved breathing space.

Even more striking than the increase of domestic work in this era was the emergence of the tourist industry. Tourism was a partner for regional anti-Communism. A country which could be made hospitable to North American and Western European tourism, it was imagined, was less open to the appeals of leftist revolutionaries and their Soviet sponsors.

In the 1980s, tourism became the Caribbean response to the world's declining demand for cane sugar. Sometimes the shift was explicit, as in the mid-1980s in the Dominican Republic, where Gulf and Western, the hydra-headed American conglomerate, sold off more than two hundred thousand acres of sugarcane fields to American entrepreneurs, who planned to turn their newly purchased land into tourist havens. By 1984, tourism had leapt ahead of sugar to become the Dominican Republic's top earner of foreign exchange.

Typically, this rapid rise of foreign-capitalized tourism was condemned by critics for turning the countries of the Caribbean into "nations of busboys." The very character of these sprawling Holiday Inn chains, in this vision, deskilled their workers; it institutionalized racism and kept crucial decision-making prerogatives in the hands of overseas executives. Furthermore, the lengths to which Holiday Inn or Club Med managers would go to make their American, Canadian, French, and British patrons feel comfortable, with imported foods and familiar decor, could only siphon off whatever foreign exchange the friendly regimes may have hoped to keep for themselves.

But was it a "nation of busboys" that was replacing the region's plantation society? Was this the most accurate way for us to make sense of the kind of transformation that was taking place in Grenada, Jamaica,

Barbados, the Dominican Republic, and other countries that the Reagan administration was trying to draw into its security orbit? Fear of becoming a "nation of busboys" may have raised masculine anxieties to the status of a nationalist cause, but it may not have reflected the actual gender dynamics of tourism.

Observers who bothered to put on their gender glasses noted that tourism was a blatantly feminized industry in its lowest ranks. Approximately 75 percent of the 250,000 Caribbean tourism workers in the 1980s were women.[6] Many of these women sought hotel jobs in the wake of agricultural decline. Cash income had become a desperate necessity for women because it was women, even more than men, who had to find daily ways of coping with their government's decisions to succumb to IMF pressure to cut public services and raise food prices.[7]

In other words, one way we can make sense of how the Reagan administration transformed U.S. influence in the Caribbean is to trace the connections between the decline in foreign-funded agribusiness, the growth of tourism, and the imposition of U.S. control. It appears that each of these trends required that Caribbean women play certain roles— as workers, as "copers." When they refused to play those roles, Washington's security plan for the region faltered.

"NIMBLE FINGERS" FOR THE COLD WAR

Light industry was the newest economic sector to be opened up in the Caribbean and Central America during the last decade. Much of this development was based on the lessons derived from Puerto Rico's earlier Operation Bootstrap, a formula that depended in no small measure on forced sterilization and making women's wages cheap. If observers concerned with the militarization of the Caribbean paid any attention to Puerto Rico, however, they usually concentrated on its American military bases, such as Roosevelt Roads. But such a focus may have defined U.S. Cold War security policy too narrowly. Military basing always needs to be understood through its connections to a security-driven political economy. And to make sense of feminized industrialization as a theme in the United States government's security scenario for the region, we need to learn a lot more about the political history of Puerto Rican women.

"Light industry," such as was first promoted in Puerto Rico, usually encompasses labor-intensive forms of manufacture such as toy- and garment-making, food processing, and electronics assembly. Taking a page out of the textile industry's history book, contemporary executives of light industry have defined assembly jobs as "unskilled"—requiring "merely" a high tolerance for repetition, without loss of precision—and thus low-waged. The ideal job for a woman.

Obsessed with a Cold War and imagining Nicaragua and Cuba to be mere front men for Soviet power, the Reagan administration urged friendly regimes of what they began, misleadingly, to call the Caribbean Basin (which included Central America and Colombia) to accept more light-industry foreign investment. The aim of the Caribbean Basin Initiative (CBI) was not so much the promotion of Caribbean economic development or even of U.S. corporate profits as the guarantee of a security alliance between those weaker regimes and the United States. The glue? Economic dependency.

Yet this security scheme ultimately could not work unless the local regimes and U.S. investors could attract women workers. Attracting them would depend, in turn, on sustaining myths of masculinity, femininity, motherhood, skill, and family. Together, these five conceptions, if properly controlled, could make and keep women's labor cheap. In contrast, women who wrote plays about battering, women who risked overseas migration, women who unionized, women who demanded more training, and women who saw single motherhood as a political category were not the sorts of women who would guarantee the success of Reagan's Caribbean Basin Initiative and the security objectives the CBI was designed to serve.

Thanks to the wonders—and the cost-effectiveness—of satellite communications, U.S. executives during the Reagan era began to look outside the United States for office workers. International lending agencies such as the World Bank and the IMF were enthusiastic. A Washington-based organization called the "Free Zone Authority" urged Jamaica's Seaga regime to open up a word processing export facility, a "teleport," at a location that had the added attraction of being only a stone's throw from Jamaica's tourist mecca, Montega Bay. In nearby Barbados, a hundred women were sitting at rows of computers entering three hundred thousand ticket reservations that flowed in from a single U.S. airline every day. In the same building, other women were processing telephone books, insurance claims, and pornographic novels for foreign companies. Their average wage was only $2.50, which was $7.00 less than the wage paid to women in the U.S. doing comparable work. But to many of the Barbadian women, not only did the wage seem attractive compared with the wages available in other sectors of the Barbados economy, but also the job seemed like work that would earn more respect for a woman than, for instance, being a chambermaid for a tourist hotel.[8]

It was the feminization of cheap labor, plus the legacy of the English language in the postcolonial countries of the Caribbean, that made this extension of America's global reach attractive. As one of the boosters of offshore office work told a journalist, "These workers are really good. . . . Typing skills are impressive, and accuracy is about 99 percent."[9]

Diana Roos, researcher for the national office of the 9 to 5 organization, however, reported that American executives hadn't stopped siteshopping. They continued to compare the costs, productivity, and controllability of three groups of women office workers: American women employed at the companies' own offices; American women contracted to do office work as home work in the suburbs (without the costs of overhead and in a setting that is harder to unionize); and, finally, Caribbean and Asian (especially Indian) women working offshore.[10]

For American feminists, these corporate strategies presented at least two interlocking challenges. First, politically active office workers and their supporters had to find ways to understand these global maneuvers that didn't play into the hands of divide-and-rule union busters. Second, office workers and their supporters here and in countries such as Barbados, the Bahamas, and Jamaica had to try to get the attention of women and men active in the peace and anti-intervention movements.

Activists in those campaigns would have to mobilize their energies with an awareness of how women in the United States and other countries of the region were being linked to one another in ways that could serve to smooth the way for Caribbean militarization; recognizing those links could permit them to work together to subvert Washington's grand security scheme.

BASE INSTINCTS

A foreign military base shares some striking similarities with a multinational company's overseas branch. Both camouflage their functional interests with talk of "family" and "community." Both rely on the energies of local residents but use alien cultural presumptions to organize their work lives. And both, while concentrated in compact physical spaces, spill their gendered consequences far beyond the base or factory gates.

Feminists in the Philippines, South Korea, and Thailand have described in detail just how U.S. military bases distorted the sexual politics of the countries. A military base wasn't only an installation for servicing bombers, fighters, and aircraft carriers or a launchpad for aggressive forays into surrounding territories. It was also—and always had been—a package of presumptions about male soldiers' sexual needs and about the local community's resources for satisfying those needs. Massage parlors had, over the years, become as integral to Subic Bay (the mammoth, recently closed U.S. naval base in the Philippines) as its dry docks. We have yet to possess comparable sexual histories of the U.S. military bases at Roosevelt Roads, in the Panama Canal Zone, at Guantánamo Bay, and at Key West. Until we have such histories, we won't have a realistic picture of just how militarization of the Caribbean and Central America has been entrenched in the twentieth century. We won't know how sexuality was used to wage the Cold War in this corner of the globe.

Still, we have some clues. In the 1980s, Honduras was the newest regional site for a U.S. military base. If Honduran women had met with

Thai and Filipina women, what common stories would they have had to tell? What light would those stories shed on what it takes to militarize international relations?[11]

Lucy Kosimar, a freelance reporter, wrote an account of how sexual politics in Honduras were being fashioned so as to meet the alleged needs of the U.S. military there.[12] In 1985, Kosimar went to visit the shanty town of brothels that had grown up near Palmerole, one of the bases used by the U.S. military in its series of "Big Pine" joint maneuvers, which were intended to preserve U.S. Cold War control over Central America. She found Honduran women serving as prostitutes to both Honduran and U.S. soldiers. Her report revealed in a microcosm what Honduran public health officials have noted more generally: that there had been a notable rise in the cases of sexually transmitted diseases in Honduras in the three years since the start of U.S. military buildup. Hondurans refer to a particularly virulent form of STD as "Vietnam Rose." While the nickname once again wrongly blamed the victim, it suggested that Hondurans saw the Vietnamization of their country in terms of sexuality as well as in terms of anti-Communist ideology, money, and weaponry.

Lucy Kosimar let us hear from some of the people behind the statistics. First there were the Honduran women—as young as sixteen years old—who had been virtually kidnapped and brought to the brothels as captives. One woman who tried to escape was caught and returned by Honduran policemen. There were other women who, on the surface, seemed to have come to the brothels freely, although in fact they had been driven by their need for money. These women split their fees with the owners of the shabby cantinas where they conducted their business. But many of the women living on the fringes of the U.S. base fell somewhere in between these two groups. They had been drawn so deeply into debt to the men who supplied their food and minimal housing that they were never able to pay off their debts and thus regain their freedom.

Kosimar found that local policemen acted as enforcers of the prostitution system. The police, in turn, were controlled by Honduran army officers. This control reflected the country's then-growing militarization, the increasing capacity of the military to intimidate other Honduran officials. The U.S. soldiers involved were from both the enlisted and officer ranks. It may have been the construction of militarized masculinity that was most responsible for U.S. enlisted men's belief that one of the prerogatives due an American male GI overseas was the sexual services of local women. However, whereas in Vietnam most American military women were nurses, in Honduras the U.S. field units included several dozen women soldiers. It is not clear whether their presence affected the men's assumptions of sexual prerogatives. The most common complaint from the women soldiers was that they had not been issued proper sanitary supplies. But where did these women soldiers go for their R and R when their male comrades headed for the cantinas?

It would be wrong to imagine that the sexual exploitation of local women was sustained solely by Honduran military intimidation and diffuse U.S. patriarchal culture. As is true in other base towns around the world, the system of militarized sexual relations required explicit American policy-making. Kosimar reported, for example, that U.S. army doctors from the Palmerole base routinely conducted medical exams on Honduran women working in the nearby brothels. Their job was to ensure that American male soldiers would have access to sex without jeopardizing the army's operational readiness.

COLD WAR RAPE

In our attempt to discover to what degree militarization is a gendered process—that is, how much of militarization is a process that won't work unless men accept certain norms of masculinity and women abide by certain strictures of femininity—we need to think more internationally about rape. About rape and the waging of the Cold War. Coupling them is no more far-fetched than coupling rape with World War II. The relationship is only unexamined. We also need to look closely at military recruitment, not only as it reveals masculinity, racism, and poverty at home, but also as it supports or weakens particular policies abroad. Third, we have to dig deeper into ideas about and roles of women in the

very ideology of national security. In what ways exactly was the gendering of each of these necessary for the U.S.-sponsored militarization of the
Caribbean and Central America in the 1980s?

I can only be suggestive here, but doing so might raise our level of
genuine political curiosity. For instance, there was minimal political
questioning about why rapes of civilian women by male soldiers became
so widespread in Central America. Typically, rape was listed among an
assortment of repressive acts, as if rape were not qualitatively different
in both its motivations and its repercussions. We still know surprisingly
little about why the government's male soldiers in Guatemala or the
contras' male insurgents in Nicaragua engaged in sexual assault on
women so insistently. These assaults might have been one more product
of masculinity militarized. Or they might have been the result of a
conscious command policy of intimidation. Were we witnessing men out
of control or men under control?

Women in countries as different as Guatemala, Bosnia, and Uganda
now have begun to ask questions: If rape was being used deliberately as
a tactic of intimidation, who was the ultimate target of that intimidation? Was rape used to intimidate the women themselves, or was the real
military target the rape victims' husbands, sons, and fathers, whose sense
of male honor is tied up in their capacity to protect "their" women?[13]

Guatemalan army commanders were quoted as saying that killing
Indian women and children was part of a deliberate strategy of counterinsurgency. The foundation of the Indian guerrillas' organization was
seen to be the family nucleus; therefore, whole families had to be mur-
dered or intimidated if the insurgency was to be crushed.[14] Perhaps there
was also a third target: the new male military recruit. Both the Guatemalan government forces and the Nicaraguan contra units depended on
unwilling young men. Were new recruits pressed to participate in rape
during military maneuvers as a technique for socializing them into a kind
of brutality, thereby severing their ties from their civilian compatriots?

During the past decade some Latin American feminists began to
theorize that masculinity was being reconstructed by some of the region's regimes in order that men would tolerate extreme forms of violent

behavior, and not simply to control particular women or particular men. Masculinity was being remade for the sake of controlling the society at large. Anti-Communism for these regimes, many of which are funded and advised by the U.S. government, implicitly required a form of patriarchy based on brutal misogyny.[15] Cold warriorism and rape were being woven into an intimate alliance.

To make sense of this form of anti-Communism, we have to listen more carefully to women who have been raped and the men in their families. We need to know when it was that rape politicized and mobilized women or men, and when it served instead to intimidate and silence—even shame—them. We have been much more comfortable analyzing when and how landlessness or plantation exploitation has politicized rural Central Americans. We have imagined sexual assault as either too horrifying or too "private" to be discussed in the same political breath as peasant impoverishment. It may well be that a woman who has herself suffered rape by a government soldier, or who has seen her mother or sister raped, will have thoughts about power and injustice that are rather different from those of her male comrades who either have not been politicized by rape at all or who have been only indirectly, as failed protectors, failed proprietors.

Then there are the gendered politics of military manpower. Upon hearing that, in the wake of the Grenadan invasion, the Barbados government was expanding its military "manpower," I found myself wondering about some things that in my prefeminist years might have appeared far removed from the Cold War or regional militarization. For instance, cricket: I wondered how it was that Barbadian standards of masculinity could be so transformed that the cricket player was overshadowed by the soldier (or the militarized policeman). Not all societies, and certainly not all of those in the Caribbean or Central America (e.g., Costa Rica) have so merged soldiering and manhood that they have become indistinguishable. True, it makes the military recruiter's task easier if most women and men in one's country believe that being a soldier proves a man's masculinity. But the two are analytically and historically separable. If they weren't, governments would not need to waste their legitimacy by trying to enforce conscription laws.

So when the Reagan administration set out to urge governments in the Caribbean and Central America to increase their numbers of soldiers, it was asking them to engage in some tricky cultural maneuvers. Unless those regimes could count on young men to accept conscription or enlist simply to escape the despair of unemployment or the threat of repression—and both of these motivations are available to Caribbean and Central American recruiters—they would also have to convince their male citizens that soldiering was the ultimate proof of manhood after all. They would also have to convince women in their countries that men who joined newly expanding armies were more genuinely "real men" than were the men who were able to get decent civilian jobs. What happened in the 1980s to Barbadian and Costa Rican women's beliefs about masculinity? Were they changing in ways that would grease the wheels of Washington's militarizing operations? If women in these countries resisted such cultural changes, then they may have become more alienated from their governments, and possibly from the men in their lives as well.

Finally, we could perhaps understand militarization of any region in any era better if we looked at how "national security" is gendered there and then. Feminists who have studied European and North American societies in wartime and militarized peacetime have discovered that men and women occasionally differ sharply about what they need to feel safe. These studies have also revealed how governments intent upon legitimizing their expanded powers have used propaganda emphasizing women's need for protection and men's duty to serve as protectors to win that legitimation.

There is strong reason to believe that some of the same efforts may have been needed in order for Caribbean and Central American regimes to gain their people's acceptance of larger "manpower" quotas, greater security budgets (for police as well as the military), wider emergency powers, and more foreign bases on their soil. Does this mean that the U.S.–fueled militarization of these countries depended on an even more entrenched version of machismo? This may not have been easy to guarantee in the 1980s. By that era, there were more women in these countries controlling their own fertility, raising children on their own, farming on their own, learning how to read and write for themselves, and joining crafts cooperatives.[16] These are not the sorts of experiences that encourage women to accept national security doctrines that portray them as mere objects of male protection.

Sometimes during this era when I thought of U.S. efforts to militarize Central America and the Caribbean I imagined a big map showing women in all these countries with arrows arising from some of us directed toward others of us. It was a diagram charting how the militarism of the United States and other countries needed us all to behave as women. But our "womanly" behavior had to be of several different, though complementary, sorts. To fulfill the goals of militarizers of the Cold War era, some women in the U.S. needed to feel protected by a massive arms buildup and by their sons and husbands in uniform. Wives of soldiers needed to accept the extra duties of household maintenance when their husbands were on maneuvers in Honduras, without worrying too much about the rumors they had heard about Honduran brothels. Other women in the U.S. (but not too many) needed to view the military as the place to prove their equality with men. And the bureaucratically sophisticated women inside the military did indeed use the invasions of both Grenada and Panama to expand the opportunities for American women soldiers. Militarizers depended on still other women in the U.S.—Latinas, maybe new arrivals from war-torn Central America—to work in Silicon Valley's electronics factories making the latest electronic weaponry, and needed these women to see their husbands and boyfriends answer the U.S. Army recruiter's invitation as a step toward acculturation.

In Central America and the Caribbean, militarization required women to work for low wages for foreign companies or to support those companies' low-paid male workers by performing family work that was rewarded with no pay at all. It also relied on women to do the stress-inducing juggling of household budgets so that the governments could cut their social service budgets in order to live up to agreements with the IMF. If local poor women couldn't manage these demanding tasks, or if they refused to privatize their economic struggles and chose instead to take to the streets, then U.S.–fostered militarization would be jeopardized by faltering local governments.

The more I concentrated on this imagined Cold War map, the denser the arrows became, and the subtler and more complex grew the connections between this hemisphere's women. We have just begun to understand which particular relations between women, and between women and men—in movements, in families, on military bases, on plantations—were the prerequisites for American-promoted military expansion in the name of anti-Communism.

MAKING FEMINIST SENSE OF A PEACE ACCORD

In 1991 Nicaraguan voters elected Violeta Barrios de Chamorro and her fourteen-party coalition, the National Opposition Union (UNO). Voters believed Chamorro's claim that only she, and not the ruling Sandinistas, could bring the country's civil war to an end. The following year a peace accord was signed in El Salvador. Each event has been seen as a landmark on the road to Central America's demilitarization. The U.S. government, newly confident in the wake of its successful invasion of Panama, its war in the Persian Gulf, and the fracturing of the Soviet Union, also seems less preoccupied with arming allies in its backyard. But demilitarization is always problematic. It calls for feminist monitoring as close as that required for militarization. Men and women do not turn into blandly ungendered "citizens," "peasants," "officials," "investors," and "workers" simply because the shooting has (almost) stopped.

There is a feminist lens through which to read any peace agreement. The El Salvador agreement reached in January 1992 between the military-supported government of President Alfredo Cristiani and the leadership of the Farabundo Martí National Liberation Front (FMLN) has three pledges at its center: first, to legitimate the rebels' political participation; second, to reduce and reform the government's military; and third, to reorganize the police. All three processes could potentially be carried out in ways that demasculinize Salvadoran public life. All three

could also be carried out in ways that *re*masculinize Salvadoran public—
and private—life.[17]

First, the police. Police are typically neglected by political commentators, especially those claiming to make sense of international politics.
However, feminists from India to France have made it abundantly clear
that women's relationships both to the state and its foreign allies and to
the individual men in their lives are shaped in large measure by the ways
in which police forces and policing operations are gendered. Precisely
because the intimidation and repression of women have been so central
to the Salvadoran government's waging of its eleven-year-long war
against the leftist insurgents, the postwar reorganization of the police
should be a process that empowers women. But will it be?

"Goodbye Treasury Police, goodbye National Guard," leftists and
their supporters sang in January 1992. They were bidding a joyful fare-
well to two of the most repressive and misogynist arms of the Salvadoran
police.[18] Following the peace accords, both forces have been legislated
out of existence. Six months after the signing of the accords, however,
there were reports that most of the eight thousand men who had formed
the two disbanded forces have now been incorporated into two new
units, the Border Police and the Military Police, which will form part of
the army.[19] There is no evidence that these men are being pressed to
rethink their masculinized relationships to the state or to its male and
female citizens. Creating a new, civilian-controlled, demilitarized police
force is a process that might recreate the links between masculinity and
the state—or, in an optimistic scenario, could loosen those links. The
architects of the new peace accord envision the majority of new police
officers as Salvadorans who have not been combatants on either side in
the civil war, although members of the existing police as well as members
of the FMLN guerrillas will be eligible to join. Women as well as men
can apply. Whether women will be seen by the government as appropriate, much less desirable, members of a new, demilitarized police remains
uncertain. But the implementation of a fresh policing policy might be a
useful gauge to employ in the feminist monitoring of the country's
demilitarization.

Second, a feminist might take a close look at how the new police training program is fashioned. Reportedly, six hundred police officers (the *New York Times* refers to "policemen") from other countries are being sent to El Salvador under United Nations auspices to help train the new, postwar police.[20] Will that training force be conscious of the relationships between rape and policing? Will the governments selecting the foreign trainers to be sent to El Salvador choose at least some policewomen or men who understand the importance of the prevention of domestic violence in postwar policing?

Guatemalan indigenous women have reported that domestic violence increased during the long years of civil war in their country. "Before the army and the so-called civil self-defense patrols came, my husband and I shared all our ideas and dreams," one rural woman recalled. "But now everything's changed. Now he doesn't share anything with me, and when he talks to me he yells. He always asks me who I talk with and what people are saying. . . . He's always depressed. The children are afraid of him because he hits them . . . I don't know my husband anymore."[21] As feminist commentators living under other repressive Cold War regimes have noted, governments that wield policing powers in a spirit of generalized suspicion tear apart the fabric of local relationships, and the shredding can take the form of domestic violence. Nowhere is men's violent behavior toward the women and children in their households merely private. As Central American women are making clear, nowhere is such behavior merely national, either. Domestic violence is international insofar as it has become integral to any regime's attempt to assert its control over those sectors which may want their society to develop quite a different relationship to the international order. Thus, to reform any country's police force to make it part of a genuine international peace process will require placing domestic violence on the agenda of new police training and deployment.

Which brings us back to rape. In the same month that the El Salvador peace accord was signed, Amnesty International issued its very first report on rape and sexual abuse.[22] Although it was a modestly slim pamphlet, its publication broke new ground. For never before had Amnesty or most other international human rights groups seen the sexual abuse of women as a distinctive form of illegitimate state action. Using careful documentation, the report's authors laid out the ways in which governments have employed rape and other forms of sexual abuse to intimidate female citizens suspected of criminal behavior. The Amnesty pamphlet laid much of the blame at the doors of senior police and military officers. These officers either have refused to prosecute low-ranking police and soldiers who have engaged in such sexual abuse of women in custody or have prosecuted alleged assailants but have handed down mild reprimands for those few men declared guilty.

Thus, Central American feminists bestow considerable significance on the rape behavior of regimes claiming today to be demilitarizing. They will be watching for new disciplinary policies as police forces and militaries are being reconstructed in Panama, El Salvador, Nicaragua, and Guatemala. Before celebrating a peace, they will wait to see if a male police officer who rapes a woman is treated by his superiors as a normal male who is just a bit out of control or even as worthy of congratulation for successfully silencing a troublesome woman activist.

In this context, the current investigation into accusations that men in the security forces have raped U.S. and local Catholic nuns takes on added significance. Sister Diana Ortiz, a member of the Kentucky-based Ursuline Sisters, agreed to return to Guatemala in April 1992 to testify in a trial of men in the security forces accused of rape, but only after months of therapy designed for victims of torture and only after U.S. authorities had reassured her that the regime, eager for international legitimation, was now serious about bringing the perpetrators to justice. Yet the government of Jorge Serrano nonetheless seemed most comfortable operating in the mode of those governments described by the Amnesty investigators: dragging its feet, not seeing women as credible witnesses, and acting reluctant to hold accountable a military or police official accused of rape.[23] And the rape of a nun, at that. For nuns have been essential symbols of idealized femininity in Central America. As such, they have played important roles in perpetuating the existing sexist political order. Thus, the decisions of many nuns during the 1980s to reimagine not simply their religious vows but also their institutionalized feminine identities sent political ripples throughout the region. As the nuns became politically active, they became allies of many poor women and thus threats to elitist anti-Communist regimes. The outcomes of trials for the state-sanctioned rape of nuns, consequently, should provide more than a few clues as to what demilitarization will mean for the relationship of femininity to state authority in post–Cold War Central America.

The Salvadoran trials and the remaking of the country's police force are occurring at a time when feminists are coordinating an international effort to insert domestic violence and rape into the formal discourse on human rights. Feminist activists and legal scholars have mobilized their arguments to present to the first World Conference on Human Rights in twenty-five years, scheduled to be held in Vienna in 1993. These women are taking the United Nations seriously. They are seeing it not only as an overseer of peace accords in war-torn countries like El Salvador and Somalia, but as a site for redefining power relations between women and men in postwar societies.[24]

Specifically, these feminist advocates of the internationalization of the politics of domestic violence call for the following measures: first, the staff of the Convention on the Elimination of All Forms of Discrimination Against Women (CEDAW) should be moved from Vienna to Geneva, the heart of international agency operations. Second, individuals and groups, not just governments, should have the right to initiate CEDAW investigations. Third, the UN Declaration of Human Rights should be amended to protect women from police rape and domestic violence.[25]

The second pledge calls for the demobilization of the rebels' troops and the reduction of government military personnel. While each side has been reluctant to reduce its soldiers, the process has been revealing. The FMLN leadership initially devised a way to fulfill at least part of its pledge while retaining what it considered as its military capacity. It chose to demobilize only those guerrilla fighters it believed were peripheral to its mission. Thus, in the first ten months of the peace accords, it sent back to civilian life the children, older men, and women of all ages. For the first eleven months of peace, what the FMLN leadership held onto was a remasculinized core of combatants.[26]

To demilitarize any country often calls for the sharp reduction or total elimination of myriad institutions which have been designed to militarize masculinity:

- militarized police forces
- torture units
- state intelligence agencies
- civil patrols and home guards
- death squads
- militias
- regular military units
- insurgent guerrilla units

Each of these institutions may have become dependent over the years on a quite distinct form of masculinity: men in torture units might look either up to or down on men in militias. Thus, the process of political reconciliation in Central America may provide a sense of relief to peasant men demobilized from civil patrols, a feeling that they have been freed from the burden of molding themselves to a kind of ill-fitting masculinity that made them outsiders in their own communities. By contrast, many men who have spent months or years operating in death squads or guerrilla units may believe that their manhood is being shrunk when those organizations are disbanded.

The Salvadoran peace agreement's land redistribution pledge may affect its success in demilitarizing masculinity. Distributing land is a time-worn strategy for assuaging the anxieties and resentments of male soldiers who are being demobilized. Little has been written about the consequences of such a strategy for women's landholding in postwar eras. The Salvadoran plan calls for three- to twelve-acre plots to be purchased by the government and distributed to 7,500 rebel combatants, 25,000 peasants from villages that supported the rebels, and 15,000

Fig. 7. Photos of Salvadoran women kissing babies in celebration of the 1992 peace accords seemed to presage the remasculinization of the country's military. (AFP Photo)

ex-soldiers from the government's own forces. Most of the recipients will
be men. Some may find that their manhood is reconfirmed in their new
control over land. Even three acres can provide some men with a reassurance of patriarchal dignity. Little has been spelled out to ensure that this
demilitarizing formula does not entrench women's inequality in the
politics of land.[27]

To understand just how thoroughly a man's masculine identity has
been transformed by his enlistment in or conscription into one of these
militarized units, we first need to be curious about masculinity. Then we
need to trace varieties of masculinity as they served to foster civil strife.
Shari Truiz, for example, has described how an ordinary Guatemalan
military recruit was socialized to become a torturer. "To use torture as
a tool against the civilian population, the soldier has first to be dominated himself. And so, during training, any violation of the norms of
military life is severely punished. If a new recruit does not understand an
order, does not carry it out correctly, gets out of the shower late, fails
to shout with enough enthusiasm, or fails to make his bed properly, he
is likely to be punished with various cruel methods of torture."[28] Only
when it is known how any particular form of masculinity has been
militarized will one be able to devise personal and state strategies for
reversing that transformation.

The men who have served in the multitude of militarized organizations will not all have become equally imbued with militarized forms of
masculinity; nor will all forms of militarized masculinity be identical. A
Nicaraguan contra who feels naked without his gun, a pro-Sandinista
soldier who is fearful of losing his livelihood, a Nicaraguan man who
thought his masculinity was assured by his participation in an armed unit
on either side but who now faces the Chamorro government's postwar
anti-gay law, a Guatemalan male peasant conscripted into the regular
army, his brother who has been pressed into a torture unit, a Panamanian National Guard commander used to the privileges not only of
masculinity but also of class—these men may pose quite different problems for demilitarizers. And for their lovers, wives, and mothers.[29]

If the years of violent conflict have depended upon varieties of militarized masculinity, then successful demilitarization will require the reconstitution of each of these varieties into a form that fosters social reconciliation. This gendered transformation has not been recognized in the recent Central American accords. So it is being left to women to accomplish the task. More than likely it will be women, in their roles as mothers, lovers, and wives, who will be expected to socialize men, one by one, into new masculine identities that rest more on cooperation and respect for women, and less on violence and sexism. If they fail, it is more than likely that they, the women in these still-militarized men's lives, will bear the brunt of persistent contempt and violence. Will the United Nations peacekeepers monitor misogyny?

It remains unclear how postwar civilian political competition will be shaped by this problematically gendered process of demilitarization. Some of the evidence is not encouraging; some is. Feminists in Chile have given fair warning. Despite the essential part played by activist women in bringing down the Pinochet regime, when it came time for democratic elections in 1988, the candidates selected were overwhelmingly male. Those few important women candidates who competed successfully for seats in the revived national legislature owed their victories at the polls more to the concentrated campaigns of women's groups on their behalf than to the backing of male party leaders. As a result, in the first freely elected, postmilitary Chilean legislature, women hold a mere 8 of the total 158 seats. This is a smaller proportion than they held in the pre-Pinochet legislature. Moreover, the new president, Christian Democrat Patricio Aylwin, felt free to ignore the activism by women's groups which helped bring him to power; he appointed only one woman to his cabinet, and she was not given a ministry.[30]

Therefore, it may not be a mere photographic fluke that those FMLN leaders who are pictured descending from a plane after successful negotiations in New York are uniformly male. What the photographer seemed intent on showing was that the former Salvadoran guerrillas had traded in their camouflage fatigues for jackets and ties—and that they could disembark in full public view, without fear of being shot or arrested. What the photographer unintentionally suggested as well was that Salvadoran women's activism in support of antimilitaristic trade unions, peasant groups, antidisappearance campaigns, and guerrilla combat itself had not translated into prominence in the new civilian leadership.

Demilitarization is thought by many observers to be part and parcel of the creation (or revitalization) of electoral competition. Such open competition is generally organized around at least two legalized political parties. A lot of faith is being invested in political parties as vehicles for demilitarization—not only in Central America, but also in Eastern Europe, Africa, and Asia. Thus, a feminist becomes immediately curious about how the demilitarization of masculinity relates to the potential masculinization of political parties. Where are the women in these revitalized political parties?

All too often, men have presumed that patriarchy is the social system most effective for running competitive electoral political parties. Women are welcomed as supporters, canvassers, symbols, wives, and widows. They are not welcomed as leaders, candidates, platform writers, or strategists. The more that men imagine party competition as a form of warfare without guns, the more parties become sites for the reprivileging of masculinity in a postwar society.

As oppressive as the militarized era was for Central American women, it provoked new kinds of political action, fresh approaches to consciousness-raising and organizing. For example, widows became a political class, a social sector whose actual needs could be addressed in ways that underscored their importance to the larger antimilitarism effort. So did women peasants, the mothers of disappeared sons and daughters, and women garment workers. A postwar return to the politics-as-usual of patriarchal parties threatens to marginalize these innovative forms of political intervention. It is conventionally presumed that demilitarization automatically widens the political space; but it could also shrink it. Much of the responsibility for preventing such a shrinkage in El Salvador will fall on women activists in all of these sectors. It will be left to women to stop both leftist and conservative men from constructing a postwar civilian party system that ignores the remarkable political mobilization of women that has occurred in the past decade.

For Nicaraguan Sandinistas, the transition from being a party in control of a besieged state to being a party in opposition during a period of demilitarization has created new pressures. Despite having to pour a disproportionate percentage of their national budget into defense expenditures, the Sandinistas did use state authority to improve women's lives. Pressured by Sandinista women of AMNLAE, the Luisa Amanda Association of Nicaraguan Women, the wartime regime passed laws recognizing common-law marriages and legalizing the status of children born outside marriage; it encouraged fathers and sons to share domestic work; it funded literacy, legal advice, and health programs directed toward women; and, although it excluded women from military conscription, it encouraged women to join the militia.[31] Nonetheless, since the party's electoral loss, the Sandinista leadership has been faced with a new independence on the part of women both inside and outside the party who, during the 1980s, had lent it their support during the war against the contras.

These women's critique of political parties on both the right and the left has given rise to a nascent autonomous women's movement. It has also made the women's caucus inside the Sandinista party more impatient. During the first two years of the Chamorro administration, women began to break out of the double boxes of mothers-mobilizing-to-save-the-revolution and mothers-as-protectors-of-sons-about-to-be-conscripted boxes which had been built by the Sandinistas and the U.S.–funded counterrevolution. Sexuality became a topic of more open public discussion. Luz Marina Torres, a director of one of Managua's Casas de la Mujer, for instance, criticized both Chamorro's UNO government and the Sandinista leadership for shying away from public discussions of abortion. Torres spoke for many of the women active in the new autonomous women's groups when she explained that, beyond just abortion, "We want sex education and birth control. . . . Our struggle now is laying the foundation for the day we have laws and health centers which protect our right to decide about our bodies."[32]

So demilitarization in itself may not undermine patriarchal ways of conducting political life. But it may, as in Nicaragua, allow for the continuation and even the spread of nonparty forms of political mobili-

zation among women, mobilization less constrained by the need to
protect an insurgent movement or a revolutionary regime from an out-
side-supported military threat. In the short run, such mobilization may
not have a decisive impact on party politics. It may even leave male party
members the space they need to remasculinize political party life.

The first National Conference of Nicaraguan Women was held in
January 1992. Organizers were surprised that eight hundred women
came to the meeting, which had been called to create a movement
embracing academics, health workers, trade unionists, and students, and
lesbians as well as straight women. Participants voted to eschew national
leaders and a national agenda and instead build locally rooted networks.
They also agreed that what women need now is a political home that is
independent of all of the existing political parties, even the parties which
are the principal players in the nation's postwar electoral politics.[33]

In fact trade unions, rather than parties, may indeed be the centers of
many Central American women's activism in the postwar era. Among
Washington policymakers' chief incentives for demilitarizing America's
"backyard" in the wake of the Soviet Union's dissolution has been the
desire to turn the region into part of an American-directed economic
zone that can compete with Japan and the European Community. In
1992, the administration of George Bush called for an "Enterprise for the
Americas Initiative," which was designed to reinforce the postwar sexual
division of labor throughout the continent.

Canadian women were the first women in the hemisphere to hoist
warning flags over the Free Trade Agreement (FTA), Washington's vehicle for its post–Cold War "continentalism." During 1988–89, Canadians
engaged in a debate that tore their society apart, while most of their
neighbors to the south looked the other way. Wives and husbands,
friends and workmates argued with each other over the implications for
Canadian identity, Canadian jobs, and Canadian social welfare programs of signing the FTA with the United States. A sufficient number of
voters—43 percent, which translated into a majority of Conservative
seats in the federal parliament—eventually were persuaded by Prime
Minister Brian Mulroney's prediction that if Canada refused to sign the

FTA, it would be left out in the economic cold. Canadian feminists analyzed the probable effects of the FTA on women during the 1989 debate and continue today to monitor its consequences, charting especially Canadian women's loss of jobs—most notably in garments, textiles, and telecommunications—directly traceable to the FTA.[34]

Canadian and Central American women's relationships to each other are rarely weighed when trying to unravel the meanings of Central American demilitarization. But the Republican vision of an economic market that will encompass the entire continent, a market made more viable by demilitarization following immediately after hyper-militarization, has made that long-distance relationship salient. Following on the heels of the Canada–U.S. FTA were negotiations between the U.S. trade representatives and their Mexican counterparts for a similar Mexico–U.S. treaty. By the time of the U.S. presidential campaign of 1992, the North American Free Trade Agreement (NAFTA) had become a popular issue. At stake, Republicans argued, was the shape of the post–Cold War world. Women packaging strawberries and assembling Ninja toys in Juarez, women sewing jogging outfits in Tennessee, and women working for insurance companies in Toronto were encouraged to believe that, for the sake of a post–Cold War order, they must see each other as competitors. The new continentalism depended on it.

Women trade unionists from Mexico, the U.S., and Canada began meeting in 1991 to construct a feminist analysis of and strategy for responding to the NAFTA negotiations and the new continentalist vision of women's threat to one another. The role of Canadian women has been crucial in these tripartite meetings because they have felt the effects of the FTA and, far more than their U.S. feminist counterparts, have developed a political analysis of the FTA's gendered dynamics. Mexican women have contributed to the strategy sessions their experiences of working for U.S. corporations, developing feminist consciousness while working inside unions still run by males, and creating autonomous women's trade unions that have raised issues such as neighborhood pollution and domestic violence.[35]

Demilitarization can take a variety of forms. Not all paths toward ending militarism's influence on politics lead to easy acceptance of the free trade model. Thus, the demilitarization of Central America is being promoted by Washington policymakers and by governing elites in El Salvador, Panama, and Guatemala in such a way as to lay the groundwork for the spread of the NAFTA model southward. That is, to foster conditions hospitable to acceptance of the NAFTA, demilitarization must be of a particular sort. This was well understood by American foreign policy and security officials, who in the 1980s pressured the field staff of the U.S. Agency for International Development (AID) to entice American companies to invest in the Caribbean and Central America. While this policy only became well known to unemployed women garment workers in Tennessee and to the American public in the heat of the 1992 presidential debate, it had been the subject of considerable concern both inside and outside of AID several years earlier.[36]

A demilitarization process designed to produce a society congenial to NAFTA would not break up export plantations or deprive them of the labor they need to operate profitably. Nor would it allow local environmental grassroots organizations entry into the corridors of national policymaking. Demilitarization would be fashioned to encourage small farmers to grow export crops such as broccoli and mangoes and to accept marketing arrangements with such multinational agribusinesses as Green Giant. Formulas intended to halt civil war would not permit organized labor to gain effective economic or political influence. And power-sharing accords would reserve senior posts in the ministry of finance and in the central bank for officials who shared the NAFTA architects' presumptions about reducing public spending. Finally, although demilitarization might contain within it the seeds of reducing masculinist privileges, it would be accomplished in ways that would continue to devalue women's labor. Given the level of popular mobilization that has occurred in Central American countries during the last decade, however, none of this would be easy.

Some Central American analysts fear that perhaps worse than being drawn under the NAFTA tent is the prospect of being left just outside it: becoming, as one feminist sociologist described it, the place for the "quick-and-dirty" investment.[37] Multinational corporations already operate in El Salvador, Honduras, Panama, Costa Rica, and Guatemala. J. Crew, the popular American mail-order company, currently has Panamanian women sewing its 100 percent cotton, turtleneck jerseys. Whereas in 1986 Guatemala hosted a mere 10 garment factories, five years later the Guatemalan government, still fighting a civil war, had licensed an estimated 250 garment factories, employing a mostly female work force of 50,000.[38] Foreign investment has become a sign of a national regime's political legitimacy. Many observers consider multinational investment to be a sign that the local regime is making progress toward ending a destabilizing civil war. Such investment has been heralded as a reflector—and, many argue, a creator—of international confidence, social stability, and global belonging.

The factories most often located in these countries are precisely those that maximize profits by using foreign and local constructs of femininity to devalue women's labor. This is not a new situation. It is as old as the dilemma of a woman who must choose between an unlivable farm income, a position as a domestic servant, or a factory wage, on the one hand, and a demeaning and risky but occasionally more lucrative income from prostitution, on the other.[39] What is new in the 1990s is the prospect that entire economies built on gendered as well as class- and race-dependent presumptions of skill and worth will be integrated through treaty arrangements into a hemispheric market. What is also new for this hemisphere is that this treaty-based continentalism is being legitimized as a formula for (a) coping with the new conditions of a world without competition between two superpowers, and (b) ending local military conflicts fueled in large part by that superpower rivalry.

Suddenly, stylish Van Heusen shirts have taken on a distinctly post–Cold War look. Garments have become Guatemala's second leading export, after coffee. Even while the civil war continued, the government of President Vinicio Cerezo worked with agencies of the U.S. government to entice foreign investors to return to Guatemala. Foreign-owned and jointly owned factories assembling products for export—*maquiladoras*—were seen by both the nervous civilian regime and Washington's security-minded aid officials as an engine for postwar economic development that would not upset Guatemala's traditional landed elite.[40] Companies such as Levi-Strauss, Guess, Bugle Boy, Phillips–Van Heusen, Sears, K-Mart, and Montgomery Ward decided in the late 1980s and early 1990s that it served their interests to accept the invitation to invest directly in Guatemalan operations or to contract indirectly with Korean companies that now have factories in Guatemala or with locally owned manufacturers. Managers who have set up their factories in the countryside hire as many men as they do women, preferring Indian men. In the cities, 80 percent of the workers whom factory managers hired were women, mostly young, single women between the ages of 14 and 24.[41] Some of these women told interviewers that they were going to work as daughters, leaving school or quitting work on farms or as domestic servants, in order to support their parents and siblings. A fifteen-year-old girl working in a *maquiladora* explained: "I would not be working in this horrible factory for this demanding manager unless it was absolutely necessary. My father does not have a job and so we—the girls—had to find work. I went to the *maquila* because I knew they would hire me. I want to be in school but I am here. I do not like it but what can I do?"[42]

Phillips–Van Heusen executives, headquartered in New York City, were not expecting Guatemalan women to be assertive, organized, or militant. Like the designers of post–Cold War continentalism, these executives presumed that established notions about femininity would survive demilitarization and continue to ensure a compliant work force. They hoped to keep their factories union-free. But in 1991, workers—primarily young women—began to organize in Phillips–Van Heusen's two Guatemalan factories. They threatened to strike unless they gained the right to unionize and better wages; they also called for an end to unsafe working conditions and sexual abuse.[43] Naming sexual harassment was unsettling to the postwar continentalist project. This organizing grew not only out of conditions experienced in the Phillips–Van Heusen plants, but also out of autonomous women's consciousness-raising and organizing begun earlier as a direct response to Guatemala's militarization. In late 1992, the Guatemalan government recognized the union.[44]

.   .   .   .   .

So demilitarization is a process that can take more than a single route. It can follow a path leading to the remasculinization of civil life. Or it can be nudged along a road that leads toward the reduction not only of organized violence but also of masculinity's civic privileges. If the designers and monitors of formal peace processes ignore the diverse ways in which masculinity provided fodder for earlier militarization, the prospects for taking the latter route will remain dim. On the other hand, if the feminist question "Where are the women?" is taken seriously, men's notions about themselves will be recognized as problematic, and thus political. Masculinity—in policing, in political parties, and in trade negotiations—will be charted as a necessarily contested zone. How this zone is constructed and occupied during the next decade will determine in large measure how Central America's women and men experience the post–Cold War world.

Chapter Five

It Takes More Than Two

THE PROSTITUTE, THE SOLDIER,
THE STATE, AND THE ENTREPRENEUR

> *Since U.S. occupation troops in Japan*
> *are unalterably determined to*
> *fraternize, the military authorities*
> *began helping them out last week by*
> *issuing a phrase book. Sample utility*
> *phrases: "You're very pretty" . . .*
> *"How about a date?" . . . "Where*
> *will I meet you?" And since the sweet*
> *sorrow of parting always comes, the*
> *book lists no less than 14 ways to say*
> *goodbye.*
>
> Time, July 15, 1946

On a recent visit to London, I persuaded a friend to play hooky from work to go with me to Britain's famous Imperial War Museum. Actually, I was quite embarrassed. In all my trips to London, I had never visited the Imperial War Museum. But now, in the wake of the Gulf War, the time seemed ripe. Maybe the museum would help put this most recent military conflict in perspective, mark its continuities with other wars, and clarify its special human, doctrinal, and technological features. I was in for a disappointment.

Only selective British experiences of the "great" wars were deemed worthy of display. Malaya, Aden, Kenya, the Falklands—these British twentieth-century war zones didn't rate display cases. In fact, Asia, Africa, and the West Indies didn't seem much on the curators' minds at all. There were two formal portraits of turbaned Indian soldiers who had won military honors for their deeds, but there were no displays to make visible to today's visitors how much the British military had relied on men and women from its colonies to fight both world wars. I made a vow on my next trip to take the train south of London to the Gurkha Museum.

The only civilians who received much attention in the Imperial War Museum were British. Most celebrated were the "plucky" cockney Londoners who coped with the German blitz by singing in the Underground. Women were allocated one glass case showing posters calling on housewives to practice domestic frugality for the cause. There was no evidence, however, of the political furor set off when white British women began to date—and have children with—African-American GIs.

Our disappointment with the museum's portrayal of Britain's wars served to make us trade hunches about what a realistic curatorial approach might be. What would we put on display besides frontline trenches (which at least showed the rats), cockney blitz-coping lyrics, and unannotated portraits of Sikh heroes?

Brothels. In my war museum there would be a reconstruction of a military brothel. It would show rooms for officers and rooms for rank and file soldiers. It would display separate doors for white soldiers and black soldiers. A manikin of the owner of the business (it might be a disco rather than a formal brothel) would be sitting watchfully in the corner—it could be a man or a woman, a local citizen or a foreigner. The women serving the soldiers might be white European, Berber, Namibian, or Puerto Rican; they might be Korean, Filipina, Japanese, Vietnamese, African-American, or Indian. Depending on the era and locale, they could be dressed in sarongs, saris, or miniskirts topped with T-shirts memorializing resort beaches, soft drinks, and aircraft carriers.

In this realistic war museum, visitors would be invited to press a button to hear the voices of the women chart the routes by which they came to work in this brothel and describe the children, siblings, and parents they were trying to support with their earnings. Several of the women might compare the sexual behavior and outlook of these foreign

men with those of the local men they had been involved with. Some of
the women probably would add their own analyses of how the British,
U.S., French, or United Nations troops had come to be in their country.

Museum goers could step over to a neighboring tape recorder to hear
the voices of soldiers who patronized brothels and discos while on duty
abroad. The men might describe how they imagined these women were
different from or similar to the women from their own countries. The
more brazen might flaunt their sexual prowess. They might compare
their strength, chivalry, or earning power with that of the local men.
Some of the soldiers, however, would describe their feelings of loneli-
ness, their uncertainty of what it means to be a man when you're a
soldier, their anxieties about living up to the sexual performance expectations of their officers and buddies.

War—and militarized peace—are occasions when sexual relations
take on particular meanings. A museum curator—or a journalist, novelist, or political commentator—who edits out sexuality, who leaves it on
the cutting-room floor, delivers to the audience a skewed and ultimately
unhelpful account of just what kinds of myths, anxieties, inequalities,
and state policies are required to fight a war or to sustain a militarized
form of peace.

A letter from a former CIA analyst, now an academic, suggests one
reason why prostitution is so invisible, not only in military museums, but
also in "serious" official discussions of security. He noted that in a recent
book I had surmised from a Rand Corporation report that Soviet commanders had banned prostitution from their bases in Afghanistan during
the counterinsurgency of the 1980s. He warned me not to jump to
conclusions. While working as a CIA analyst in the 1970s, he had conducted a classified study of morale and discipline among Soviet forces.
During the course of the study, he had interviewed an émigré who had
been a conscript on a remote Soviet air force base in Russia's Far North.
In reply to the analyst's inquiry about the presence of women on the
base, the former conscript recalled that there had been approximately
one hundred. What were their functions? *"Prostituki!"* The U.S. analyst
found this pertinent and included the information in his report. But when

the official CIA version came out, this was the only information excised by his superiors from the original draft. The analyst, looking back, speculated: "Since the U.S. military represses its bases' dependency on sexual access to local women, the organizational incentive is to avoid mentioning the Soviet problems for fear of drawing attention to the issue in the U.S. The tendency," he went on to explain, "to use information about the USSR as a means of discussing U.S. problems was something I commonly encountered in the CIA."[1]

It is for this reason that feminist ethnographies and oral histories are so vital. They help us to make sense of militaries' dependence on—yet denial of—particular presumptions about masculinity to sustain soldiers' morale and discipline. Without sexualized rest and recreation, would the U.S. military command be able to send young men off on long, often tedious sea voyages and ground maneuvers? Without myths of Asian or Latina women's compliant sexuality, would many American men be able to sustain their own identities, their visions of themselves as manly enough to act as soldiers?

Women who have come to work as prostitutes around U.S. bases tell us that a militarized masculinity is constructed and reconstructed in smoky bars and sparsely furnished rented rooms. If we confine our curiosity only to the boot camp and the battlefield—the focus of most investigations into the formations of militarized masculinity—we will be unable to explain just how masculinity is created and sustained in the peculiar ways still imagined by officials to be necessary to sustain a modern military organization.

We will also miss just how much governmental authority is being expended to insure that a peculiar definition of masculinity is sustained. Military prostitution differs from other forms of industrialized prostitution in that there are explicit steps taken by state institutions to protect the male customers without undermining their perceptions of themselves as sexualized men.

"Close to 250,000 men a month paid three dollars for three minutes of the only intimacy most were going to find in Honolulu."[2] These figures come from records kept in Hawaii during 1941 and 1944. Historians have these precise figures because Honolulu brothel managers, most of whom were white women, had to submit reports to Hawaii's military governor. American soldiers' sexual encounters with local prostitutes were not left to chance or to the market; they were the object of official policy consideration among the military, the police, and the governor's staff. Two hundred and fifty prostitutes paid $1.00 per year to be registered merely as "entertainers" with the Honolulu Police Department because the federal government had passed the May Act in 1941, making prostitution illegal, to assuage the fears of many American civilians that mobilizing for war would corrupt the country's sexual mores.[3] Hawaii's military governor disagreed. He had police and military officers on his side. They saw a tightly regulated prostitution industry as necessary to bolster male soldiers' morale, to prevent sexually transmitted diseases, and to reassure the Hawaiian white upper class that wartime would not jeopardize their moral order. The navy and the army set up prophylaxis distribution centers along Honolulu's Hotel Street, the center of the city's burgeoning prostitution industry. The two departments collaborated with the local police to try to ensure that licensed prostitutes kept their side of the bargain: in return for the license, women servicing soldiers and sailors up and down Hotel Street had to promise to have regular medical examinations, not to buy property in Hawaii, not to own an automobile, not to go out after 10:30 at night, and not to marry members of the armed forces. The objective was to keep prostitutes quite literally in their place.

The effort was only partially successful. Women working in the most successful brothels, white women, many of whom came by ship from San Francisco to work as prostitutes, made enough money to violate the official rules and buy homes outside Honolulu. They kept $2 of the $3 from each customer. Out of their earnings they paid $100 per month to the brothel manager for room and board, plus extra for laundry and $13 for each required monthly venereal disease test.

Before the war, most Hotel Street brothels had two doors, one for white male customers and one for men of color, most of whom were Asian men who worked on the island's pineapple and sugar plantations.

Brothel managers believed this segregation prevented violent outbursts by white men who objected to the women they were paying for servicing men of any other race. As the wartime influx of white soldiers and sailors tilted the brothels' business ever more toward a white clientele, most managers decided that any risk of offending white male customers was bad business; they did away with the second door and turned away men of color altogether.

Opening time for the typical Honolulu brothel during the war years was 9 A.M. It operated on an efficient assembly-line principle. From prostitutes and soldiers recalling the arrangement, we learn that most of the brothels used what was called a 'bull-ring' setup consisting of three rooms. "In one room a man undressed, in a second the prostitute engaged her customer, in a third a man who had finished put his clothes back on."[4] Prostitutes learned to tailor their services to the sexual sophistication of their military clients. They offered oral sex to the more nervous and inexperienced men. A senior military police officer in the middle of the war speculated before an audience of local citizen reformers that those sailors who performed oral sex with the Honolulu prostitutes were those men most likely to engage in homosexual behavior once they were back on board ship. The U.S. military's policymakers tried to think of everything.

Today British and Belize officials work hard together to develop a complex policy to ensure a steady but safe supply of military prostitutes for the British troops stationed in that small ex-colony perched on the edge of Latin America.[5] A new nine-hundred-man batallion arrives every six months. British soldiers have special brothels designated for their patronage, although they slip out of the carefully woven policy net to meet local women in bars and discos in Belize City. Most of the women who work in the officially approved brothels are Latinas, rather than Afro-Belize women; many have traveled across the border from war-torn Guatemala to earn money as prostitutes.

The government-to-government agreement requires that every brothel worker, with the cooperation of the owners, have a photo identification card and undergo weekly medical examinations by a Belizean doctor. Prostitutes are required to use condoms with their military customers, although it is not clear how many women may be paid extra by their customers to break the condom rule. If a soldier-patron does show symptoms of a sexually transmitted disease or tests positive for HIV, it is assumed that the prostitute is to blame. The infected soldier gives his British superiors the name of the prostitute who he believes infected him. On the basis of the soldier's word as well as on test results, on a first "offense" the woman is reprimanded by the brothel owner; on a second offense she is fined; on a third she is fired.

British-born soldiers and their Nepali Gurkha comrades, both in Belize under a Belize-British defense pact, have rather different racial/sexual preferences. Whereas the former are likely to frequent both Latina and Afro-Belize women, the Gurkhas reprotedly prefer Latina women, which means that the Gurkhas are more likely to stick to the government-approved prostitutes. The fact that any Gurkha troops go to prostitutes at all, however, contradicts the long-standing British portrayal of Nepali militarized masculinity: though white British men's masculinity is presumed by their officers to require a diet of local sex while overseas, Nepali men's masculinity is constructed as more disciplined, faithful when home and celibate while on assignment abroad.[6] With the end of the Cold War and the relaxation of political tensions between Belize and Guatemala, the future of the government-to-government prostitution agreement has become uncertain. But in early 1992, Britain's Chief of Defence Staff, Field Marshal Sir Richard Vincent, made it known publicly that the Conservative government of John Major was hoping that the British troop rotation in Belize could be continued. Though no longer needed to defend Belize, the British army, according to the field marshal, now finds Belize's climate and topography especially attractive for jungle warfare training.[7] Do the field marshal and his superiors back in London perhaps also find the Belize government's willingness to cooperate in the control of local women's sexuality a military attraction?

The United States fashioned a rather different policy to regulate soldiers' relationships with prostitutes around major U.S. bases such as Clark and Subic Bay in the Philippines. Like the British, the Americans supported compulsory medical examinations of women working as prostitutes. Similarly, women without the license issued with these examinations were prevented from working by the local—in this case Filipino—municipal authorities. U.S. soldiers who contracted sexually transmitted diseases (STDs) were not required to report the woman whom they believe gave them the disease. Nonetheless, it was the practice of the Angeles City and Olongapo health authorities to pass on to U.S. base officials the names of sex workers who had contracted STDs. The base commanders then ordered that the photographs of infected Filipinas be pinned upside down on the public notice board as a warning to the American men.[8]

Apparently believing that "stable" relationships with fewer local women would reduce the chances that their personnel would become infected, base commanders allowed Filipinas hired out by bar owners to stay with their military boyfriends on the base. U.S. officials occasionally sent out a "contact" card to a club owner containing the name of a Filipina employee whom the Americans suspected of having infected a particular sailor or air force man. However, they refused to contribute to the treatment of prostitutes with sexually transmitted diseases or AIDS and turned down requests that they subsidize Pap smears for early cancer detection for the estimated one hundred thousand women working in the entertainment businesses around Clark and Subic.

The closing of both Clark Air Force Base and Subic Naval Base in 1992 forced many Filipinas in precarious states of health into the ranks of the country's unemployed. Their few options included migrating to Okinawa or Guam, or even to Germany, to continue working as prostitutes for U.S. military men. They may also have been vulnerable to recruiters procuring Filipina women for Japan's entertainment industry, an industry that is increasingly dependent on young women from abroad.[9] Olongapo City's businessman mayor, with his own entertainment investments now in jeopardy, has been in the forefront of promoters urging that Subic Bay's enormous facilities be converted into private enterprises, although the Filipino military is also eager to take over at least part of the operations for its own purposes. Military base conversion is always an intensely gendered process. Even if women working the entertainment sector are not at the conversion negotiation table, they will be on many of the negotiators' minds. For instance, the above-mentioned mayor, among others, has urged not only that privatized ship maintenance be developed at Subic Bay, but also that tourism development be high on the new investment list.[10] In the coming years, the politics of prostitution in Olongapo City may take on a civilian look, but many of the tourists attracted may be slightly older American men trying to relive their earlier militarized sexual adventures with Filipina women.

There is no evidence thus far that being compelled by the forces of nature and nationalism to shut down two of their most prized overseas bases has caused U.S. military planners to rethink their prostitution policies. Shifting some of the Philippines operations to Guam or Singapore or back home to the United States does not in itself guarantee new official presumptions about the kinds of sexual relations required to sustain U.S. military power in the post–Cold War world. The governments of Singapore and the United States signed a basing agreement in Tokyo in mid-1992. But, despite popular misgivings about the implications of allowing U.S. Navy personnel to use the small island nation for repairs and training, the basing agreement itself was kept secret. Thus, Singapore citizens, as well as U.S. citizens, are left with little information about what policing formulas, public health formulas, and commercial zoning formulas have been devised by the two governments to shape the sexual relations between American and Singapore men and the women of Singapore.[11]

The women who have been generous enough to tell their stories of prostitution have revealed that sexuality is as central to the complex web of relationships between civil and military cultures as are more talked-about security doctrines and economic quid pro quo. Korean and Filipino women interviewed by Sandra Sturdevant and Brenda Stoltzfus for their oral history collection *Let the Good Times Roll* also remind us of how hard it is sometimes to map the boundaries between sexual relations and economics.[12] They found that the local and foreign men who own the brothels, bars, and discos catering to soldiers are motivated by profit.

These men weigh the market value of a woman's virginity, her "cherry," as well as her age. They constantly reassess their male clients' demands. Thus, by the early 1990s, bar owners and procurers concluded that AIDS-conscious U.S. soldiers were competing to have sex with younger and younger Filipinas, and so the proprietors sought to supply them, driving down the value of the sexual services supplied by "older" women—women in their early twenties.[13]

Over the decades, U.S. Navy veterans stayed in the Philippines and set up bars and discos, both because they liked living outside the United States (often with Filipina wives) and because they could make a comfortable livelihood from sexualized entertainment. Australian men immigrated to launch their own businesses in the base towns and eventually made up a large proportion of the owners of the military-dependent entertainment industry.[14] Local military personnel, especially officers, also used their status and authority in the rural areas to take part in the industry. Some men in the Philippines military have been known to supplement their salaries by acting as procurers of young rural women for the tourist and military prostitution industries.[15] Similarly, among the investors and managers of Thailand's large prostitution industry are Thai military officers.[16] Militarized, masculinized sexual desire, by itself, isn't sufficient to sustain a full-fledged prostitution industry. It requires (depends on) rural poverty, male entrepreneurship, urban commercialized demand, police protection, and overlapping governmental economic interest to ensure its success.

Yet military prostitution is not simply an economic institution. The women who told their stories to Sturdevant and Stoltzfus were less concerned with parsing analytical categories—what is "economic," what is "social," and what is "political"—than with giving us an authentic account of the pressures, hopes, fears, and shortages they had to juggle every day in order to ensure their physical safety, hold onto some self-respect, and make ends meet for themselves and their children.

The stories that prostitutes tell also underscore something that is overlooked repeatedly in discussions of the impact of military bases on local communities: local women working in military brothels and discos mediate between two sets of men, the foreign soldiers and the local men—some of whom are themselves soldiers, but many of whom are civilians. Outside observers rarely talk about these two sets of men in the same breath. But the women who confided in Stoltzfus and Sturdevant knew that they had to be considered simultaneously. The Korean and Filipina women detailed how their relationships with local male lovers and husbands had created the conditions that initially made them vulnerable to the appeals of the labor-needy disco owners. Unfaithfulness, violent tempers, misuse of already low earnings, neglectful fathering—any combination of these behaviors by their local lovers and husbands might have launched these women into military prostitution. Children, too, have to be talked about. Most of the women servicing foreign soldiers sexually have children, some fathered by local men and others fathered by the foreign soldiers. Prostitution and men's ideas about fathering: the two are intimately connected in these women's lives.

In deeply militarized countries such as the Philippines, South Korea, Honduras, and Afghanistan, a woman working in prostitution may have to cope with local as well as foreign soldiers who need her services to shore up their masculinity. Because it is politically less awkward to concentrate on foreign soldiers' exploitation of local women, local soldiers' militarized and sexualized masculinity is frequently swept under the analytical rug, as if it were nonexistent or harmless. And in fact the local soldiery may have more respect for local women, may have easier access to noncommercialized sex, or may have too little money to spend to become major customers of local prostitutes. But none of those circumstances should be accepted as fact without a close look.

For instance, Anne-Marie Cass, an Australian researcher who spent many months in the late 1980s both with the Philippine government's troops and with insurgent forces, found that Filipino male soldiers were prone to sexualizing their power. Cass watched as many of them flaunted their sexualized masculinity in front of their female soldier trainees, women expected from respectable families to be virgins. She also reported that many Filipino soldiers "expect to and receive rides on civilian transport, and drinks and the services of prostitutes in discos and bars without payment."[17]

This is not, of course, to argue that local men are the root of the commercialized and militarized sex that has become so rife, especially in countries allied to the United States. Without local governments willing to pay the price for the lucrative R and R business, without the U.S. military's strategies for keeping male soldiers content, without local and foreign entrepreneurs willing to make their profits off the sexuality of poor women—without each of these conditions, even an abusive, economically irresponsible husband would not have driven his wife into work as an Olongapo bar girl. Nonetheless, local men must be inserted into the political equation; the women who tell their stories make this clear. In fact, we need to widen our lens considerably if we are to fully understand militarized prostitution. Here is a list—probably an incomplete list—of the men we need to be curious about, men whose actions may contribute to the construction and maintenance of prostitution around any government's military base:

- husbands and lovers
- bar and brothel owners, local and foreign
- local public health officials
- local government zoning board members
- local police officials
- local mayors
- national finance ministry officials
- national defense officials
- male soldiers in the national forces
- local civilian male prostitution customers
- local male soldier-customers
- foreign male soldier-customers
- foreign male soldiers' buddies
- foreign base commanders
- foreign military medical officers
- foreign national defense planners
- foreign national legislators

Among these men there may be diverse forms of masculinity. Women in Okinawa, Korea, and the Philippines described to Sturdevant and Stoltz-fus how they had to learn what would make American men feel manly during sex; it was not always what they had learned would make their Korean, Japanese, or Filipino sexual partners feel manly.

Sexual practice is one of the sites of masculinity's—and feminin-ity's—daily construction. That construction is international. It has been so for generations. Tourists and explorers, missionaries, colonial offi-cials and health authorities, novelists, development technocrats, busi-nessmen, and soldiers have long been the internationalizers of sexualized masculinity. Today the U.S. military's "R and R" policy and the industry it has spawned function only if thousands of poor women are willing and able to learn those sexual acts that U.S. military men rely on to bolster their sense of masculinity. Thus, bar owners, military commanders, and local finance ministry bureaucrats depend on local women to be alert to the historically evolving differences between masculinities.

Korean women have been among the current historical investigators of militarized prostitution. Korean women petitioners, together with a small, supportive group of Japanese feminists and Japanese historians, recently pressed the Japanese government to admit that the Japanese military had a deliberate policy of conscripting Korean, Thai, and Bur-mese women into prostitution during World War II.[18] In the past, Japa-nese officials insisted that any Asian women pressed into servicing Japa-nese soldiers sexually during the war were organized and controlled by civilian businessmen. The military itself was institutionally immune. Senior officers had simply accepted the prostituted women as part of the wartime landscape. This defense is strikingly similar to that employed by U.S. officials when asked about the Pentagon's current prostitution pol-icy. Their Japanese counterparts, however, have had to give up their long-time defense in the face of convincing bureaucratic evidence uncov-ered by Yoshiaki Yoshimi, a professor of history at Chuo University. In the Self-Defense Agency's library he found a document entitled "Regard-ing the Recruitment of Women for Military Brothels" dating from the late 1930s, when the Japanese army was moving southward into China.

It ordered the military to build "facilities for sexual comfort." The official rationale was that brothels would stop Japanese soldiers from raping Chinese and other women along the route of the army's invasion. Eventually, an estimated 100,000 to 200,000 Asian women were forcibly conscripted to work as *Karayuki-san,* "comfort women," in these military brothels.[19]

Although the uncovering of the document evoked a formal apology from Prime Minister Kiichi Miyazawa, the issue is not resolved. Kim Hak Sun, one of the survivors of the "comfort women" program, and other elderly Korean women are calling on their government and the Japanese government to reach a settlement that will include monetary compensation for the hardships they suffered.[20]

Furthermore, the internationalizing dynamics which have shaped military prostitution in the past grind on. Thus, the uncovering of 1930s and 1940s Japanese policy on prostitution led to a spate of articles in the U.S. media at a time when many Americans were in search of evidence that they were morally superior to, albeit economically lagging behind, Japan. Thus the story was set in a Pearl Harbor context by many U.S. readers, even if not intentionally by its authors. It could have been quite a different story. The research by Yoshiaki Yoshimi, Nakahara Michiko, and other Japanese historians about their country's military's prostitution policies could have been written—and read—so as to draw attention to U.S., British, French, and other militaries' past and present prostitution policies.

This possibility was what inspired Rita Nakashima Brock to write to the *New York Times* in the wake of the discovery of the Tokyo document. A researcher studying the sex industries in Southeast Asia, she is also an Asian-American woman who spent her childhood on U.S. military bases in the United States, Germany, and Okinawa. She recalls that, as a girl, "I faced the assumption that any woman who looked Asian was sexually available to soldiers. I was often called 'geisha-girl' or 'Suzy Wong' (soldiers usually couldn't tell Japanese from Chinese). Every base I ever lived on . . . had a thriving red-light district near it." When she was older, Brock began to wonder about official military policies that led to the prostitution she had witnessed as a child. "A former Navy chaplain who served in Japan during the post–World War II occupation told me that when he protested the American base commander's efforts to set up prostitution centers using Japanese women, he was reassigned state-side."[21]

Thanh-Dam Truong, a Vietnamese feminist who has investigated the political economy of Thailand's prostitution industry, also reminds us to view sexuality historically. Thai women working in prostitution, she discovered, had to learn new sexual skills in the 1980s that they hadn't needed in the 1960s because by the 1980s their male customers, now mainly local and foreign civilians, had acquired new tastes, new insecurities, and new grounds for competing with other men.[22] Similarly, around the U.S. Navy base at Subic Bay in the late 1980s, bar owners, still dependent on military customers, introduced "foxy boxing." These entrepreneurs believed that having women wrestle and box each other on stage would make the American sailors in the audience more eager for sex with the Filipina employees. Women, in turn, learned that they would be paid for their performance only if at the end of a bout they could show bruises or had drawn blood.[23] At about the same time, women in the bars were instructed by their employers to learn how to pick up coins with their vaginas. This, too, was designed as a new way to arouse the American customers.[24]

Each group of men involved in militarized sexuality is connected to other groups by the women working in the base town bars. But they also may be connected to each other quite directly. At least some Filipino male soldiers are adopting what they see as an American form of militarized masculinity. The men most prone to adopting such attitudes are those in the Scout Rangers, the elite fighting force of the Philippine Constabulary. They act as though Rambo epitomizes the attributes that make for an effective combat soldier: "a soldier in khaki or camouflage, sunglasses or headbands, open shirt, bare head, and well armed, lounging in a roofless jeep traveling down a Davao City street, gun held casually, barrel waving in the air."[25] One consequence of this form of borrowed masculinized intimidation is that local prostitutes servicing

Filipino soldiers perform sexual acts that they otherwise would refuse to perform.

A woman who comes to work in a foreign military brothel or disco finds that she must negotiate among all of these male actors. She has direct contact, however, with only some of them. She never hears what advice the foreign base commander passes on to his troops regarding the alleged unhealthiness or deviousness of local women. She never hears what financial arrangements local and foreign medical officials devise to guarantee the well-being of her soldier-customers. She rarely learns what a soldier who wants to marry her and support her children is told by his military chaplain or superior officer. She is not invited into the conference room when U.S., British, or French legislators decide it is politically wise not to hold hearings on their government's military prostitution policy. The Latina woman working as a prostitute in Belize or the Filipina woman working in the Philippines or Okinawa makes her assessments using only what information she has.

Much of that information comes from the women with whom she works. The women who told their stories to Sturdevant and Stoltzfus did not romanticize the sistership between women working in the bars. The environment is not designed to encourage solidarity. Women *have* engaged in collective actions—for instance, bar workers in Olongapo protested against being forced to engage in boxing matches for the entertainment of male customers. But, despite growing efforts by local feminists to provide spaces for such solidarity, collective action remains the exception. Most women rely on a small circle of friends to accumulate the information necessary to walk the minefield laid by the intricate relationships between the various groups of men who define the military prostitution industry. The women teach each other how to fake orgasms, how to persuade men to use a condom, how to avoid deductions from their pay, how to meet soldier-customers outside their employers' supervision, and how to remain appealing to paying customers when they are older and their valued status as a "cherry girl" is long past.

Women are telling their prostitution stories at a time when the end of the Cold War and the frailty of an industrialized economy are combining to pressure governments in North America and Europe to "downsize" their military establishments. The U.S. Department of Defense has announced the closing of military bases at home and abroad. One of the apparent lessons of the Gulf War in the eyes of many American strategists is that the United States now has the administrative capacity to deploy large numbers of troops overseas rapidly without maintaining a costly and often politically risky base in the region. Simultaneously, Mount Pinatubo spewed its deadly ash so thickly over Clark Air Force Base that even this facility, which until 1991 the Bush administration had deemed vital to American national security, was classified as uneconomical. The Philippine Senate, for its part, rejected Corazón Aquino's requests that the Subic Bay Navy Base agreement be renewed.

Base closings have their own sexual consequences. U.S. military and civilian men and their Filipina lovers had to discuss the possibility of marriage, perhaps each with quite different fears and expectations. There were reports of a number of quick marriages.[26] In March 1992 Pat Ford, National Public Radio's reporter in the Philippines, described the departure of the last U.S. ship from Subic Bay. Filipina women from Olongapo's bars cried and hugged their sailor boyfriends and customers at the gates of the base.[27] What sexual expectations would the American men take home with them? Perhaps the Filipinas' tears and hugs prompted many men to imagine that they had experienced not commercialized sex but rather relationships of genuine affection. What were women shedding tears for? Perhaps for the loss of some temporary emotional support. Or maybe for the loss of their livelihoods. How many women who have lost their jobs around Subic Bay will seek out the employment agencies that, for a fee, will send them to Kuwait to work as maids?[28] Despite the efforts of the Filipino anti-base campaign, the government had no operative base conversion plan ready to launch that would put women's health and autonomy high on its list of objectives.[29]

It might be tempting to listen to Asian women's stories as if they were tales of a bygone era. That would, I think, be a mistake. Large bases still exist in South Korea and Guam. Over forty thousand American military personnel were stationed in Japan (including Okinawa) at the end of

Fig. 8. November 24, 1992. After eighty-nine years, the American flag is lowered at Subic Bay Naval Station in the Philippines. Foreign journalists see a Filipina woman hugging a departing marine. But what is it she is really grieving—the loss of an income, child support, money to send to her landless parents? (Reuters/Bettman)

1991; even more will be redeployed from Clark and Subic Bay. In early 1992, the U.S. government made agreements with officials in Australia, Singapore, and Malaysia to use facilities in their countries for repairs, communications, and training. Even with some cutbacks, the number of American men going through those bases on long tours and on shorter-term maneuvers will be in the thousands. Governments in Seoul, Tokyo, and Manila have made no moves to cancel the R and R agreements they have with Washington, agreements that spell out the conditions for permitting and controlling the sort of prostitution deemed most useful for the U.S. military. The no-prostitution formula adopted to fight the Gulf War—a no-prostitution formula not initiated by Washington policymakers, but rather imposed on the United States by a Saudi regime nervous about its own Islamic legitimacy—has not been adopted anywhere else. What discussions have U.S. military planners had with their counterparts in Singapore, Canberra, and Kuala Lumpur about morale, commerce, health, and masculinity?

Listening to women who work as prostitutes is as important as ever. For political analysts, listening to them can provide information necessary for creating a more realistic picture of how fathering, child-rearing, man-to-man borrowing, poverty, private enterprise, and sexual practice play vital roles in the construction of militarized femininity and masculinity. For nonfeminist anti-base campaigners, listening to these women will shake the conventional confidence that has come from relying only on economic approaches to base conversion. Marriage, parenting, male violence, and self-respect will all have to be accepted as serious political agenda items if the women now living on wages from prostitution are to become actors, and not mere symbols, in movements to transform foreign military bases into productive civilian institutions. Listening is political.

Chapter Six

The Gendered Gulf

A DIARY

Most of us are still trying to make sense of the Gulf War. Its meanings are as multilayered as a Mesopotamian dig. For instance, I realize now that I know nothing—nothing—about Kurdish women. Consequently, I have an inherently faulty understanding of how Iraqi Kurdish national-ism is being conceptualized; and I don't know how either the Peshmerge guerrilla forces or the noncombatant Kurdish refugee communities are organizing their lives as they face threats from the governments of both Iraq and Turkey. The six entries that follow, therefore, are best read as incomplete, time-anchored attempts to bring a feminist sensibility to bear on what was initially described as the "Gulf Crisis" and later labeled the "Gulf War." Nowadays one also hears it referred to as the "first post–Cold War war."

My first entry was written in mid-September 1990, only a few weeks after I returned from my first visit to the South Pacific. I was in the Cook Islands when I heard on the BBC World Service the news of the Iraqi military's invasion of Kuwait. The South Pacific was nudging me to imagine this post–Cold War world in new and surprising ways. I was seeing Australia as an emerging and militarizing regional power, and New Zealand as not only an antinuclear renegade but also once a colo-nizer. Small islands no bigger than pin pricks on a world map were turning out to have dynamic and complex international relations their citizens barely had the resources to monitor, much less control. And women's relationships to men in each of these small societies—Fiji, Vanuatu, the Cook Islands, Tahiti—were as much the stuff of political myths, alliances, and anxieties as they were in any other society.

So when I first heard the news of what was instantly called the Gulf Crisis, I tried, not always successfully, to think about what the invasion and its ripple effects meant for Cook Islanders, Australians, and Fijians: higher petrol and kerosene prices, plummeting tourism, and a further rationale for expanding Australian military presence. Each would have its own distinctively gendered causes and consequences.

Perhaps it was these mental aerobics that encouraged me a month later, now back on the East Coast of the U.S., to set off on a trial run at analyzing the crisis by imagining it from the vantage point of one of its apparently least significant participants: a Filipina working as a maid in Kuwait City. Although I didn't have all the analytical ends neatly tied together, I had been taught by feminists over the last twenty years to be wary of presuming that the political actors with the most power—and the most media coverage—were the most useful starting points for figuring out exactly how politics work. I might get back to George Bush, François Mitterrand, King Fahd, and Saddam Hussein eventually. But coming to their ideological outlooks and uses of state power by way of particular groups of women, and the relationships of those women with other women, would prove more fruitful than taking the masculinist shortcut. That was the path paved with presumptions that powerful men would reveal the most about why a crisis had developed and why it was following its peculiar course.

The second entry in this diary was written almost five months later, in February 1991. The Bush administration and its allies had launched their massive air bombardment on Iraq under the umbrella of the United Nations and were in the opening stages of what would be an alarmingly brief ground war. I had been following the protest by a few Saudi women against the prohibition on women driving automobiles; I was watching for the consolidation of military prostitution policies which would rely

on Third World women and scanning the European press (more promis-
ing than that of the U.S.) for any signs that the feminist, prodemocracy
Iraqi Women's League would be listened to among the exiled opposition
coalitions. Yet, back in February, I felt most compelled to turn my
attention directly toward women closer to home. Yellow ribbons were
sprouting in my neighborhood like daffodils in spring. They seemed to
be spontaneous expressions, especially expressions by women; only later
did the press and Washington officialdom impose their own meanings on
them.

To this day I am not at all sure I know what each woman was saying
when she put a ribbon on her winter coat lapel or on her secretarial
in-tray or on her hospital staff association notice board. That is something we still had better be curious about. But in the midst of the ground
war I felt that women had suddenly become invisible. During the tense
months of the "prewar" autumn, women had at least served as valuable
"human interest" stories—as wives, soldiers, girlfriends, mothers, or
even alien veiled women. Now that the serious business of combat had
begun, women had slid further down the page; only their yellow ribbons
caught the public eye. Yet it seemed clear that the yellow ribbon phenomenon (which occurred, to a lesser degree, in Canada and Britain as
well) was drawing U.S. women into the Bush administration's larger
global scheme in ways we needed to understand—not just because any
change in the world order would affect women, but also, more radically,
because any configuration of international relationships can be fashioned by government leaders only if they can devise ways to harness
women's compliance.

The third entry was written in June 1991. The regime of Saddam
Hussein, although weakened, remained in power. British and U.S. troops
were being pulled out of northern Iraq, where they had been protecting
Kurdish refugees.

The governments of George Bush and John Major wanted the refugees to return to their homes in Iraq, less because the Kurds were now
secure than because a lingering U.S. troop presence might remind voters
back home of a Vietnam-like "quagmire"; also, if Iraqi Kurds stayed in

southern Turkey, they might destabilize that ethnically less-than-harmo-nious NATO partner. At that point the Soviet Union still existed, but NATO was beginning to look like an alliance without a mission. Rum-blings in the Balkans were still too faint to catch the world's attention.

Oily smoke continued to hang over Kuwait City, though only the most committed environmental investigators were charting the spills threatening Persian Gulf marine life or the aftereffects of the bombing of Iraq's chemical plants on the health of women and men dependent on the local water supply. There was no date set and no list of invitees yet agreed upon for an Israeli-Palestinian peace conference, and in the mean-time new Soviet Jewish immigrants were being settled on the disputed West Bank. Arms dealers were doing a brisk business in the Middle East; disarmament seemed to have few genuine advocates. Even with Saudi Arabia and Israel as willing showcases for its Patriot missiles, however, Raytheon Corporation was laying off hundreds of women and men back in recession-plagued Massachusetts. Wearing yellow ribbons and host-ing the president back in February hadn't saved these defense workers their jobs in June.

Despite all these signals that the war—wars, actually—had not ended for Iraqis and Kuwaitis, most North Americans and Europeans were acting that summer as though they were living in a "postwar" era. Those who had come to support the U.S.–led warmaking, however reluctantly (as a majority of women had), were going to victory parades; those who had opposed the warmaking were going to conferences.

The fourth and fifth entries were written a year later. It felt then like I was writing about a war that had evaporated eerily from the public consciousness—almost. Election campaigns in the U.S., Britain, Canada, France, and Japan were preoccupied far more with domestic economic problems than with foreign affairs. Being on the winning side in the Gulf was not guaranteeing the leaders of any of these governments victory at the polls. Still, the Bush administration rattled swords in the form of joint military maneuvers with Kuwaiti soldiers, helping to forge a revised and rearmed Kuwaiti masculinity in the process. It was this masculinity that was allowed expression in Kuwait's own limited election in mid-1992.

Rare was the journalist who seemed curious about how the return of so many Asian women to domestic servant jobs might affect the relationship of public to private politics in postwar Kuwait. Why didn't they interview some of the two thousand maids who had sought refuge in their ill-prepared embassies to escape from women employers who had hit them and male employers who had sexually assaulted them, in part to make sense of 1992 electoral politics?[1] And what had happened to the Kuwaiti women's suffrage movement in the aftermath of the war? Only a few writers covered the story of the Kuwaiti women who participated in October 1992 election rallies and pressured male candidates to commit themselves to votes for women if they won seats in the revived parliament. The network news reporters didn't interview the male leaders of the surprisingly successful opposition party to see how their agendas incorporated women's demands. They didn't tell of some of those men's willingness to allow women to vote but staunch refusal to allow them to hold public office. Television screens didn't show Kuwaiti women picketing the polling stations and carrying signs.[2]

Next door, in Saudi Arabia, King Fahd introduced a few postwar political reforms, taking modest steps to rein in the religious police who had so energetically enforced Saudi women's decorum and quietly reinstating to their jobs the middle-class women who organized the driving protest, without addressing any of their substantive demands. At the same time, the king's U.S. allies became more nervous about his Islamic fundamentalist opposition. Thus in mid-1992, U.S. commanders ordered women soldiers still on duty in Saudi Arabia to stop driving cars and trucks so as to stop critics' charges that the king's alliance with the United States was jeopardizing the Saudi moral order.[3] As Asian women returned to the Gulf countries to work again as maids, as vulnerable as ever to sexual abuses, North Americans and Europeans coming back from their summer holidays turned on their television sets to find that once again the screens were full of "womenandchildren"—this time trying to escape wartime havoc in Bosnia and Somalia, countries without the oil fields and without the potent Orientalist imagery that spurred international mobilization during the Gulf Crisis.

Wartime and post-wartime were evolving simultaneously. While wars raged in Bosnia and Somalia, the Gulf War was being subtly but perhaps significantly reconstructed in the postwar collective psyches of the Americans and the British. A group of British women and men politicized their parental grief and sued the U.S. government for killing their soldier sons in the desert with "friendly fire." American women soldiers at the same time were beginning to tell what they had experienced in the Saudi desert: sexual assault by fellow soldiers and contempt from commanding officers. These unpleasant revelations would somehow have to be incorporated by the public into the unblemished portrait of the post–post-Vietnam U.S. military.

Postwar periods are dangerous times. They are times when lessons—sometimes the wrong lessons, and sometimes lessons that are useful for some but harmful to others—are hammered out. A postwar period is a time for feminists to keep their eyes wide open. It is a time when masculinity and femininity will be reconsidered, and perhaps reconstructed, by warmakers and peacemakers alike.

SEPTEMBER 1990: "WOMENANDCHILDREN"

In the torrents of media images that accompany an international crisis, women are typically made visible as symbols, victims, or dependents. "Womenandchildren" rolls easily off network tongues because in network minds women are family members rather than independent actors, presumed to be almost childlike in their innocence about international *realpolitik*. Rarely do journalists look to women to reveal any of the basic structures of a dangerous confrontation.

If there is an image that defines television's Gulf Crisis, it's a disheveled white woman coming off a Boeing 747, an exhausted baby on her shoulder. States exist, this media story implies, to protect womenandchildren. U.S. intervention in the Gulf would be harder to justify if there were no feminized victim. The real diplomatic wives, the British and American women who in the last decade have created formidable lobbying organizations to press their interests, don't fit into this scenario.

It follows that the Gulf Crisis story must also ignore the female attaché at the U.S. embassy in Kuwait, negotiating with the Iraqis for the release of these very same womenandchildren. Passing over State Department women's organizing, which opened up the previously masculinized foreign service, the media treats the attaché as merely an honorary man: capable, able to take care of herself—and Others. Her existence is not allowed to disturb the womenandchildren-protected-by-statesmen script.

Though you don't see them on the evening news, there are an estimated seventeen thousand Filipina women today working as domestic servants in Saudi Arabia. Thousands of others have been cleaning, washing, and minding children in Kuwait and the United Arab Emirates. Together, there are over twenty-nine thousand Filipina domestic servants in the Middle East. Government officials, not only in the Philippines but also in Sri Lanka, Indonesia, Jamaica, and Ethiopia, have been counting on the paychecks that maids send home to lessen their nations' imbalance of payments and to keep the lid on politically explosive unemployment. These Asian women, now trapped in occupied Kuwait or crowded into Jordanian refugee camps, have been crucial players in reducing the global tensions generated by international debt.

After the 1970s oil boom, Kuwaiti and Saudi women became employers in their homes. But their relationships with their Sri Lankan or Filipina maids had to be devised in ways that met with their husbands' approval and kept the foreign workers at least minimally content. When stories began to filter back home of abuse that some—not all—Asian domestic servants were experiencing, the Sri Lankan and Philippine governments were pressed by their own women's advocates to take steps to protect their nationals working abroad. The regimes acted ineffectually, in part because they were afraid of offending the Gulf states on whom they depend for oil, in part because they have rebellions and other worries closer to home diverting them, and in part because they have concluded that they need to satisfy the men from the IMF more than they need to win the support of their own women's movements.

Caryl Murphy, the *Washington Post* reporter who sent out clandestine reports from Kuwait in the days following the Iraqi invasion, described how some Filipina maids were taken by their Kuwaiti employers to the Philippine embassy so that they would have some modicum of protection. Other Kuwaitis, she reported, fled in front of the invading troops leaving their Filipino employees to fend for themselves. Filipinas in Kuwait City told Murphy that they had heard stories that Iraqi soldiers had raped domestic workers. Rape in war is never simply random violence. It is structured by male soldiers' notions of their masculine privilege, by the strength of the military's lines of command, and by class and ethnic inequalities between women. As a rich Kuwaiti woman you would have less chance of being raped than you would as an Asian maid.

To make sense, then, of the Iraqi occupation of Kuwait, we have to talk about soldiers' ideas of manliness, middle-class women's presumptions about housework, and the IMF's strategies for handling international debt. Debt, laundry, rape, and conquest are understandable only in relation to each other.

Though we have a hard time understanding it, to many Jordanians, Palestinians, and other Arabs, Saddam Hussein is a potent symbol of nationalist aspirations, fueled by a resentment of European and U.S. attempts to impose their values and their priorities on the societies of the Middle East. To many Arab men, women appear most vulnerable to Western corruption and exploitation. This conviction has infused debates over women's attire and women's education with political passion.

But Middle Eastern women are not mere symbols. First, they are diverse, distinguished by ethnicity, ideology, class, and nationality. Second, since the turn of the century many have been active participants in their countries' freedom movements. Arab feminists have criticized many of their male compatriots for trying to fashion a nationalism which camouflages male privilege under the legitimizing mantle of "Arab tradition." Being an Arab nationalist feminist is a risky enterprise (although one might say that being a feminist nationalist in any community is a daunting project). A women's rights advocate in these countries is always open to nervous men's double-barreled charge that she is succumbing to alien Western bourgeois values, while splitting the nation at a time when it needs unity above all else.

The current Gulf Crisis, defined largely by massive U.S. military posturing, has radically complicated the task of local feminists. Arab women activists, who walk a tightrope between male nationalists' patriarchy and Western policymakers' cultural imperialism, have the most to lose when an international crisis polarizes internal debate. Western male officials who claim their policies are supporting "civilized" politics are, in fact, painting Arab women into a tight corner.

But many observers, nonetheless, are portraying wartime mobilization as good for women. Saddam Hussein—a secular, not a religious, nationalist—has made wide use of women in his military buildup. During the Iran-Iraq war, Saddam Hussein encouraged the Iraqi Women's Federation to channel women into nontraditional jobs in order to free men to fight. A Saudi feminist stationed with the United Nations in Baghdad during that war even wondered aloud whether it didn't further Iraqi women's emancipation. The more devasting the war became, she recalled, the more Saddam Hussein's all-male Revolutionary Council called on women to lend their efforts to the nation (without ever forsaking their primary responsibility of producing more children). Her wondering would sound familiar to many U.S. feminists: the U.S. government followed the same course during World War II. Of course, the Iraqi cousins of Rosie the Riveter also discovered, once the war had ended, that male government officials—and their own fathers and husbands—expected women to return to the more restricted, domestic feminized roles that bolstered male egos and made space for the employment of demobilized male soldiers.

Today there is evidence that once again Iraq's Women Federation is being called upon to mobilize women, this time to put in place the consumer rationing programs which will be key to the Hussein regime's ability to withstand the UN embargo. It would not be surprising if many Iraqi women activists saw in the crisis yet another opportunity to use wartime mobilization to demonstrate their public capabilities. Now, however, in search of Muslim allies, Saddam Hussein is beginning to refer to his campaign as a holy cause. The more he couches his brand of Arab nationalism in religious terms, the less likely it is that even the exigencies of wartime mobilization will produce long-term gains for Iraqi women.

There are reports out of Saudi Arabia this week that King Fahd has instructed his ministries to encourage Saudi women to volunteer for war-related jobs until now closed to them. Saudi women nurses who have been restricted to caring only for women patients are now to be permitted to attend wounded men. Though the Western media is heralding this announcement as evidence that the wartime mobilization may benefit Saudi women portrayed as benighted, there has been scarce curiosity about the history or current thinking of those women.

In fact, U.S. coverage of the Gulf Crisis has been framed by a contrast between the liberated U.S. woman soldier and the veiled Arab woman. It is striking how consistent this current media preoccupation is with the Western tradition of Orientalism, that package of often ambivalent ideas about the presumed backwardness and allure of Arab culture. The harem has been at the center of this Western preoccupation. In the past it was the daring Victorian lady traveler who posed the stark contrast with the secluded Arab woman. The former's presence served to reassure the self-satisfied Western man that his society was the more "civilized" and thus within its natural rights in colonizing the Middle East. The European woman traveler also tempted many of her homebound sisters to imagine that they were a lot more emancipated than they really were: even if they were denied the vote, couldn't control their own reproduction, and couldn't divorce a violent husband, at least they weren't pent up in a harem. The imperialist enterprise relied on the feelings of both its women and its men that they were superior to the patriarchal Arabs.

Today, television and print journalists are substituting the U.S. woman soldier for the Victorian lady traveler, but the political intent remains much the same. By contrasting the allegedly liberated American woman tank mechanic with the Saudi woman deprived of a driver's license, American reporters are implying that the United States is the advanced, civilized country whose duty it is to take the initiative in resolving the Persian Gulf crisis and in leading the international community into a new world order. Women of both countries are being turned into the currency with which men attempt to maintain the unequal relations between their societies.

Yet Arab women, even in the conservative societies of the Gulf, are more than passive victims of purdah. There are Saudi women who have a university education, who have founded women-only banks, who practice medicine in women-only hospitals, and who earn wages in newly established garment factories. One need not overstate the political and economic freedom of these women to argue that Saudi women are diverse and offer authentic analyses of their own.

There are Kuwaiti women who have organized neighborhood-level protests against the occupying Iraqi army. Susan Shuaib, a Kuwaiti-British feminist writing in the latest *New Statesman and Society*, puts this surprising news in the broader context of Kuwait's changing political relations between women and men. Just this past July, according to Shuaib, women became more visible as activists pressing for parliamentary government. They organized petition drives and took part in public rallies.

The second problem with the neo-Orientalist interpretation adopted by so many American reporters is that it treats the "advances" made by U.S. women soldiers outside any consideration of militarism. There are daily stories now about women soldiers coping with life in the desert. Approximately 6 percent of all U.S. forces in Saudi Arabia are women, a little more than half their proportion in the military as a whole. In the U.S. and British media, the woman flying a giant C-141 transport is portrayed as the natural descendant of Susan B. Anthony.

It is true that many women in the military do see themselves as feminists, breaking down formidable sexist barriers. For them, the Persian Gulf operation is not part of Middle East political evolution, with its volatile mix of imperialism and nationalism; it is part of a political struggle that began with the American women in Vietnam and was carried into the U.S. invasions of Grenada and Panama. Each U.S. military intervention has provided a chance for women to hone their bureaucratic skills, to perfect end runs around chauvinist field commanders, and to turn up the heat on Pentagon officials still dragging their feet in opening up military career opportunities to women soldiers.

If, however, winning first-class citizenship depends on American women's gaining full acceptance in the military, what does that mean for the very concept of citizenship? In all the coverage of U.S. women soldiers' advances, there is the implication that the military defines citizenship.

The always-artificial categories of "combat" and "noncombat" may indeed be crumbling in the desert. But few women are talking yet about what sorts of sexual harassment they are likely to experience as the weeks pass with male soldiers who have none of their usual access to foreign women while overseas. Which country will play host to the thousands of U.S. soldiers on R and R? Not Saudi Arabia. Whichever government agrees to serve as a rest and recreation site will make agreements with the Pentagon to ensure that U.S. male soldiers have direct access to local women without endangering the men's health. Buried in the fine print of government-to-government R and R agreements are stipulations about public health and police authority that directly affect local women's relations with GIs. These agreements, in turn, support a military culture that nurtures misogyny and homophobia. According to the Pentagon's recently released study, 64 percent of women in the military say they have been sexually harassed. A woman soldier who won't pay attention to a male colleague is always vulnerable to lesbian-baiting. And exposure to this risk is made doubly intimidating when the Pentagon persists in its policy of forcing suspected lesbians out of the service.

The Persian Gulf crisis is not built out of relations between ungendered presidents, kings, foreign ministers, oil executives, and soldiers. If we pay attention to the experiences and ideas of the women involved, two realities come into sharper focus. First, this international confrontation, like others before it, is being played out in part by governments attempting to confine women to roles that, even if they briefly shake conventional social norms, nonetheless serve those governments' interests. Those government attempts to control women, however, are not always successful. Second, men's sense of their own masculinity, often tenuous, is as much a factor in international politics as is the flow of oil, cables, and military hardware.

FEBRUARY 1991: TIE A YELLOW RIBBON 'ROUND THE NEW WORLD ORDER

On the eve of the Gulf War, polls in the U.S. revealed a startling gender gap: American women were far less likely than American men to support going to war with Iraq. Less than one week before the fighting began, the ABC News/*Washington Post* poll showed that only 58 percent of the women surveyed, compared with 82 percent of the men, thought that war was the best way for the U.S. government to respond to Saddam Hussein. For pollsters, a 24-point difference is a gender gap of monumental proportions. Then, on January 16, U.S. bombs began falling on Baghdad. As the bombs rained, the gender gap began to shrink. It wasn't American men who were changing their minds; it was the women. By January 20, the gender gap had shrunk to a mere 10 points: 71 percent and 81 percent.

George Bush has justified using force against the Iraqis to protect a "New World Order." Whereas, under the oversimplified banner of the old order, East was pitted against West, in the new, also unrealistically dichotomized post-1989 order, the North is pitted against a South personified by Saddam Hussein. Yet this allegedly new order remains stuck in the old presumption that military power must be the principal tool for wielding international influence.

Bush's world order depends on its own kind of gender gap: George Bush, Colin Powell, John Major, Saddam Hussein, Yitzhak Shamir, the Iraqi Republican Guards, and British Tornado and U.S. B-52 pilots are all part of a state elite, their masculinity unquestioned. Their wives, as well as M-16–toting U.S. women soldiers and Saudi women driving protesters, are of course discussed as women but are consequently treated as trivial. Yet, as feminists have revealed in the last decade, every public power arrangement has depended on the control of femininity as an idea and of women themselves as workers, caregivers, and sexual partners. We cannot make sense of any government's hoped-for world order in a gender vacuum. The post-August U.S. gender gap, and its recent dramatic shrinkage, must be explained precisely because the not-so-new, militarized *pax Americana* won't work unless women cooperate. The current world order is "orderly" only if national security officials can imagine their responsibilities to be "manly," diplomats can be served by unpaid diplomatic wives, nationalist men can count on their women to pay homage to the nation's gendered culture, multinational corporations can feminize and thereby cheapen labor, indebted governments can send maids overseas to mail home paychecks, and technocrats can celebrate supermoms as models of modernity.

A militarized world order needs women to find rewards in a militarized femininity. Wives who refuse to behave like self-sacrificing "military wives," mothers who reject military service as their sons' avenue to manhood, and young women who will not see enlistment as a guarantor of "first-class citizenship" jeopardize Bush's global design. For the United States to wage a war successfully in the Gulf, the gender gap had to be closed. A lot of women had to be persuaded to move across the opinion divide without throwing overboard their notions of femininity.

Turning U.S. soldiers into "our troops" seems to have been the key. It was when U.S. soldiers in the Gulf were subjected to the dangers of actual combat that the gender gap collapsed. In "tying a yellow ribbon 'round an old oak tree"—or a car antenna, a porch pillar, or a shop sign—most women probably do not see themselves as endorsing something as grandiose as a new world order. More likely, they see themselves as providing moral support to particular sons, daughters, neighbors, and friends. But as far as the U.S. national security elite is concerned, these women are voluntarily constructing a feminized "home front" to complement a battle front that—thousands of American women soldiers notwithstanding—is thoroughly masculinized. As well-meaning and as profoundly humane as every ribbon-tying gesture may be, each one makes it harder than ever to preserve that earlier distinction between caring for particular soldiers, on the one hand, and objecting to the Bush policy, on the other.

Patriotism has always been an arena that women have found especially difficult to enter. It has always been easier for an Oliver North to gain entrance than for a Betsy North. For many women, the only path is through the narrow doorways marked "mother" and "wife." If a woman cannot become a recognized patriot on her own merits, then she may try to become a patriotic mother or a patriotic wife—real or vicarious. Governments encourage women to imagine that being a loyal female member of a family is synonymous with being a patriot. For women in wartime, the nation becomes a family.

The Gulf War has made this myth of the wartime family even more potent. The U.S. military today has daughters as well as sons; it includes single parents and husband-soldiers married to wife-soldiers. Yet the spiritual soul of the institution, male "combat," remains intact. So long as the allies continue to rely on an air war, the imagery of U.S. global power will be of male top guns, not female ground mechanics.

At the same time, the military's reliance on two hundred thousand women in uniform has given the U.S. military a new cloak of legitimacy. The institution doesn't seem such an anachronism. It can even claim to be a means for American women to achieve full political status as people who can "die for their country." To many American women, whether or not they themselves are considering signing up, today's military is no longer "other." The military looks every day more like General Hospital. That makes it an even better instrument for building and entrenching a U.S.–designed not-so-new world order.

Not only U.S. society, but also Saudi, Egyptian, Kuwaiti, Israeli, Iraqi, British, Japanese, and German society are waging this war at a sexually specific historical moment. For instance, this war has sparked new debates among Saudi men about just what constitutes Saudi nationalism: can Saudi nationhood withstand dependence on other countries' men to fight its battles? Thus, news of a Saudi fighter pilot's first victories in the air has consequences for women. The wartime coalition between U.S. senior partners and Saudi junior partners may create a new, more militarized form of Saudi nationalist masculinity. In postwar Saudi Arabia, will Saudi women, just now reaching out for political rights, be faced with patriarchal barriers that are not only sanctified religiously but also blessed militarily?

Similarly, Americans have named the gender gap only during the past two decades, as women have developed their own perspectives on many public policies, have become more organized in articulating those perspectives, and have voted into office more women willing to give authoritative voice to those perspectives. The Gulf War itself has been launched by a president who wielded masculinity nervously in his 1988 electoral campaign, at a time when U.S. collective manliness appeared to be jeopardized by the country's slide in global economic competitiveness.

The Gulf War is being waged in the shadow of the sexual politics of another war. The Vietnam War left a cultural legacy of gendered guilt: the betrayed male vet. He has taken fifteen years and a lot of celluloid and paper to create, but today he is a potent figure inspiring complex emotions. While there are at least seventy-five hundred female American Vietnam veterans, it is the unappreciated, alienated male Vietnam vet whose image looms over the present war. It is for him as much as for the U.S. soldiers actually in the Gulf that many women seem to be tying yellow ribbons around their trees and antennas. This war is about masculinity, just as all wars have been; but it is a historically and socially specific masculinity. Without the feelings of guilt inspired by the image of the betrayed Vietnam male vet, without a public discourse that permits the stories of male soldiers to blot out discussions of government policy errors, perhaps it would have been much harder to convert the women against a war on January 15 into the women supporting it on January 20.

JUNE 1991: "POSTWAR" PATRIARCHY

As I walked home yesterday in the 100-degree heat of a June afternoon, I noticed yellow ribbons still tacked up on my neighbors' front porches. They drooped now in the heat, their color drained by months of rain and wind. Most of the houses that had proudly flown American flags had taken them in, but somehow the yellow ribbon seemed best left to age naturally in the New England elements.

We are now officially in the "postwar" era. Though the fate of Iraq's Kurdish minority hangs precariously undecided and, according to medical experts' reports, wartime embargoes are causing scores of infant deaths in other Iraqi communities, we have adopted a postwar emotional and political stance. We are thinking retrospectively. We are generating "lessons."

The Gulf War lasted less than a year, but this postwar period is as fraught with lessons as the ones that followed on the heels of longer conflicts have been. Just as atheism is defined by reference to a god, so any postwar era is marked by its relationship to the war it succeeds. In that sense, this is a militarized time, not a time of peace. And thus it is a time for vigilance. Many of those horrified by their inability to prevent the massive use of military power, or perhaps even by their inability to withstand the seductive attractions of technological wizardry and post-Vietnam patriotism, will use these postwar months to take a close look at the failings of their country's peace movement. But it is also critical to watch how other players in the Gulf War use this postwar era to fashion lessons. For the lessons that are presumed to have been taught by the war against Iraq will become the basis for militarizing the next international conflict. Many of those lessons are specifically about the relationships between women and men.

After every war, governments—on the losing as well as the winning side—take stock of how gender either served or undermined their war efforts. The Crimean War offers a striking example of the postwar politics of gender. Every government involved in this mid-nineteenth-century Middle Eastern conflict came away unhappy about its own performance. The British military command and its parliamentary masters, for instance, were convinced that British soldiers had been ill-prepared to fight in the Crimea. Like military strategists today, they devoted their postwar energies to pinpointing what ensured that male soldiers had high morale and physical well-being. And, like their counterparts today in Washington, London, Riyadh, and Baghdad, they paid special attention to masculinity—and to the ways that different groups of women might be controlled so that they would not jeopardize the sort of manliness deemed best suited for waging the government's military campaigns. In practice, this meant that British officials launched two fierce debates: first, should the rank and file be allowed to marry? (Were women as wives a drag on a military, as long supposed, or were they potential protection against venereal disease and debt?) Second, was the rampaging venereal disease among male soldiers controllable? (Was it more effective and honorable to impose police restrictions on women in British garrison towns than to humiliate military men by making them undergo compulsory genital examinations?) Britain's first national women's political campaign—the Anti-Contagious Diseases Acts Campaign—was prompted by the nineteenth-century postwar lessons drawn by worried military planners.

Marriage, morale, sexuality, discipline—these are the arenas for lesson-forging that still produce postwar attempts to refine the relations of women to the government's mostly male soldiery.

The first post–Gulf War attempt to change the U.S. military's relationship to mothering has already been concluded; the military won. Representative Barbara Boxer, a progressive California Democrat, was dismayed by the stories published during the war of dual-military families that had both parents called up and deployed far from their very young children. For several weeks the media carried pictures of infants being tearfully left behind with relatives while their mothers and fathers donned their fatigues and headed for the Gulf. No one should have been surprised. During the past decade the military had been relying more and more on the reserves in their global planning. The Pentagon had deliberately been using women to compensate for the decline in the pool in eligible young men (high school graduates, drug-free, nonfelons); after an initial reluctance, it had come to see dual-career military couples as promoting reenlistment and deepening whole families' loyalty to military service. But for the media, much of the public, and the Congress, it came as a rude shock to see this military personnel formula translated into the apparent abandonment of infants.

Barbara Boxer thus saw as one lesson of the Gulf War the need to put limits on military deployment; the parenting of very young American children should take priority over the Pentagon's need for soldiers. Yet her bill barely survived its initial hearings. Defense Department officials, not surprisingly, raised immediate objections. In the Bush administration's vision of the new world order, the U.S. military will have fewer overseas bases, though not necessarily reduced responsibilities. In personnel terms, this combination will be feasible only if the military can have absolutely free rein in calling up reserves and moving those reserves, as well as active-duty soldiers, anywhere at any time, at a moment's notice. Mobility has always been the sine qua non of an effective military. And it has always required military commanders to have control over women, as service workers, as wives, as mothers, and as girlfriends. Bush's conception of the post–Cold War world makes this need for control over women acute. They must not be allowed to slow future mobilizations.

Barbara Boxer's bill was a very real threat to reliance on this smaller but more mobile force. Nonetheless, the politics of parenting—especially of mothering—is at least as potent in the early 1990s as is the strategic imperative for a mobile military. So why did the Boxer bill never get off the ground? It would appear that it was killed not only by the Pentagon's opposition but also by the cool reception it received from many women military careerists. They feared, perhaps rightly, that although the bill sought to restrict deployment of "parents" of young children, if passed, it would be used to restrict the deployment of *mothers* in uniform. The Boxer bill, many canny women lobbyists predicted, would create a military mommy track.

"Women in combat" achieved an even higher profile in this postwar America than military mothering did. What lessons did the Gulf War generate about women's capacity to engage in combat and militaries' willingness to use them for combat? The Canadians had carried on this debate several years before their government sent women and men to fight Iraq. As the result of a court case brought by women's rights advocates under the country's new Charter of Rights, women soldiers no longer could be excluded from combat. But neither they nor Dutch women, also theoretically eligible for combat, actually served in officially designated combat roles during the Gulf conflict. The British and Australian forces had banned women from whatever they deemed to be "combat" (the definition is arbitrary in any military), but observers in both of these countries watched as the much larger and more visible U.S. contingent became the site for this latest skirmish in the long struggle over femininity, masculinity, and the changing landscape of high-technology warfare.

Again, it was women members of the House of Representatives who took the lead in raising this postwar issue. Patricia Schroeder, Democratic representative from Colorado, and Beverly Byron, Democratic representative from Maryland, interpreted the Gulf War as proof that the nature of contemporary warfare made the conceptual divide between combat and noncombat irrelevant. Despite the U.S. ban on women in combat, thirteen U.S. women soldiers were killed in action in the Gulf, and two were taken prisoner by the Iraqi forces. The sight of "women returning in body bags" turned out not to have seriously undercut the legitimacy of the Bush administration's war policy. The Pentagon itself was divided over the political and logistical wisdom of ending the ban. According to the astute Pentagon-watcher Linda Grant De Pauw, editor of the journal *Minerva,* older military professionals concluded that the Gulf operations had not demonstrated decisively whether allowing women access to combat roles would jeopardize the fighting morale of men in the now-masculinized infantry, armored, fighter plane, and bomber units. Morale has always been the sticking point: a military cannot afford to take any step that undermines the morale of its mainly male force, and morale among men is dependent in large measure on esteem derived from their sense of manliness.

But a younger generation of Pentagon officials, civilian and uniformed, had come of age professionally since 1973, the start of the military's deliberate efforts to compensate for the end of the male draft by recruiting large numbers of women. These officials were willing to let the postwar lessons be honed by public representatives. If the U.S. public would legitimate women in combat, the military would have even more flexibility in deploying personnel according to its own needs. Women officers publicly backed the Schroeder and Byron legislative initiative. They had become convinced that the combat ban was a major stumbling block on their path toward senior promotions.

According to De Pauw, however, the actors most notable for their silence in this postwar debate were organized feminists. When the legislation reached the Senate in May 1991 (sponsored by Bill Roth, Republican from Delaware), no broad-based feminist organization submitted testimony. Although during the war the National Organization for Women had issued a declaration calling simultaneously for support of women in the Middle East and for an end to all forms of sexism in the U.S. military, its leaders, like other women who had spent years working for the Equal Rights Amendment, remembered how anti-ERA forces had manipulated women-in-combat anxieties to defeat the amendment. Also, as in the past, many U.S. feminists—even those who had adopted a liberal feminist approach which assigns priority to equal opportunity—were profoundly ambivalent about making women's access to combat jobs a political priority. The debate, coming as it did in the wake of a war which frustrated many women whose activism had been devoted to unsuccessful campaigning for peace, seemed to leave no space for a more complicated dialogue about women's relationship to a militarized state.

So it was without a civilian feminist presence that on May 22, 1991, the overwhelmingly male House of Representatives passed the 1992–93 Defense Authorization Bill as amended by Byron and Schroeder to permit the civilian secretaries of the U.S. Navy and U.S. Air Force for the first time to assign women soldiers to fly combat aircraft. The amendment—which formally repeals Section 512 (the army's combat exclusion policy is dictated not by law but by the service's administrative policy)—is expected to pass the Senate later this year.

Farther away from the floors of Congress and from the public limelight, Defense Department officials were assessing how well they had done in ensuring that military wives and girlfriends stayed supportive not only of their men in uniform but also of the military cause at large. The Gulf War had provided the department with a chance to try out its

revised family strategies. Since the early 1970s, partly in response to
vocal military wives, the military had taken a far more activist and
interventionist role in military family affairs. The once autonomous
Military Family Resource Center, originally run by the Young Men's
Christian Association (YMCA), was integrated into the Pentagon. Child
abuse and wife abuse became issues to be discussed administratively,
inside the Defense Department. Men's antiviolence groups reported
being asked to visit bases to give training sessions to men returning from
Operation Desert Storm, men likely to have inflated expectations of
wifely welcomes, men likely to be quick to resort to physical abuse when
confronted with the messier realities of ordinary domestic life. Military
social workers and military spouses learned that if they could show that
dysfunctional families threatened "military readiness," they could get
even under-secretaries of the military to sit up and take notice. During
the Gulf War, the Pentagon authorized the creation of family support
groups for girlfriends and partners as well as spouses. Although officers'
wives had recently become more resistant to pressures to perform unpaid
labor on military bases, in many cases a woman married to a senior
officer served as the hub of each support group. While many family
members found the authorized groups helpful in everything from sharing
fears to figuring out how to deal with creditors, others who took part
said the groups seemed to be intent upon ensuring that women stay
supportive of the Bush policy and that they pour their energies into
reducing soldiers' worries, not their own.

Even farther from public attention in the U.S., militaries that had been
U.S. allies thought about the lessons of a war fought without prostitutes.
The Saudi regime of King Fahd had made a no-brothels policy one
stipulation of its acceptance of foreign forces. As its harsh suppression
of the apparently modest women's driving protest later revealed, the
regime was being challenged by male Islamic fundamentalists. Each
group of men—those supporting the monarchy and the emergent opposition—held up its ability to control Saudi women as the litmus test of
political legitimacy. We still know almost nothing about what the consequences of the prostitution prohibition were for militarized masculine

sexuality. In Central America, Vietnam, the Philippines, South Korea, Japan, Puerto Rico, the mainland United States, Germany, and Italy the Pentagon has operated as if prostitution were a necessary and integral part of U.S. military operations. It has not always been easy to control that prostitution, of course; it has meant the spread of AIDS; it has produced marriages not wanted by the military; it has caused friction between local police and military police; it has threatened the morale of American women in the services. But not until this war did the U.S. Defense Department believe it could sustain the masculine morale needed to ensure motivated, disciplined soldiering without prostitution. Perhaps the intensity and brevity of the Gulf conflict will mean that the absence of prostitution will be viewed as merely an anomaly, generating no institutional policy revisions. Or perhaps the policy resulted in delayed male sexual behaviors known only to waiting girlfriends and wives back home, or to those Thai women working as prostitutes who greeted some of the first U.S. ships as they made a deliberately scheduled stop at Pattaya, Thailand, on their route from the Persian Gulf to Japan. We don't know. What we do know, based on years of experience, is that somewhere in the military someone is trying to figure out whether this war provided lessons for a better way to control sexuality for the sake of more effective warmaking.

What are those lessons? Women's relationship to their government's military remains one that is *not* fashioned primarily by broadly based women's organizations, in large part because the relationship is a source of much confusion. Is the military chiefly a public institution that distributes valuable benefits (pride, skills, salaries, influence, independence)? Or is the military best understood as a vehicle for state violence? What should feminists' stand be if the military has become both?

The yellow ribbons and the push to end the exclusion of women in combat seem to be intimately connected in the United States of the 1990s. Women inside and outside the country's military are insisting that they have their own thoughts, their own aspirations. But so long as women have so little control over the terms of debate, even their genuine efforts to voice those ideas and press for those aspirations are likely to produce short-sighted gains (more media coverage, more military promotions) without actually changing the basic ways in which public power is used. For their part, many men working in peace groups have barely conceded that the issue of women's relationship to state power, confusing as it is, is worthy of serious political attention. Few of these men asked women exactly what thoughts they were expressing when they put ribbons on their secretarial in-trays; few monitored with genuine concern the congressional debate over women in combat. In this sense, male peace activists have yet to recognize that militarization cannot be reversed until the politics of femininity's relationship to both masculinity and the state are taken seriously.

It may be that the U.S. military—along with, perhaps, the militaries of other NATO governments—has learned how to absorb just enough of the changes in women's expectations and influence to permit it to use women without drastically altering its own political mission. It may be that the military has come out of the Gulf War more thoroughly integrated into the social structure than it has been in the last two centuries. If so, the end of the Cold War will not mean the end of the militarization of women's lives.

AUGUST 1992: RAPES IN THE DESERT

It's so tempting to begin here with Army Specialist Fourth Class Jacqueline Ortiz. She seems to hold a vital clue to rethinking the war. Her testimony to a Senate committee last month recalling how she had been sexually assaulted by her own sergeant during Operation Desert Storm strongly suggested that this was not, as so many Americans wanted to believe, the war that would blot out the tawdriness of Vietnam.

But Jacqueline Ortiz is an American. The twenty-four other military women who have told Army investigators how they were sexually abused by their fellow soldiers on the Saudi desert are also American. Is this really the best place to start the next phase of postwar rethinking? It is surprising how much sustained, conscious mental effort it takes to think of this war from a vantage point outside one's own society. But if two years ago it was useful to try to make sense of what was then labeled the Gulf Crisis by imagining the experiences of a Filipina woman working as a maid in Kuwait City, that analytical stance probably remains valuable today.

Filipina and other Asian women are back in the Gulf states doing other people's housework. Their return, which was not anticipated, sheds some light on the processes by which postwar Kuwaiti society is being constructed. As there is after most wars, there was considerable public and private debate over just what had "gone wrong" that had made the country so vulnerable to aggression and so ineffectual in defense. And as in so many other countries, this postwar self-inspection generated judgments of local femininity and masculinity. Had the country's men sacrificed their masculine military competence on the altar of effeminized degeneracy? Had the country's women frayed the threads of the country's social fabric by neglecting their home duties? The oily smoke was still hanging over the city of Kuwait when people began to criticize the prewar dependency on foreign domestic servants. If Kuwaiti women started to do their own housework, perhaps the entire social order could be strengthened and made ready to repel future military invasions. Many Kuwaiti women active in the wartime resistance and in the movement for women's suffrage concurred. They were concerned less with postwar militarization, however, than with reconstructing Kuwaiti womanhood so that it incorporated a sense of self-reliance.

The return of Asian women to work as domestic servants, then, provides one piece of evidence that the initial postwar attempt to reorder notions of gender fell short of some reformers' hopes. But other things *have* changed. More Asian women working as maids appear unwilling now to remain silent in the face of sexual abuse by their male employers. Since early January there have been press reports of Filipina women who have taken considerable risks in order to leave abusive employers, taking refuge in the Philippine embassy. It is not clear whether the Filipinas now seeking work overseas are more self-confident and aware of their rights or whether, in the wake of the war, many Kuwaiti men are more violent in their domestic expressions of manliness.

On May 3 *USA Today* reported, "The number of women being raped
by Kuwaiti soldiers has risen to as many as 20 a day, according to
hospital records and officials." Nadia Ghaleb, a nurse at Kuwait City's
Maternity Hospital, estimated that "now there are more rapes than there
were during the occupation." The women being assaulted have included
both Asian emigrant women and local Kuwaiti women. Most have
reported that their assailants were men in Kuwaiti military uniforms.
There is official disagreement over whether the cause lies in the continuing lack of firm government control, which allows some men to do
what they want to do without fear of reprisal, or whether it lies buried
in the frustrated postoccupation sense of bruised masculinity that some
Kuwaiti men have converted into rampant misogyny.

Unfortunately, Kuwaiti women who experienced the oppression of
Iraqi occupation have not necessarily drawn from it the lesson that
women need to make alliances across class and race. Raymond Bonner,
writing for the *New Yorker,* was told by Filipinas taking refuge in the
Philippine embassy that their bruises were as often inflicted by their
female as by their male employers. Thus, some Kuwaiti women seem to
be treating their domestic servants as they themselves are often treated.

Other Kuwaiti women are coming forward to tell of the rapes they
endured by Iraqi soldiers during the occupation. One Kuwaiti psychia-
trist who has been trying to assist these women estimates that perhaps
as many as thirty-two hundred women were raped by men of the occupying forces between late August 1990 and February 1991. The Kuwaiti
women had waited six, nine, even eleven months to tell of their ordeals.
The *New York Times* reporter provided a cultural context for this
August 4 story: Kuwaiti women, he explained, had found it especially
difficult to come forward as victims of wartime rape because Arab
culture put so high a value on feminine sexual honor and purity that any
woman subjected to assault, even though against her will, would likely
be rejected by her husband and family.

While this cultural explanation for the still-unfolding sexual politics
of postwar Kuwait may be valid, the rape victims' long silence does
not set Kuwait aside as distinctly non-Western. Consequently, such an

Fig. 9. Some of the 130 Filipina women who sought refuge in the Philippine embassy in Kuwait City in January 1992 after being abused by their Kuwaiti employers. (NYT Pictures)

explanation does not, or should not, serve as fodder to sustain the ideology of Orientalism, that package of gendered ideas which proved such a potent wartime mobilizing tool for the U.S.–led alliance two years ago.

The unsatisfactoriness of the Orientalist explanation was underscored in June and July when U.S. women soldiers began to break their own silence about the sexual abuses they had endured during the Gulf War. It had taken these allegedly liberated American women as long as it had taken their Kuwaiti and Filipina counterparts to come forward publicly and identify themselves as victims of men's sexual violence. The silencing of women to preserve the honor not only of individual men but of a nation turns out to be an integral part of the processes of war and postwar order in societies as seemingly different as Kuwait and the United States.

The U.S. women soldiers whose stories of sexual abuse are being told this summer do not have identical stories to tell; nor are they being treated by editors and officials in identical ways. The story that has received the most coverage has been that of Major Rhonda Cornum. Though serving as a flight surgeon, a job legally defined as noncombat, she was captured by Iraqi troops after her helicopter was shot down. She was one of two American women soldiers who became prisoners of war (POWs) during the conflict, and as such she was subjected to intense scrutiny when she was released as part of the eventual cease-fire agreement. A principal argument used by all governments who exclude women from any job they categorize as a combat position is that as combatants women would be likely to be captured and that in captivity they would become victims of sexual assault. That possibility, these defenders of combat exclusion insist, is one that citizens on the home front would not tolerate, and thus its very likelihood would erode civilian confidence in any war effort. Major Cornum's reassurance upon her release that she was not sexually abused by her Iraqi captors was taken as evidence by some women's advocates that the combat exclusion rested on false assumptions.

At about the time when Kuwaiti women were finding their voices in order to describe their victimization by Iraqi men during the war and Kuwaiti men after it, Rhonda Cornum broke her silence as well. She told the Presidential Commission on Women in the Military that, contrary to her earlier public account, she had indeed been sexually abused by one of her Iraqi captors. She said that she had witheld this information from the media for so many months because she believed that it would be blown out of all proportion, and perhaps even be used by those in the Congress and the Pentagon who wanted to bolster the now-weakened rationale for keeping combat an all-male preserve. Rhonda Cornum's story was sold to a publisher, and she appeared on prime-time television as well as respected public radio interview shows. Despite her own attempts to play down the incident, it had too many enticing ingredients for the media to ignore. Most appealing was the fact that Rhonda Cornum had been assaulted by an enemy male. When interviewer Terry Gross asked her on August 7 whether "manual rape" would be an accurate description of what the soldier had inflicted on her, she reluctantly replied yes, although, she said, she preferred to think of herself as having been "manually molested." With Iraq's regime in mid-1992 still defying the insistence of the United Nations and the United States that it disarm and cease attacks against Kurds and Shiites, the portrayal of an unnamed and thus generalizable Iraqi male as brutal (Rhonda Cornum was suffering from two broken arms when she was assaulted) might have appeared an easy ideological fit for journalists and editors covering this story.

Major Cornum was correct, however, in her prediction that opponents of U.S. women soldiers' entry into combat positions would interpret her experience as validation for their policy stand. The dispute over combat eligibility, which had been so quietly settled several months earlier in a legislative compromise, once again burst into the open. A month after her testimony, on August 17, Patrick Buchanan delivered a nationally televised speech intended to boost the sagging morale of Republican Party delegates at their Houston convention. He listed "women in combat" as one of the planks in the radical feminist–inspired platform of the rival Democrats. Abortion on demand, women in combat, and homosexual rights—these were the reforms that the nation had to look forward to if the Democratic ticket was elected in November, Buchanan warned. The only way to prevent these changes, which would subvert the American society in this dangerous postwar era, was to reelect a Republican president. His speech was met with enthusiastic cheers from the floor of the Houston Astrodome.

Specialist Jacqueline Ortiz's testimony before Senator Alan Cranston's Senate Committee on Veterans' Affairs received far less media attention than Major Rhonda Cornum's testimony. On June 30, Ortiz, a twenty-nine-year-old army reservist, described to the senators how she had been "forcibly sodomized" by her own sergeant in broad daylight in a U.S. desert camp on January 19, 1991. Her testimony suggested that it was not combat engagement with an enemy that posed a threat to women; it was service in any predominantly male organization whose institutional culture remained imbued with misogyny.

Ortiz went on to tell how her male army superiors had dismissed her complaints and how, months later, now discharged, she had watched her requests for psychological counseling go unmet at a string of Veterans Administration hospitals which had made no preparations for assisting women soldiers who had been the victims of sexual assault. Her experience, furthermore, appeared to be part of a more general pattern of male abuse and bureaucratic neglect. In late July, the Army's Criminal Investigation Command began to release its still-tentative findings. As reported to the *Washington Post*, "at least 24 U.S. Army servicewomen were raped or sexually assaulted while serving in the Persian Gulf region during Operations Desert Shield and Desert Storm."

Maybe these revelations were too painful or simply too difficult to absorb for a public which wanted so deeply to hold on to one of the few positive legacies of the war: the transformation of a tainted post-Vietnam soldiery into a soldiery that Americans could be proud of. At any rate, the reports of sexual assault by American military men on American military women hardly caused a ripple in the popular culture. What would Americans and CNN viewers around the world have thought of the U.S. military's claim to have transformed itself into the exemplar of a post–Cold War military if Ortiz and her fellow women soldiers had been able to get their experiences onto the front pages in January 1991 instead of August 1992? By summer 1992, critiques of the media's willingness to subject itself to Defense Department management were beginning to appear. But only a few observers noted what the media's processes of self-censorship, combined with government manipulation, had done to distort the gendered politics of the Gulf War. Now, in the wake of the Ortiz testimony, syndicated columnist Molly Ivins recalled her own frustration. In her column printed July 5 in the *Boston Globe,* she wrote, "I know that quite a few people in the press knew about the rapes of servicewomen in the Gulf almost 18 months ago, because I tried to get the story out myself. The network of women in the military was buzzing about the rapes, and the concern was strong and vocal."

Ivins described what seemed to her to be the two editorial roadblocks to getting these stories into print so that the reading public could have a more realistic understanding of how the American military operated in this alleged "good war." The first barrier was an institutional reluctance to publish a report "so controversial and upsetting" without its being confirmed by an official source. The fact that the very heart of the story was the unwillingness of military officers to take rape and sexual harassment seriously evidently was not comprehensible or else not important to most editors. Second, according to Ivins, some women reporters with knowledge of the assaults of American male soldiers on American servicewomen were prevented from printing those accounts by their editors' personal investment in the portrait they were helping to draw of the new U.S. military as "fearless, peerless and without fault." And there was, Molly Ivins remembered, a final obstacle. Although the women soldiers were willing to tell at least some of their colleagues about their experiences, they were afraid to tell their stories for the record. They were silenced by a (probably realistic) fear that "the Pentagon would use it as an excuse to keep women out of combat zones, out of chances for promotion and out of the ranks."

As the end of this summer is being marked by the Republican Party convention in Houston, it seems as though the Gulf War victory is not important enough in many Americans' minds to be decisive in their presidential voting choice; on the other hand, it has taken deep enough root in the collective culture to withstand a serious challenge from Jacqueline Ortiz and other American women who did not experience the U.S. military as a postsexist institution. Perhaps for most Americans, consequently, this war did nothing more—or less—than sanitize their state's armed forces by showing it as a place where honorable men can handle hardship and deadly technology with competence and aplomb and where women can take a more active role in defending their country.

There are connections, of course, between Filipina, Kuwaiti, and American women's experiences of wartime and postwar sexual assault. As these women find their voices—the Filipina maids raped by their Gulf employers, the Kuwaiti women raped by Iraqi soldiers, the Kuwaiti women raped by Kuwaiti men, an American woman soldier raped by an Iraqi captor, and the American women soldiers raped and harassed by American male colleagues—the entire meaning of this deceptively brief war will become clearer. But connecting the dots between these women's experiences—and between their silences—already suggests that there are serious flaws in the widespread assumption that the U.S. "won" the Cold War in large part because of the superiority of its social order, an order whose twin flagships have been its consumerist culture and its state military. The Orientalist convictions that two years ago elevated the confident, camouflage-attired American woman soldier to the status of a global model of liberation—and, by inference, raised the American male soldier to the status of a model of the New Man—have turned out to rest on a foundation of desert sand.

OCTOBER 1992: TAILHOOKERS
AND DRAFT-DODGERS

The *New York Times,* in its cultural wisdom, once summed up Somerville, Massachusetts, as an "unsavory Greater Boston backwater." But even backwaters, savory or not, like parades. As the presidential campaign was grinding on in early September, Somerville celebrated its 150th anniversary with a parade. It was a beautiful, warm autumn day, bringing residents out to sit on the curbs or on their plastic lawn chairs along the full length of the parade route. Neighbors greeted each other; vendors plied balloons and iced cherry slush.

Parades: culture in linear motion. The Grand Marshal of Somerville's anniversary parade was a marine general. He strode out in front with a long-legged, easy gait. Clearly known to a lot of the people sitting in the sun along the curb, he was greeted by many spectators as a neighbor who had come home. His mother and sisters, two of them nuns, rode several yards behind him in a chrome-and-polish 1950s classic.

For the next several hours the nature of this solidly Democratic community unfolded as the parade advanced. There was a "Somerville Recycles" float and a Dixieland quartet; there were high school majorettes and a bevy of local elected officials. But every other contingent was military: the National Guard unit, the Veterans of Foreign Wars branch, its women's auxiliary, Vietnam War veterans, Gulf War veterans, a young black man dressed in a Revolutionary War uniform, POWs and MIAs (missing-in-action) represented by a man crouching in a simulated bamboo cage carried on the back of a flatbed truck. The sheer variety was striking.

Military service seems woven into the very fabric of American popular culture. And it appears so benign, so homegrown that it takes an act of perverse imagination to connect these smiling, waving, motley-uniformed neighbors to something as grandiose and ominous as "militarism"—a dependence on the military for a sense of pride and security. Thinking about militarism in this way reminds us that we all can be militarized, as girlfriends, fathers, factory workers, or candidates. Thinking about it this way allows us to make connections, and making connections is what political consciousness is all about: connecting sexual harassment to congressional culture, connecting the North American Free Trade Agreement to child care, connecting heroines of situation comedies to political party platforms.

This is America's first post–Cold War presidential campaign. It is a noticeably demilitarized campaign. Bill Clinton and the Democrats do appear to be effectively steering public discussion away from weapons systems and external threats, topics that have dominated presidential contests repeatedly since 1948. Even George Bush's "victories" over Manuel Noriega and Saddam Hussein appear to be like the Russian ruble: nonconvertible.

Yet the military service record of every presidential and vice presidential candidate is held up to excruciating public scrutiny. And no two careers are identical. George Bush was of a generation, class, and race that enabled him to enlist as an officer and see combat in the U.S. Navy during the "good war," World War II. Dan Quayle enlisted in the National Guard, then 98 percent white, during the "bad war" in Vietnam. Bill Clinton and his vice presidential choice Al Gore shared Dan Quayle's dilemma of having come to manhood during an unpopular war. Though both had the money to attend college and both acted out of an ambivalence about the war, Clinton worked the Byzantine selective service system in a way that preserved his educational deferment; Gore, defining his young manhood in large part as the loyal son of a senatorial father, went into the regular army in a noncombat role. Ross Perot, who chose a retired vice admiral for his running mate, had himself served in the navy, although he requested a transfer from sea duty, scandalized by sailors' harsh language.

Masculinity's relationship to any military has never been simple. The historical evolution of citizenship, the state's military, racial politics mixed with class politics, the articulation of women's public roles, the global competition for resources and prestige—all have played their parts in shaping young men's dependence on military service to affirm their manliness in their own eyes and in the eyes of their mothers, fathers, buddies, lovers, and potential voters.

The militarization of masculinity proceeds in grand isolation from other militarizing—or demilitarizing—processes. Thus, the discussion of the presidential and vice presidential candidates' ambiguous relationships to military service seems quite odd in the current national campaign. It's as if the issue were stranded on its own discourse island. In reality there are other military worries and puzzles that are also structuring electoral choice. But, viewed from the discourse island, these issues appear only as faintly perceived sails shimmering on the far horizon. If one got out the binoculars, one could just make out the words painted on their canvas: "Tailhook," "Combat," "MIAs," "UN Peacekeeping," "Defense Jobs," "Base Closings."

Connecting the discussion of military service to each of these concerns, and all of them to each other, is what will develop a political consciousness about the role of the military in post–Cold War American society that can inform our electoral choices. And making those necessary connections isn't going to be possible if we don't take seriously the subtle and not so subtle meanings of militarism.

Take, for instance, the lines running web-like between the candidates' military service, combat, and what is now referred to as the Tailhook scandal. Tailhookers are navy carrier pilots; they take their name from the hook that catches their planes as they land on the deck of an aircraft carrier. Since these pilots' jobs have been defined by defense officials as combat positions, only men can be tailhookers—at least for now. There is a heated debate going on in Washington over whether women will be allowed in combat in the future. A presidential commission will issue its recommendations just two weeks after the election. The majority of the fifteen commissioners appointed last March by the president are Buchanan Republicans, from the party's right wing; they seem more upset about the one American woman assaulted by a single Iraqi captor than about the twenty-four American army women assaulted in the Saudi desert by their own officers.

Though nominally private, the Tailhook Association has been deemed a useful extension of the U.S. Navy. The navy has routinely supplied the association's members with transport, and senior uniformed and civilian navy officials have regularly attended its gatherings in fraternal solidarity. Its annual conventions are all-male affairs.

Well, not quite. Because of the government's current gendered conception of combat, the conventioneers are men, and the ethos is masculine; but *for that very reason* women's participation has been an essential ingredient in the celebration. Without women to objectify, the story suggests, these men's military service would be less confirming of their manhood, perhaps even of their citizenship. Then, last autumn, there was the end of a post–Cold War war to celebrate. The fifteen hundred aviators and former aviators who attended the group's 1991 convention at the Las Vegas Hilton seemed to need to wrap up their post–Gulf War euphoria in a flag of misogyny.

Paula Coughlin, a thirty-year-old lieutenant, helicopter pilot, and admiral's aide, was one of the women forced to run the tailhookers' frightening and humiliating hotel corridor gauntlet. Initially, she remained silent about the incident. Coughlin recently told reporter Katherine Boo that when a month later she watched Anita Hill trying to make male senators see why a woman subjected to sexual harassment would choose to remain silent for so many years, *she* "got it" all too quickly. She had learned from her years in the navy that a woman who rocked the boat could find her career torpedoed. It is still uncertain how many women over the years had endured the annual carrier pilots' assaults in silence. Men anonymously interviewed during the Pentagon's own investigation of the affair reported that there had been a gauntlet at every convention since at least 1986. It had become "an honored tradition." But this time Paula Coughlin decided to take the risk and break the silence, connecting the dots between Anita Hill's experience and her own. Heads finally began to roll at the top: three admirals disciplined, a civilian Secretary of the Navy dismissed, naval appropriations cut by angry Congressional committees. Still, to date, not a single one of the ungentlemanly officers who manned the tailhookers' gauntlet has been formally charged.

This is the same navy, the same culture of militarized masculinity, that has provided George Bush the high ground in the campaign debate over military service as an indicator of presidential competence. The point is not that George Bush might have manned such a gauntlet during World War II. Nor is it that Bill Clinton, by avoiding fighting in a war he disapproved of, is more free from the temptations of sexual harassment. Rather, it is that the military is not simply a site for performing selfless public service. In the American experience, pre–Cold War, during the

Cold War, and now post–Cold War, this military's institutionalized relationships have infused a culture that has distorted individual men's sense of their own manliness and have bound that distortion to the very nation-state itself.

Any postwar era is more than a set of dates on a calendar. To mean anything politically, it has to be a state of mind, a consciousness of threats dissolved, opportunities recognized, and relationships reimagined. Next month's presidential election will not live up to its promise as the first post–Cold War election if we continue to treat military service as if it has nothing to do with the American version of militarism. Militarism is a package of ideas. Looking at any person's military involvement with a sharp eye for the culture of militarism requires seeing the military as more than an institution with its own budgets, bases, rituals, and myths. It is also the inspirer of civilians' expectations, values, silences, pleasures, and memories. The Tailhook gauntlet was an "honored tradition" for five years, and no one in Washington raised a public eyebrow. And even when the scandal was finally out in the open last month, no one who sat with neighbors on the curb in the Somerville sunshine seemed to stifle cheers or hesitate in waving when the military contingents marched by. The friendly marine general, followed by the recycling float, followed by the MIA in his bamboo cage, followed by the fire engine—this remains grassroots America, post–Cold War–style.

FEBRUARY 1993: SUCH A FRAGILE THING, AMERICAN MASCULINITY

When we first heard that the U.S. government was once again bombing Iraq, the news seemed to come to me down through a long tunnel: the events seemed very far away, and yet the words gave off eerie vibrations. Ten of us were sitting at a banquet table in a grand though now frayed colonial-era hotel in Hanoi. We were coming to the end of two wonderful weeks of discussions with Vietnamese women's studies researchers in both the north and the south. In Ho Chi Minh City it had been hot, but here in Hanoi it felt like Seattle in midwinter. Out on the streets residents paused amid their New Year's shopping errands to warm themselves with a bowl of noodle soup or a cup of mud-dark coffee at micro-cafes comprising a table, three stools, a charcoal brazier, and a single kerosene lamp. Inside, all of us around the table that night, Vietnamese and Americans, were unwilling to let the news of the Bush administration's eleventh-hour attack in the name of United Nations sanctions dampen our spirits. We continued to toast each other with the local "333" beer, with a potent spiked eggnog, and with rice wine. We wished for the new Clinton administration's lifting of the devastating American postwar economic embargo against Vietnam; we wished for each other's happiness in the forthcoming Year of the Rooster; we wished for livelier exchanges between women's studies researchers everywhere.

It was only two days later, in the departure lounge of the Bangkok airport, that we heard the details of the bombing of Baghdad. Gathered around the television set, we listened to CNN's reporter tell of Kuwait's reorganized military put on alert, of Washington's other Arab supporters raising objections, of the British and French governments' initially supporting Washington, only to become cooler when the number of civilian casualties became known. Our own clothes still carried the aroma of Hanoi's charcoal fires, and our heads were still filled with images of vegetable gardens amid rubble where, until 1968, the grand imperial city of Hue once stood. It made the news of more American bombing of someone else's city harder to hear, even if it was coated with soothing CNN blandness.

Now, three weeks after George Bush has flown off to a Texas retirement and the White House has been occupied by a thirteen-year-old schoolgirl, her cat, and her parents, Iraq has slipped again to the back pages of the American dailies. The conflicts over the fate of the country's Kurds and Saddam Hussein's weapons program remain unresolved. But now it is a different sort of issue that is keeping the American military in the morning headlines. Clinton's announcement that he plans to keep his pledge to end the ban on gay men and lesbians serving in the country's all-volunteer military has been treated by many commentators and senior defense officials as if it were a greater threat to U.S. national security than a nuclear-armed Iraqi dictator.

The two worries, of course, are not unrelated. In the afterglow of the Cold War, the world's most potent military institution is searching for a new role. And new roles can call into question old notions of militarized masculinity. Even more importantly, far from the banks of the Potomac the citizens whose taxes, their sons, daughters, pride, and fears have underwritten this American military power seem unsure about just what they want in a soldier. Do they want a young woman who can join her brother on the front lines of a high-tech battlefield? Do they want a young man who can derive professional military pride from cradling a Somali refugee infant in his camouflaged arms? Do they want a man who sees heterosexuality as part of his arsenal when he flies his jet in all-male formation over Baghdad?

By early 1993, questions of military doctrine and militarized gender had become exquisitely intertwined. Marine fighter pilots serving aboard the USS *Tarawa* last week voiced their own comingled frustrations. They told a *Boston Globe* reporter, Brian MacQuarrie, that they were fast losing the confidence in themselves that had been born two years before almost to the day. *Then* they knew what it was to have a mission; *then* they knew who was the enemy; *then* they trusted their commander in chief; *then* they were secure in their manliness. It all had come together in their flights off the decks of this aircraft carrier. But today they didn't feel like real marines when they supplied logistical support for the relief operations in Somalia: "I didn't come in the Marine Corps for that type of thing," explained a thirty-nine-year-old pilot, Peter Coz. "Not that I have any problem with it, but it's not what makes me tick." Some of his flying comrades saw the Somalia operation, however, as even more worrisome: if the U.S. military began focusing its attention on helping the beseiged Kurds, the starving Somalis, the flood-ravaged Bangladeshis, wouldn't it quickly lose its capability to do what it was really designed for, to fight wars? Helping people might be admirable, these men told the reporter. But it didn't foster aggressiveness and personal competition, the sorts of qualities that had been so essential for Cold War military preparedness. And wasn't this doctrinal danger consequently heightened if gays were permitted to openly enlist in this military? Their presence would as surely remake the American military as would assigning priority to United Nations humanitarian missions. Wouldn't it?

Chapter Seven

The Politics of Constructing
the American Woman Soldier

More American women fought in a war zone during the 1990–91 Gulf War than had fought in any American war since World War II. The forty thousand white, African-American, Asian-American, and Hispanic-American women who were deployed to Saudi Arabia during the nine-month military buildup amounted to four times the number of American military women sent to Vietnam over the entire decade of U.S. involvement in that country. Three-fourths of those women were deployed by the army. By contrast, only 3 percent of Canada's forces sent to the Gulf were women (although they constitute 10.6 percent of Canada's entire active-duty force), and 1.5 percent of Britain's units were women (although they comprise 5 percent of its total military). France deployed thirteen women in its force of ten thousand soldiers. Kuwait included nine women among the 250 Kuwaiti volunteers sent to the U.S. for military training in 1991.[1]

During the period from August 1990 to March 1991, when the Gulf War was prepared for and waged, there was a torrent of American public attention aimed at "women in the military." This attention sparked a national discussion strikingly akin to the discussions that have occurred in virtually every U.S. war since the eighteenth century. Even when women were used only marginally—for example, as civilian nurses in military medical services during the 1860–65 Civil War—their participation inspired public anxieties and hopes quite disproportionate to their actual numbers. So, too, in the Gulf War: American women sent to the Gulf constituted only 7 percent of the total U.S. uniformed contingent, and that 7 percent underrepresented the 11 percent women in the total U.S. uniformed, active-duty force worldwide.

Thus, it does not seem to be numbers or proportions that determine whether the American public becomes conscious of the gendered stakes in a given war. Rather, it appears to be women's proximity to the institution of war that is critical. Many Americans appear to view war as the institution where more than in any other, (a) the *state* and the *nation* converge, and (b) that convergence is suffused with both organized *violence* and selfless *sacrifice*. Violent sacrifice under state discipline in the name of the nation—this seems to get very close to what many Americans still today, at the dawn of the post–Cold War era, understand to be the essential criterion for first-class citizenship. Such a criterion makes the doorway into that desired realm narrow indeed.

It also makes that desired realm of citizenship gendered. For violent sacrifice and state-disciplined service have been imagined in American culture to be masculine domains.[2] What reconciles the unresolved national debate over women's proper place in wartime with the cultural inclination to associate true citizenship with militarized sacrifice? It may be professionalization. If American citizen-soldiering became professionalized—if it could be liberated from its traditional need to be associated with minuteman amateurism—*and* if professionalization could bestow on American notions of femininity a new coat of protective respectability, then perhaps women could attain first-class citizenship without jeopardizing the still-gendered political culture. Transforming the feminized meaning of respectability has been a major goal of virtually all women's rights movements, in countries as different as Brazil, Russia, and the United States. The transformation of gendered, militarized respectability seems to be what occurred in U.S. culture between 1972 and 1993.

The participation of women inside the U.S. military invested the very idea of femininity with extraordinary political salience. The peculiarities of both how femininity is constructed and how the state's military tries to organize relationships between masculinity and femininity may be distinctively American. But in the dozens of societies for which we have comparable evidence, one can see a similar tendency: when the state's military—or an insurgent military aspiring to replace the state—comes to rely on women inside its uniformed ranks, that military provokes wide public concern about the meaning and uses of femininity. This provocation, in turn, makes the content and function of masculinity more problematic.[3]

．　．　．　．　．

Post–Cold War popular and elite discussions in the United States about how to use women and men differently to serve military purposes have a significance that extends beyond filling out a cross-national comparative analysis. First, the United States military's gendered manpower formula has had an exceptional influence on other militaries. American military thinking over the past two decades has encompassed not only nuclear strategic doctrine and standardized weapons production, but also ideas on how best to use women in ways that optimize human resources and relegitimize the military during an era of disintegrating power blocs and changing relations between women and men. Given NATO's structure of inequality, these American military ideas have insinuated themselves throughout the sixteen member states in the alliance in a way that, say, Dutch or Italian military thinking has not. Having said this, however, it is important to confess that we know all too little about the internal cultural dynamics of institutions such as NATO. This ignorance prevents us as analysts of internationalized political culture from determining whether and how genuinely new concepts of "enemy," "threat," and "security" are trickling though the alliance's bureaucratic layers. Nor can we tell how (I don't believe we need an "if") these possible cultural transformations are reshaping NATO's own gendered culture. We need feminist anthropologists to imagine their "field" as lying inside NATO's Brussels headquarters.

But NATO is not the only structure that produces the American military's disproportionate influence on ideas about gender. Literally thousands of foreign military officers, especially those tagged by their own superiors for senior promotion and thus policy responsibilities, are trained by American military institutions: the School of the Americas in Panama; Fort Bragg in South Carolina; the Army War College in Carlisle, Pennsylvania; the Navy War College in Newport, Rhode Island; and, of course, the three service academies at Annapolis, West Point, and Colorado Springs. Each of these training institutions has turned out explicit and implicit lessons about how to ensure bonding and morale, how to enforce discipline, how to cultivate leadership, and how to optimize human resources in different sorts of warfare. And all of these preoccupations—bonding, morale, leadership, discipline, and human resources management—are profoundly gendered, even if there is not a single woman in the platoon.

Second, the globalization of communications and culture has made American military and civilian commentators' reassertion or redefinition of presumptions about what is possible within the ideological confines of femininity and masculinity disproportionately influential. Bombay, not Hollywood, is the world's most prolific producer of films. Yet Hollywood's films are the most widely distributed. It is therefore Sylvester Stallone's Rambo, not a Hindi actor's portrayal of a singing warrior prince, that is affecting diverse societies' ideas about militarized masculinity. Similarly, Goldie Hawn's Private Benjamin has spread the image—we do not know how persuasively—of the modern single woman who finds fitness and self-assurance in her country's military.[4]

More recently, U.S.-controlled satellite television companies have internationalized the image of the militarized American woman. CNN's role in the Gulf War has been much discussed, but its impact on popular constructs of the woman soldier has been virtually unanalyzed. There were, in fact, several hundred Australian, British, French, and Canadian women soldiers deployed in the Gulf on the allied side of the conflict. But they were rendered almost invisible, not only to the rest of the world but even to their own compatriots, because of the dominance of U.S.-generated news. It was the portrayal of American women's military roles—a sanitized portrait, we are now learning—that became the basis for most of the international discussion of "women in the military" during the war.

This portrait would have been distorted even if the news coverage had been immune to government censorship and manipulation. But despite CNN's occasionally subversive operations, American news coverage was deeply influenced by the U.S. Defense Department's efforts to get the sort of coverage that would serve its own priorities. Thus, whereas the Pentagon had deliberately restricted news coverage during the 1983 Grenada invasion and the 1989 Panama invasion, in part to keep the public at home from becoming alarmed about the already growing utilization of American women in "near-combat" positions,[5] in the Gulf conflict the same defense officials decided that much expanded (though less than candid) coverage of women sent abroad would bolster popular support for the war. What the American—and the British, Portuguese, Egyptian, and Indian—public sees of American women soldiers in this or any other war is thus largely dependent on what the U.S. officials at the time deem most ideologically palatable and supportive of their own foreign policy objectives.

For all of these reasons—the U.S. government's influence in training and inside NATO and U.S. television's global reach—the ideological construction of the American woman soldier generates multiple consequences. It doesn't have to be this way. In the decade of the 1990s, NATO could be reorganized so that the U.S. notion of what legitimizes a military carries less weight throughout the rest of the alliance. Or, after European Community integration, NATO might even fade into security insignificance compared to the now hollow, but perhaps soon to be invigorated, Western European Union (WEU) or the increasingly active United Nations peacekeeping force. At the same time, alternative news and entertainment outlets might challenge the international influence of the U.S. media giants. But until such transformations occur, the image and reality of American women soldiers call for special attention, not because the women are especially admirable but because their images produce such far-reaching, cross-national ripples.

.   .   .   .   .

The 1990–91 Gulf War may have surprised a lot of Americans who had not paid much attention to the gendered transformations taking place inside their military. It even, it seems, surprised many women in uniform, especially reservists. But the developments that made headlines during the war had been in the making since 1972. That was the year that the U.S. Congress ended the male draft, made so unpopular by the long Vietnam War. Fearing that an all-volunteer force would become disproportionately reliant on African-American men, "manpower" planners inside the Defense Department and in the powerful congressional armed services committees apparently looked to other sources for military recruits. They rediscovered women.[6]

During the period between the end of World War II, when most women in uniform were deliberately demobilized, and the end of the Vietnam War in the early 1970s, when those women who were deployed were made virtually invisible,[7] women comprised less than 2 percent of American uniformed personnel. More importantly, their role in the military had little, if any, ideological salience for policymakers or the general public. Some women who managed to stay in the military—overwhelmingly, white women—report that their invisibility had its advantages: because their presence was of so little interest, they had more freedom to carve out their own niches and to outmaneuver FBI lesbian-baiters.[8] One might imagine, then, that American femininity was demilitarized between 1946 and 1972. It is more accurate, however, to see the militarization of femininity during those years as simply reconstructed upon women's postwar demobilization. During World War II there was an awkward tension between, on the one hand, femininity legitimized by direct participation inside explicitly military institutions and, on the other, femininity legitimized by supportive backstage roles as military wives, girlfriends, and daughters on the fringes of those institutions.

From 1946 until 1972 femininity was imagined by American government policymakers and nongovernment proponents of Cold War culture in a fashion that would harmonize with militarized national security goals. Loyal wives of male engineers working for defense contractors, loyal wives of male officials working in intelligence services—all were upholding forms of feminine behavior that sustained the Cold War. Likewise, women teaching elementary school children about the dangers of Communism, mothers who believed they were doing the right thing to support their sons in accepting their draft call-up, women who felt proud in doing volunteer work for patriotic organizátions such as the Veterans of Foreign Wars—all of them, as well, were fulfilling this Cold War, militarized ideal of American femininity. None of these women were making the sorts of sacrifices recognized as bestowing first-class citizenship, but they were proving that they could hold on to their respectability while serving as patriotic mothers and patriotic wives. Thus, as the hot war was replaced by the Cold War in American gendered political culture, there was less ideological confusion over, but not necessarily less militarization of, American femininity.[9]

With the U.S. government's decision to vastly increase the numbers and proportions of women in the military, to offset the end of the male draft and to forestall a reliance on African-American male volunteers, a great deal more popular as well as official attention was devoted to the tensions between these two notions of militarized femininity.

.   .   .   .   .

The history of how these tensions over American femininity emerged in the period from 1972 to 1991 was played out in several arenas simultaneously. It would be easier to make sense of this history, of course, if we could picture each of these arenas as producing ideas that flowed smoothly into and thus reinforced developments in the neighboring arenas. But we cannot take such a flow for granted. It may very well be that the politics of militarized femininity going on in one arena were relatively unconnected to, or even at odds with, the gendered trends developing in the others. Perhaps most closely monitored of the arenas where the image of American militarized femininity was being created was that of the media. But, despite all the concentration of American media power in the past twenty years, the media remains fragmented enough to require considering it in some detail, rather than as a single generator of images of militarized femininity or of the woman soldier.

Within the American media, those agents which took part in creating both images included not only the mass-market print and electronic media (news and fiction) but also the burgeoning specialized media, particularly created by and directed at African-Americans, Latinos (especially with the buildup of the wars in Nicaragua and El Salvador), feminists of all racial communities, gay men and lesbians, male military veterans and female military veterans (with their own distinct as well as overlapping magazines and newsletters). Each of these outlets carried stories about women in "boot camp" (basic training), women in the service academies, male officers training women recruits, enlisted men working alongside women as peers, women leaving home for the military, women returning to their communities as veterans, women fighting to stay in the military, and women being dismissed from the military. Each story was written or filmed with a particular audience in mind. Two stories about women in boot camp could look very different if one was constructed in order to interest a mostly male veteran readership while the other was designed to engage a feminist readership.

From 1972 to 1990, a period of growing tensions between the two constructions of American militarized femininity, there also were actors in other arenas actively trying to define issues and lessons concerning women's increasing presence in the U.S. military. Chief among those was the Congress. The congressional armed services committees—particularly the personnel subcommittees in the House and Senate—held repeated hearings on women soldiers over the last two decades. Most were initiated by three women in the House of Representatives, all Democrats and, given the Democratic majorities in both houses during the 1980s and into the 1990s, able to command considerable committee-level influence: Patricia Schroeder from Colorado, Beverly Byron from Maryland (defeated in her 1992 reelection bid), and Barbara Boxer from California (now one of California's two women senators). It matters that, while the Defense Department did not initiate its energetic recruitment of women in the 1970s because of congressional women's pressure, by the time the new generations of women recruits were being noticed by the popular media in the late 1980s, there were enough women in Congress (the great majority in the House of Representatives, only two then being in the Senate) with enough seniority to have an impact on the legislative imagining and control of women soldiers.

On the other hand, these congressional hearings did not attract coverage from the most influential television networks, the popular newsweeklies, the wire services, or big-city newspapers. When the Military Personnel and Compensation Subcommittee of the House Committee on Armed Services held its post-Panama hearings in March 1990 on women in the military, it was far from being a media event on the scale of the Clarence Thomas/Anita Hill hearings. While the 1990 hearings were monitored by some women's advocacy groups and by the Defense Department, they barely caused a stir in the news outlets that affect the political consciousness of ordinary Americans.[10]

Called to testify before these congressional committees have been representatives of high school career counselors' organizations, African-American civil rights groups, peace organizations, civil liberties lawyers, and gay rights groups. During the past two decades, when the proportion of women recruited into the military grew from a mere 2 percent to a substantial—and very visible—11 percent, these organized interest sectors paid generally sporadic and occasionally concentrated attention to issues involving women in the military. In doing so, their leaders sometimes shaped the lens through which people identifying with a particular profession or movement viewed women as soldiers. But at other times, the discussion remained relatively confined to the leaders and other specialists within each of these sectors. For instance, although a prominent black civil rights research center organized a conference in the mid-1980s to bring together civil rights leaders and Defense Department officials to discuss the particular problems facing blacks in the military, relatively little attention was directed to the rapidly growing numbers of black women enlistees, and the conference did not set off discussions among ordinary members of the black community about the black woman soldier.[11]

Most American feminist groups have paid scant attention to the issue of women in the military. Indeed, the emergence of peace activism within the women's movement in the 1970s and 1980s has made the issue of women in the military seem to be either trivial or ideologically awkward. When feminists have focused on the issue, they have been inclined to reconcile conflicting values by portraying the woman soldier as a poor woman who volunteers for military service not out of a desire to earn the status of American patriot or out of any commitment to the Reagan or Bush administration's global interventionism but out of the apolitical desire to obtain an income, training, and health benefits fast disappearing elsewhere in an era of high defense spending, public service cuts, and economic recession. While this portrait may often have been correct, most feminist groups did not feel that the image of the woman soldier was significant enough to merit using their very scarce resources to checking that image against reality. This presumption and inattention, while understandable, left many feminists who were active in antinuclear, Central American, and Middle Eastern peace work (the principal areas of American feminist peace activism during the 1970s and 1980s) unprepared for the politics of gendered image-making during the Gulf War.

It was the classically liberal women's advocacy organizations with national agendas and offices in Washington—for instance, the National Organization of Women, the Women's Research and Education Institute, and particularly the now-defunct Women's Equity Action League —that did investigate the realities of the lives of women soldiers. Each of these organizations collected data on military women and in their newsletters addressed issues concerning fairness. They deliberately intervened in judicial, legislative, and executive deliberations that shaped ideas about militarized femininity, trying to influence male state officials' perceptions of femininity. They used the concept of first-class citizenship much as the woman suffragists had done two generations earlier.

Questions about peace or militarism were less likely to be raised. These groups seemed to feel most comfortable when they could treat equality inside the institution of the military and the government's use of the military overseas as separate questions. On the other hand, these

Washington-based feminists were more curious about and sensitive to the race and class diversity of women beginning to enlist in the newly welcoming military than were other feminist groups. They were less likely to portray all women volunteers as victims of the "poverty draft." And they were more attentive to relationships between men and women inside the military, taking up issues of sexual harassment and of masculinized divisions of labor more systematically than did feminists working in the peace movement. Consequently, it was these national groups that were best prepared after the Gulf War to respond to the infamous Tailhook scandal involving sexual harassment on a grand scale. And it was the women in these Washington-based liberal women's organizations (and a handful of feminist academics known to these groups) that mainstream television and press reporters turned to when constructing images of the woman soldier in August 1990.[12]

The Department of Defense is itself a complex mesh of interlocking but not always harmonious ideological actors. In both defining and supporting the post-1972 woman soldier, DACOWITS (the Defense Advisory Committee on Women in The Services) has been the preeminent actor within the department. Created during the Korean War, when the government was using few women but wanted to reassure the public that those it did use were conforming to American Cold War conventions of feminine respectability, DACOWITS is made up of prominent civilian women—and now military officers as well—and reports directly to the Secretary of Defense. Although filled during the 1980s with Republican women appointees—women who generally rejected any affiliation with feminism—DACOWITS gradually became activist on its own terms. Its members adopted a mandate to search out and publicly report sexist barriers to women's advancement in the three branches of the military. It did so in the name of optimizing national security and military "readiness." The Cold War against the Soviet Union and the Communist threat in general could not, DACOWITS argued, be effectively waged if women soldiers' full talents were not used and rewarded. "Readiness" soon became the criterion wielded by all Washington insiders who tried to influence military personnel policies during the Reagan years.

While DACOWITS had few connections with civil rights, peace, or feminist groups and therefore had minimal impact on those groups' perceptions of the woman soldier, it did have a political status that got its members a hearing with Defense Department senior officials, Congressional armed service committee members, Washington-based liberal women's organizations, and, occasionally, the national press. DACO-WITS obtained a certain political legitimacy for women soldiers' concerns about equity. A woman soldier, in the eyes of DACOWITS, was not a victim of the "poverty draft." She was, instead, a competent female citizen whose public contributions to national defense and whose respectability as a woman were being jeopardized by male soldiers' sexual harassment, male superiors' complacency, and antiquated bureaucratic rules that were out of step with changes in technology and battlefield doctrine. In the process of working toward its goals, DACOWITS may have become an architect of the image of the American woman soldier that was disseminated at the outset of the Gulf War: the woman soldier as a still-feminine, professionalized citizen-patriot.[13]

DACOWITS engaged with a multitude of ideological players in the corridors of the Pentagon. By the 1970s, the department's equal opportunity office was fully institutionalized, though not always equipped with bureaucratic clout. The civilian, presidentially appointed under-secretary for manpower and logistics, by contrast, had ready access to the Defense Secretary and to congressional committees. Although the men filling this position were Republicans within an administration that was singularly uninterested in women's issues, they generally supported the proposition that the military needed women to enlist—and reenlist.

Unlike its Canadian and British counterparts, the U.S. military continues to be organized into bureaucratically separate, often rival, services. Thus the ideological discourses and actual policies derived from notions about militarized femininity are sometimes quite different in the navy, air force, army, and marines. For instance, many military insiders were not surprised it was the navy that was home to the men who threw the misogynist Tailhook party in Las Vegas in September 1991. Not just the navy's "tailhooker" carrier pilots, with their celebrated sense of masculine bravado, but the entire navy had the reputation of being especially protective of its exclusivist male culture.[14] One witness before the House Armed Services Committee during hearings called to investigate the Tailhook scandal noted that perhaps more indicative of the navy's institutional resistance to giving up their historically masculinized culture was what had gone on in Las Vegas *before* the much-publicized party. At what the Tailhook convention organizers billed as a professional seminar, "an admiral crawled under a table to avoid answering a female officer's question about opportunities for women pilots." The witness, Edwin Dorn of the Brookings Institution, a respected monitor of the American military's treatment of African-Americans, went on to explain to the congressional representatives that the admiral "thought the gesture was funny; and it probably was to the men in the audience who were sporting 'not in my unit' buttons. An officer who responded so dismissively to a question about a racial issue probably would have been disciplined."[15]

The deeply institutionalized defensiveness that permeated the navy was uncovered when an independent investigation was ordered of the navy's own mismanaged initial investigation of the infamous Tailhook convention. The Defense Department's Office of the Inspector General found that the navy's own effort to find out what had happened in Las Vegas and why was seriously flawed, because of senior investigatory officers' desire to protect not just particular colleagues but also their own institution from outside criticism. In a particularly damning episode— described in detail by the Defense Department's Deputy Inspector General, who conducted the review—the commander of the Naval Investigative Service, an admiral, held what witnesses described as a "screaming match" in a Pentagon corridor with a senior civilian woman official, an assistant secretary of the Navy. The civilian official had protested when the admiral, a key figure in controlling the direction of the initial investigation of the Tailhook affair, opined that "a lot of female Navy pilots are go-go dancers, topless dancers, or hookers."[16] At another time during the navy's own attempt to look into the affair, the same admiral was told by one of his own agents that a women officer assaulted during the convention had recalled saying to her attackers, "What the fuck do you think you're doing?" The admiral responded—"and [the woman NIS agent told a later investigator] I'll remember this quote forever—'Any woman that would use the F word on a regular basis would welcome this type of activity.' "[17]

Policymakers for the U.S. Air Force, which has a relatively high proportion of support roles (e.g., many mechanics and flight controllers for each fighter pilot), found that they could recruit large numbers of women without jeopardizing the masculinized construction of their combat elite. By contrast, officers of the U.S. Marines feared that even a small proportion of women in their combat-heavy service would threaten its deeply masculinized image. The Army, of course, is also combat-heavy, as it includes the combat units of infantry and armored divisions. But it also stands out because of its need for "manpower." Thus, the U.S. Army, like armies in most countries, tends to be the most ethnically and economically diverse service, though that diversity may be carefully arranged hierarchically. It has to recruit such large numbers of people that it cannot be as selective as the other services can, and its male recruits in particular tend to be immature.[18]

The male officers in the field who were commanding troops in the 1970s and 1980s often were far more ambivalent than their civilian Defense Department superiors about the wisdom of or need for deploying women in traditionally masculinized jobs. Many—though not all—of these officers were mainly concerned about the morale of their men, men who had been recruited partly with the promise that joining the military would confirm their manliness. Some of these male officers had access to the press, particularly publications aimed at veterans, and to congressional committees. They, too, wielded the potent national security concept of "readiness," but they used it to argue that women had no place at the front and that those women who wanted to be there were raising questions about their own femininity and patriotism.[19]

And finally there were the women soldiers themselves—though "soldiers" is a somewhat misleading term here. For many women who joined the uniformed forces, like many of their male counterparts, deliberately sought out jobs as administrators, computer technicians, nurses, and nutritionists, jobs that were militarized but which did not jar the masculinization of American soldiering or their own internalized feminine identities. A 1992 survey of 868 army women, which was one of the largest of its kind and was solicited by the presidentially appointed Commission on the Assignment of Women in the Military, revealed that while 60 percent of women officers and 54 percent of women enlisted personnel wanted the ban on women in combat lifted, they were not necessarily imagining themselves as combat volunteers. They themselves, like many men, wanted the training, education, independence from families, and steady income that the military provided, not the opportunity to wield instruments of direct violence. Only 15 percent of the army women surveyed in the aftermath of the Gulf War expressed a desire to serve in combat roles. What they wanted most, they said, were institutional reforms that would remove the barriers currently barring women from promotions. The combat ban, they reported, was the spikiest barrier.[20]

Women in uniform themselves did not have a monolithic image of their own femininity or of the military's impact on it. Women career officers, for instance, tended to be those most outspoken about existing bans on women in combat. These were the women who saw themselves as staying in the service for twenty years and so tagged combat exclusion as a principal barrier to their promotion. Enlisted women often were more frustrated by day-to-day harassment and by the military's inadequate medical services for women. These were the women with perhaps the biggest stake in ensuring that veterans' health and educational benefits were designed to fit women veterans' needs and were sustained by a budget-conscious Congress.

One gets the impression that it was the women careerists—the officers—who were more likely to have the confidence and the contacts to speak out when they felt they were being harassed or being denied a hearing by their immediate superiors. The women officers are the ones who have been most apt to be in contact with the liberal women advocates in Washington and most likely to be interviewed by congressional subcommittees and television talk-show hosts, thus privileging their concerns and their experiences in the complex cultural political process that was creating the image of the American woman soldier. And because only 19 percent of all women officers in the early 1990s are African-American women,[21] white women careerists' ideas have tended to receive the most visibility.

These distinct American image-making arenas do overlap. But looking at each of them separately reminds us that the ideology of militarized femininity has not been constructed through some simple or obvious process in either the Cold War or the post–Cold War era. Such an examination also prompts us to ask hard questions about how the image of the woman soldier is constructed and reconstructed in other countries as well.

- Do journalists from the mainstream national media in Japan or Norway call on field officers to voice their opinions on their women soldiers?
- Is there an equivalent of the U.S. House of Representatives Armed Services Subcommittee on Personnel in France or Turkey?
- Do women's groups with equal opportunity agendas have access to the "manpower" bureaucrats in the defense ministries in Britain or Italy?
- Have gay liberation activists turned their attention to homophobia inside the military in Israel or India?
- Do racial minority rights organizations monitor discrimination inside the military with the help of state-established agencies in Canada or Germany?
- Do Australian or Dutch base commanders agree with most American base commanders' decision to carry pornographic magazines on their base newsstands?[22]

For all the outpouring of recent feminist scholarship on World War II, we still today have only an incomplete picture of the interactive processes that redefined and/or entrenched American femininity and masculinity to suit U.S. wartime needs in the 1940s. But what we have

learned from this burgeoning work is that those earlier ideological processes involved very particular actors with their own anxieties, resources,
and limitations. It is with this awareness that we need to turn our
attention to the construction of images of American—or any other
country's—women soldiers in the Gulf War.

. . . . .

The military operations that preceded the Gulf War were the occasions for several of these ideological arenas of the 1980s to overlap in
ways that highlighted the contradictions between the two forms of
militarized American femininity. The 1983 invasion of Grenada and the
1989 invasion of Panama became—quite consciously—gendered precur-
sors to Operation Desert Storm.

Whereas DACOWITS, Defense Department civilian officials, military
male and female officers, congressional committees, specialized academic researchers, and Washington-based liberal women's advocacy
groups were the principal actors shaping the image of the woman soldier
between 1972 and 1983, the Grenada invasion opened up the regendered
military to wider popular view. This higher visibility was on the minds
of Defense Department public relations officials when they did their best
to limit the mainstream media's coverage of women's roles in the invasion. In fact, those roles were wider—and closer to the masculinized
inner sanctum of combat—than many members of the American public
had realized, due to the skillful internal lobbying of a handful of women
officers. By 1983, these women had become committed to making the
senior grades and had learned that the obstacles put in the way of their
careerist aspirations could be surmounted only by leap-frogging over
their immediate superiors.

At Fort Bragg, the main launching point for the Grenada invasion,
several women officers saw that they were about to be separated from
their assigned units and thus deprived of the chance to take part in the
Caribbean operation. These women called officials in Washington and
insisted that such a policy not only was unfair to women but also
threatened to undermine the much-valued esprit de corps within the

divided units. Eventually, 170 American women soldiers took part in the invasion—as military police, helicopter pilots, interrogators, signal corps specialists, truck drivers, and members of bomb teams.[23]

For many of these women careerists and their Washington supporters, the Panama invasion six years later was a logical next step in forcing a regendering of battle maneuvers. But this time, press and television media refused to be kept at such a safe distance. The result was much wider coverage of and hence more popular debate over women's proper roles in the military.

The discussion, however, was affected by the overall cultural politics of the Panama invasion. Women were indeed revealed to be inching closer than ever to masculinized frontline roles, but they were doing so in a war that had broad U.S. public support and was portrayed as short and "clean." The specter of Vietnam—a war that had tainted the image of the entire military, a war that was seen by many Americans as having besmirched or even corrupted any U.S. soldier who took part in it—was being exorcised in Panama. Neither soldiers taking drugs nor soldiers frequenting prostitutes made the headlines during the Panama invasion. There were no stories told of rape. Consequently, it seemed less threatening to respectable femininity for eight hundred U.S. women soldiers to be involved in this war. Military operations in 1989 would be morally just and professionally conducted. Women soldiers' femininity, in the eyes of many Americans, could be sustained even close to the front lines if they conducted themselves professionally and if their behavior increased America's respectability in the world.

The most widely reported incident treading—and defining—this fine line during the Panama invasion came when Captain Linda Bray led a small team of male soldiers to take a well-defended Panamanian military dog kennel. Was she in combat? The question was politically salient enough to require a response from the president's own press officer. The Defense Department claimed that Captain Bray's operation was not combat and that the military was upholding the long-standing ban on women in combat. The press and the general public were less sure. But there was no popular delegitimation of the war following the Bray story.

Instead, there was new activism on the part of women in Congress to dismantle the combat ban altogether, since the Panama invasion showed how artificial it was and how accepting the American public was of having women serve in frontline roles, if they did so voluntarily and with professional competence. But inside the military, in field units where so much of the daily construction of women soldiers occurs, Linda Bray experienced new pressures. She and her unit were subjected to investigations (which found no misdeeds); she was mistrusted by her troops, who resented all the media attention she had received; she tried to match physically the men she served with and ultimately broke her hip. In April 1991, Linda Bray, with no media notice, left the military.[24]

．　．　．　．　．

The stage was now set for American image-making during the 1990–91 Persian Gulf War. Women made up 12 percent of the total U.S. military active-duty force. African-American, Latina, Asian-American, and Native American women together made up 38 percent of all women in the four branches. But it was the Army that stood out: black women had signed up and reenlisted in such extraordinary numbers in the 1980s that on the eve of the Gulf War they constituted 47 percent of the enlisted women in the army—four times their proportion among women in American society.[25]

When the Bush administration deployed thousands of troops to Saudi Arabia following the Iraqi invasion of Kuwait, no attempts were made like those witnessed in 1983 to cull women from units that might serve in near-combat roles. That particular gender battle had been won. Moreover, the Pentagon seemed more confident that the military's public legitimacy would not be undermined if it allowed the mainstream mass media to cover women soldiers. It was emboldened by public opinion polls that showed a majority in favor of widening women's military roles. The policy resulted in a flood of stories about American women in the Gulf. The great majority of them were positive. Now we know that stories of rape and assault by American male soldiers on their female comrades were not reported either by field commanders or by journalists. But during the war, when the massive viewing audience assured maximum media influence, women soldiers were portrayed as doing a job and in so doing enhancing the country's military competence. They were professionals. Even women reservists and enlisted women, many of whom were not professionals in the sense of intending a military career, were portrayed as acting like professionals.

This is an accolade that carries great positive value in an American society in which formal education and publicly conferred licensing have come to be seen as guarantors of social respect and economic success. To be a "pro" means to be taken seriously. In the post-draft U.S. militarized culture, being a professional was no longer at odds with being a citizen-patriot. Professionalism also provided a protective shield, a new form of guaranteed respectability. A professional woman soldier, it appeared, was neither morally loose nor suspiciously manly. The media stories dealt with the latter anxiety, so common in World War II, by emphasizing husbands, children, and boyfriends left behind. When Major Rhonda Cornum, a year after the war, finally admitted that she had been sexually assaulted by one of her Iraqi captors, she went to great lengths to explain to journalists that she had downplayed this admittedly unpleasant incident because, as a professional soldier, a flight surgeon, and an officer, she counted other challenges she faced as a prisoner of war—for instance, protecting military information and bolstering the morale of her male subordinates—as more important than worrying about her sexual well-being.[26]

Assisting in this image-making was the seeming sexual orderliness of the Gulf War. Unlike the U.S.–Vietnam war, which was filled with stories of prostitutes, rape, and drugs, this war was under strict sexual control. But that control was insisted upon not by the U.S. government, but by the Saudi regime of King Fahd. Fearing that its internal fundamentalist opposition would exploit any rumors of sexual promiscuity to challenge the regime's political legitimacy, the Saudi government required that the U.S. government prohibit both alcohol and prostitution in its Saudi operations. This was a highly unusual—perhaps unique— agreement for the U.S. military to enter into. No other U.S. ally had managed to impose such a condition. It seemed to guarantee that American women could serve as soldiers in this war without losing their feminine respectability. Not until a year after most U.S. troops—and the camera crews—had gone home would American women soldiers begin to tell stories which made it clear that the ban on alcohol and brothels did not provide a watertight guarantee that American women in the field would not suffer indignities at the hands of their comrades.[27]

The most controversial aspect of mobilizing forty thousand women in a force of half a million Americans to fight in Saudi Arabia was motherhood. If there was one media theme that momentarily shook the legitimacy of the gendered American military, it was the story of the mother-as-soldier leaving her infant in the care of a mere father or perhaps a grandmother.

The public had not realized that the Defense Department in recent years had begun to plan for a time when the active-duty forces would be subjected to personnel cuts by an increasingly budget-conscious Congress. The department's personnel planners had started to integrate the reserves into their regular battle planning. The reserves are made up of men and women, often veterans of active-duty forces, who hold civilian jobs during the week and commit themselves to military duty several weekends each year. The reserves hold several attractions, not the least of which is extra pay. In an era when many young families could not meet mortgage and car payments without the contribution of two salaries, pay from military reserve duty had begun to look as though it would provide a welcome financial cushion—with virtually no risk. More than just a cushion, it was often a necessary source of income to make middle-class ends meet. In addition, women discovered that they could satisfy their desire to take part in unusual physical activities and perhaps acquire new skills without having to choose between military participation and having a family. With the Pentagon's blessing—since military couples reduce rival loyalties—growing numbers of wives and husbands had enlisted together in the reserves in the 1980s. By the eve of the Gulf War, women comprised 13 percent of all military reserve soldiers. So when the Pentagon began calling up whole reserve units from around the country, many young women found themselves having to leave behind very small children. The media treated this development with surprise and dismay.

But the two stories that many observers were anticipating would shatter the apparent acceptance of women in such proximity to battle—women who were taken prisoner and women who "came home in body bags"—did not have the negative effects that were expected. And it wasn't for lack of coverage. Two American women became prisoners of war, and both survived, even if they censored their own accounts of their ordeals. Thirteen women died in the war, five in combat. These events had an effect quite contrary to that foreseen by many nervous policymakers. For these women's experiences made clearer than ever that being confined to noncombat jobs did not assure protection from capture or even death given the weaponry of contemporary warfare. Feminist observers had been pointing out the mythical quality of the "front" and "rear" distinction for a decade, but now the general public could see for itself. In fact, the American military women who died had the chance to prove that women, like men, could "die for their country." Violence under state discipline for the sake of sacrifice for the nation thus remained the norm for American first-class citizenship.

The American image that came out of the Gulf War was of the professionalized, militarized woman patriot. This was an image that liberal women's advocates in the Congress, in DACOWITS, in the officer corps, and in Washington lobbying organizations had been constructing and promoting for the past two decades. The image that fit feminist peace activists' perception of the U.S. state and its role in the world—the woman joining up to escape poverty—did not gain much credence in the popular culture as a result of this war. The emergence of the militarized image must give pause to those feminists who argue that militarism is integral to American patriarchy—including feminists who supply the intellectual context and energy for campaigns and institutions all over the country.

.　　.　　.　　.　　.

In the aftermath of the withdrawal of most American forces from the Gulf, the politics of image-making have reverted to their previous arenas. Again it is the Armed Services Committee members in Congress, DACO-WITS, women military officers, women's liberal organizations, and, increasingly, gay and lesbian legal rights advocates who are the principal players. Thus, at the initiative of women in the House of Representatives and with the support of several key liberal male senators, Congress passed in August 1991 an amendment to the defense appropriations bill that would end the formal ban on women flying combat airplanes. The actual assignment of women to fighters and bombers was deliberately left by the politically savvy architects of the amendment to the civilian chiefs of the Air Force and Navy. The Congress instructed President George Bush to appoint a commission to study the whole question of women in combat and transmit its conclusions to both the president and the Pentagon.[28] None of the antimilitarist feminist groups took part in this postwar legislative process. The later revelations of Rhonda Cornum's rape while a prisoner of war might have made the bill's designers wish that they had left the White House and the armed services with less discretion. Focusing on her experience rather than on those of American noncombat women assaulted by their own fellow soldiers permitted the majority of the members of the presidential commission and conservative senior officers to dig in their heels once again.

The history of the presidential commission underscores the ways in which the concept of women in combat has been shaped and reshaped by the gendered politics of an entire political system. The congressionally legislated, presidentially appointed Commission on the Assignment of Women in the Military consisted of fifteen members. George Bush and his aides chose its appointees in early 1992, at a time when the lessons of the Gulf War seemed less salient than the rivalries between the center and the right inside the president's own political party. From the start, the liberal feminists monitoring the commission believed that several appointees were deliberately intended to assuage the ideological anxieties of the Republican party's right wing, a wing being courted in the February primaries by conservative candidate Patrick Buchanan. For instance, Bush selected nine men and only six women for the commission; among the women were Elaine Donnelly, a member of Phyllis Schlafly's Eagle Forum, and Kate O'Brien, a senior vice president of the conservative Heritage Foundation. According to a representative of the Women's Research and Education Institute, "Some of these people are really members of the ultra-right who would prefer to have women go home and bake cookies. . . . By appointing a number of these individuals, the president has preordained a decision that would preclude women from serving in combat."[29]

After six months of study costing $4 million, the commission announced its recommendations on election day, November 3, 1992, when most media attention was turned elsewhere. Only defense officials and Pentagon-watchers, among them the most stalwart civilian and uniformed advocates of women soldiers' rights, attended the press conference.[30] For many in the audience, the commission's most surprising recommendation was that women continue to be prohibited from flying combat aircraft. This recommendation was a clear rejection of the congressional women reformers' principal recommendation; they had selected it as an opening wedge that they hoped would lead to an eventual lifting of the ban on women in all combat jobs. On this first recommendation, the commission's members had split eight to seven. The vote was along ideological, not gender, lines. Donnelly and O'Brien, the two conservative women, voted against allowing women to serve as combat pilots on the grounds that women were not meant to be killers. Two of the men who voted for the lifting of this ban were the commission's head, Robert T. Herres, a retired air force general and former vice chairman of the Joint Chiefs of Staff; and Marine Corps Brigadier General Thomas V. Draude, who spoke with emotion of his support of his own daughter who was training to be a navy pilot: "I'm asked, would you let your daughter fly in combat with the possibility of her becoming a P.O.W.? . . . And my answer is yes, because I believe we should send the best."[31]

As expected, the commission's majority voted to continue the exclusion of women from ground combat jobs, such as those in the infantry and armored divisions. On the question of women's assignment to naval combat ships, the majority initially sided with exclusion. Then the commission head, General Herres, appealed to the members to give something to the reformers. If the commission didn't show a willingness to grant some new service opportunities to women, he argued, "A great number of people will not believe we credibly considered the issues." Soon afterwards, the members voted eight to six to amend their recommendation to allow women to serve on combat ships, except for amphibious vessels and submarines.[32]

One of the observers in the audience was Lieutenant Paula Coughlin. She was the admiral's aide who was the first military woman to formally charge male navy combat pilots with sexual harassment in the wake of the 1991 Las Vegas Tailhook Association convention. Upon hearing the commission's recommendations, she told a reporter, "I think the composition of the commission was predetermined and selected for just this outcome."[33]

The commission was only an advisory body. Its recommendations were to be sent to the president and to the secretary of defense. Both were about to undergo changes as a result of the Clinton victory. The Clinton White House, on the one hand, would be under no political obligation to follow the advice of conservatives and would be actively pressured to end all combat exclusion by many of the liberal women's rights groups that had backed his campaign; on the other hand, the new president was already risking high-ranking military officers' anger with his announced intention to end the ban on homosexuals in the military. In Congress, a leading proponent of women soldiers' expanded career opportunities, Barbara Boxer, had just been elected to the Senate and had the backing of many of the liberal feminist groups that supported an end to the combat ban; but she would have little seniority in the upper house. Patricia Schroeder remained in the House of Representatives and had the sort of seniority that translated into chairing an armed services subcommittee; in the new Congress she would be joined by thirty-nine other women representatives, most of whom defined themselves as feminists. With Representative Les Aspin selected by Bill Clinton to head the Department of Defense, the House Armed Services Committee chair was taken over by Ronald Dellums, an African-American Democrat who had long supported women's rights. At the Pentagon, however, Secretary Aspin nominated seven men to his first seven top policy posts.[34] Women in combat would remain fodder for political maneuvers even after Defense Secretary Aspin lifted the ban in May 1993.

In another arena, however, feminist congresswomen's inability to compel the Defense Department to revise its gendered warmaking formula failed much more quickly. Then-representative Barbara Boxer had introduced legislation to force the Pentagon to end its practice of calling up women and men with very young infants for active duty. Here, the military won the legislative day. Its counterargument that in a new era of reduced military manpower it would need optimum flexibility with *all* of its personnel persuaded Boxer's colleagues to drop her amendment from the post–Gulf War legislative agenda.

In a third arena, gay and lesbian legal rights groups stepped up their pressure to force the Defense Department to end its ban on homosexuals. They, too, used the Gulf War to make their point. These spokespeople claimed that, with educated military "manpower" in short supply, the military was doing in the 1990s what it had done at the height of World War II: in war it used all competent soldiers, conveniently turning a blind eye toward suspected gays and lesbians in the ranks. Thus, these legal activists came away from the Gulf War hoping that court actions that were slowly whittling away at the rationale for the ban, plus the support of a president newly elected with a decisive gay vote, would together move the government to end the ban altogether. Their goal was to allow homosexual Americans access to the sort of military service that remains in the United States the sine qua non for first-class citizenship.[35]

.   .   .   .   .

After the end of the Gulf War, the popular media turned its attention to the faltering American domestic economy. Meanwhile, most of the country's feminist advocacy organizations were feeling ideologically stymied by the issue of women soldiers as well as stretched thin trying to meet their primary commitments—commitments that seemed distant from military issues. Thus, it seemed likely in the 1990s that the image-making politics surrounding women in the American military would continue to be in the hands of those who felt comfortable with professionalized militarized femininity. The ideal American woman soldier of the 1990s still wears lipstick in the Pentagon advertisements. Her eyebrows are neatly plucked. But she isn't smiling. She doesn't put up with harassment. On the other hand, she doesn't have much patience with talk of post–Cold War militarism either. Under her helicopter pilot's high-tech helmet, she is a serious citizen doing her job; she's a pro.

Chapter Eight

Feminism, Nationalism, and Militarism after the Cold War

I came of age intellectually and politically (a bit belatedly) at Berkeley in the mid-1960s. It wasn't an undifferentiated "Berkeley." Like anyone coming into political consciousness, I made the journey in a very specific context. Mine was the graduate student subculture of a young comparative politics discipline, at a time when Southeast Asia was just beginning to loom on American academics' intellectual horizon. Despite the presence of large Asian-American, Chicano, and African-American communities just outside the university gates—in Berkeley and Oakland, in the nearby farming valleys, and across the Bay—the University of California was itself in the mid-1960s a largely white institution. There were few tenure-track women professors (none among the fifty in political science). It was news when the first woman was chosen to be Head Teaching Assistant. *Feminism* was not yet in the Berkeley lexicon, and neither I nor most of my friends noticed that the word *woman* scarcely ever crossed the lips of political science lecturers.

What was on our minds was nationalism. In seminars and coffee houses we friends—earnest graduate students from Vietnam, Israel, the U.S., and Sierra Leone—tried to figure out whether the Communist Party's success in China was the result of nationalist resistance to Japanese invasion or of effective mobilization of land-hungry peasants. We looked at the new African states through the lens of the nationalist movements which had given them birth. We were just starting to pay attention to the emergence of nationalist thought within the African-American community as the civil rights movement was being overtaken by the Black Power movement. When the U.S. government's involvement in Laos and Vietnam crept from political manipulation toward full-scale military intervention, we criticized a Washington establishment that didn't seem capable of telling the difference between hollow puppetry and nationalist legitimacy.

Berkeley was not, however, a milieu in which nationalist interpretations held a corner on the intellectual market. In the mid-1960s, liberal individualism informed the popular study of electoral behavior. And Marxist class analysis often made nationalist interpretations appear to us rather naive. Still, the discipline of comparative politics, arising as it did out of the proliferation of new nation-states in the wake of of the collapse of colonial empires, was infused with curiosity about how, when, why, and with what effects people in any country developed a distinctly national consciousness with effective national institutions to match. And that development, if and when it did occur, seemed to most of us a step in the right direction.

Today I'm not so sure. I've become too aware now of the ways in which men have used nationalism to silence women, too conscious of how nationalist ideologies, strategies, and structures have served to update and so perpetuate the privileging of masculinity. In recent years I've come to see how nationalism—not inevitably, perhaps, but with notable regularity—can grease the wheels of militarization, a process that ultimately marginalizes women.

At the same time, I'm wary of my own new skepticism. Many of those who, in the morning light of the post–Cold War era, are sounding the alarm against nationalist parochialism are people who seem more comfortable with centralized elites, cultural hegemony, and unequal international divisions of labor. And these critics rarely couple their critiques of nationalism with a call for the dismantling of patriarchy or pay attention to feminist analyses of masculinity inside nationalist movements. Moreover, too many women have broken out of the confines of domesticity and have carved out a space in the public arena through nationalist activism for me not to weigh carefully the antipatriarchal consequences of that activism, even if they fall short of full emancipation and are achieved in spite of, not in harmonious alliance with, patriarchal nationalist men.

My own work in those heady years at Berkeley and for the next decade and a half[1] was remarkably uncurious about gender. I was so struck, for instance, by how differently the Hmong and the ethnic Lao peoples experienced the Laotian national revolution that I didn't pause to ask whether women within each of these communities might be having quite different experiences from those of their husbands, brothers, and sons. A few years later, I was exploring how state officials wielded ethnicity to construct trustworthy state armies and police forces. But my intellectual world remained virtually ungendered. For a fleeting moment in the late 1970s, I did muse in print over how Gurkha villages were sustained when the British recruited so many of their men, leaving so many women to fend for themselves. But I didn't pursue the question. Nor did I ask whether the Nepali women whose sons and husbands joined the Gurkha regiments were themselves pressed to adopt hopes and rationales that were feminized complements to the more visible masculinized militarism.[2]

Having so little curiosity about gender, I naturally didn't see masculinity as problematic. When I looked at the Soviet military, I saw Russian, Kazakh, and Ukrainian officers and conscripts organized in ways that ensured a Russified state dominance. I didn't see men. I didn't ask about how the military's ethnic division of labor was shaping perceptions of masculinity among women and men within the Soviet Union's various ethnic communities. One result of this stunning lack of curiosity was that I was analytically unprepared for the anticonscription movement led by women-as-mothers inside the ethnic Russian community in the 1980s. Another result was my surprise at the potency of militarism's lure among men in at least some non-Russian ethnic communities in the late 1980s, derived from many men's apparent desire to assert their masculinity in the face of both rival ethnic communities and the Red Army.

Along the Massachusetts Turnpike in the 1980s, one would occasionally see the bumper sticker "Armenian Air Force." Nothing more. Presumably no more needed to be said on the bumper sticker for the drivers in cars behind to get a good chuckle. "Armenian Air Force": such an obvious oxymoron. Armenian masculinity was informed by victimization. It didn't contain the cultural "stuff" to send aloft a modern fighting force. But in the 1990s, the bumper sticker and any chuckles it once provoked seem quaint. Its humor was based on a naively limited understanding of how Armenian or perhaps any masculinized nationalism could be militarized.

Although it shouldn't give me much comfort, I was not alone in the gender-blindness of my analysis. In his 1983 book *Imagined Communities,* Benedict Anderson, for instance, left masculinity and femininity unexplored. He described how Vietnamese, Khmer, and Laotian parents encouraged "their children" to get a French education so that they could secure future jobs in the French colonial civil service.[3] Were mothers and fathers diluting their national consciousness in the hopes that their daughters would obtain colonial bureaucratic jobs? More likely, it was their sons on whom such hopes were being pinned. Daughters' futures probably were being fashioned as *wives* of colonial civil servants. Yet a person working directly for the French colonialists and a wife married to that bureaucrat would not experience identical cooptive pressures. As insightful and helpful as Ben Anderson's and other landmark books of this era were in charting new ways to think about the creation of nationalist ideas, they left nationalists—and prenationalists and antinationalists—ungendered. Our understanding of nationalism suffered. For all the variables we revealed, for all the sophistication we applied, we ultimately imagined the creation of a national community to be more simple than, in fact, it is.

A corollary: we *underestimated* the amount and variety of the power at work in the construction of a national consciousness and a nationalist movement. Consequently, we also underestimated the power it took to build a new nation-state. We thought of ourselves as specialists in power, but really we had only begun to learn where to look for it.

It is only in the last several years—thanks to the impact of feminism on scholarly curiosity—that we have begun to notice that most of the nationalists in positions to have their ideas heard and recorded have been men. We are only today wondering what exactly that fact has meant, both for nationalism as an ideology and for nationalist movements as forms of social mobilization.

Becoming a feminist in the late 1970s (again, belatedly), I began to reread some of the renowned texts on nationalism with new eyes. I began to search out the women, often finding them in the shadows or, where absent altogether, scribbling them in in the margins. I started to pay special attention to the relations between the men at stage front and the women in the chorus. For instance, while recently rereading Pierre Val-lières's classic Quebec nationalist autobiography, *White Niggers of North America,*[4] I found myself newly curious about his mother, and about her son's anger at her. To young Pierre, his seemingly apolitical mother represented the epitome of pre-1960s Québecois passivity. It was she who had dampened his father's working class Québecois spirit; it was she who had urged her uppity son to obey the conservative priests at school. Prodding French Canadians to throw off the twin oppressions of English domination and feudal French provincial rule, Pierre Vallières argued, required overcoming the parochial domestic preoccupations of women like his anxious mother.

Since the 1970s domesticity has been a contested sphere in Québecois nationalist imagining and organizing. Therefore, women's relationships to men in the domestic sphere have been politically salient.[5] One could not fix one's analytical sights only on the plaza or on the convention floor to make sense of the evolution of nationalism; one had to also look into the kitchen and the bedroom.

Feminist analyses reveal that nationalist movements are more suffused with power and evolve more erratically than most nonfeminist accounts suggest. By taking women's experiences seriously, feminists have disclosed that women and men within nascent national communities often

Fig. 10. As nationalism broke out after 1991 in virtually every former Soviet republic, these Russian women living in Moldova tried to stop the railway into the capital in order to prevent Moldavia's ethnic Romanians from pursuing their goal of reunification with Romania. (© Nistratov/Eastnet/Select)

struggle with each other over *whose* experiences—of humiliation, of insecurity, of solidarity—will define the community in its new national manifestation. Many of the struggles between women and men during the formative period occur on the floors of nationalist conferences or around strategy tables.[6] But many more occur when there is no one taking minutes. Thus, only by considering oral histories—not only of women who who have become nationalists, but also of women who held back, or of women who joined but later became disenchanted—can we uncover the actual processes by which women's relationships with men have shaped and reshaped any national community or nationalist movement.

How have so many women been persuaded that women's specific concerns could be put on the political back burner for the sake of a newly emergent or newly politicized nation? We need better answers to the question of why women's calls for an end to domestic violence, or for equality in marriage or access to land titles, or for appointment to leadership positions have been delayed or denied nationalist legitimacy altogether.

Women Against Fundamentalism is a group formed in Britain by women who include Jews, Arab and Asian Muslims, Hindus, white and Afro-Caribbean Protestants, and Irish Catholics. It was formed in 1989, in the turbulently gendered wake of the threats against Salman Rushdie's life. Its members have been developing an analysis that could be widely relevant to students of nationalism. In seminars and newsletters, Women Against Fundamentalism has been tracing the ways that the most conservative members of the women's respective communities have used nationalist anger and hopes to mobilize wide support—including support from the British state—for the perpetuation of the control and political marginalization of women. Thus, Asian British patriarchal male leaders are today using nationalist rhetoric to persuade state officials outside their communities to allow *them* to run state-funded shelters for women victims of domestic violence.[7]

African-American feminists have long struggled to carve out a political space where they could speak of violence against women perpetrated by men from both inside and outside their community without being charged by African-American men with nationalist betrayal. The 1991 Senate Justice Committee hearings delving into Anita Hill's accusations of sexual harassment by Clarence Thomas were seen by many African-American feminists as just one more instance in which they were squeezed out of a public arena. Rather than remaining silent this time, however, dozens of African-American women began to meet informally to discuss not only the hearings but also their own difficulties in having their analyses heard. Out of these spontaneous and usually intense conversations—in Boston, Detroit, Washington, Atlanta, Chicago, Ann Arbor, San Francisco, and Los Angeles—sprang the idea of raising money to take out a full-page advertisement in the *New York Times* in which African-American women would make their own statement, without the filter of any organization or any media.[8] Fifty thousand dollars were raised in small donations from women and men of diverse ethnic and racial backgrounds to pay for the advertisement's publication in the *Times* as well as in six prominent black papers. Acquiring the space to speak can be costly to women in financial as well as political terms. A total of 1,603 African-American women signed the statement. Their names—beginning with Tania Abdulahad of Washington, D.C., and ending with Deborah Zubel of Philadelphia, Pennsylvania—appeared in the ad when it was published in the Sunday *New York Times* on November 17, 1991, the week in which Clarence Thomas was sworn in as a Supreme Court justice.

"AFRICAN AMERICAN WOMEN IN DEFENSE OF OURSELVES" was the group's self-designed headline.[9] "We are particularly outraged by the racist and sexist treatment of Professor Anita Hill, an African American woman who was maligned and castigated for daring to speak publicly of her own experience of sexual abuse," the signatories explained. They continued: "We speak here because we recognize that the media are now portraying the Black community as prepared to tolerate both the dismantling of affirmative action and the evil of sexual harassment in order to have any Black man on the Supreme Court. We want to make clear that the media have ignored or distorted many African American voices. We will not be silenced." The writers objected to the effort on the part of some black nationalists to portray the Senate hearings conducted by an all-white Judiciary Committee as solely a racist event. Likewise, they took strong issue with any white feminist commentators who portrayed the hearings as solely a sexist event: "As women of African descent, we understand sexual harassment as both." The essential message the organizers and signatories insisted that readers of the *New York Times,* the *Chicago Defender,* and the *Atlanta Inquirer* absorb was that African-American women would no longer allow others to interpret their experiences, to pour their complex daily negotiations of a sexually organized racist society into a narrow, if politically comfortable, funnel. Their final sentence: "No one will speak for us but ourselves."

Which "nation's" imaginings have proved most potent in the process of persuading, silencing, or diverting women? The black women who signed the *New York Times* ad, the British white women and women of color organizing the Women Against Fundamentalism rallies, the Francophone women trying to carve out space to take part in the ongoing Quebec debates—all lead complicatedly textured lives. Perhaps many women have found formal arguments about ideas and strategies less "persuasive" than the pressures of family loyalties, sexual expectations, or sheer exhaustion.

None of these arguments that nationalist feminists find persuasive possibilities, of course, can be explored unless men in any period of nationalist mobilization are investigated in terms of their own family dynamics, sexual practices, and unpaid labor. Because we still know too little about women's experiences of nationalism, we have left ourselves ignorant of men—as men—in the histories of nationalism. If we paid as much attention to the construction of the "patriotic father" as we have (productively, one should note) to the construction of the "patriotic mother," what would we learn about the uses of masculinity in the mobilization of national consciousness?

These often difficult and private struggles between women and men over the relevance and meaning of the nation need to be charted over time. Commentators seeking to explain, for example, why nationalist concepts and agendas began to overtake older, feudal notions of Kurdish identity among Turkey's Kurds in the 1970s point to the million or more Turkish Kurds who migrated out of eastern rural villages searching for jobs in Ankara, Frankfurt, and Berlin. These urbanized migrants were the ones who created new notions of Kurdish identity no longer dependent on loyalty to clan chiefs; it was the migrants, especially those in Germany, beyond the reach of the Turkish police, who created new political organizations in which theories and skills could be honed. However, when these urbanized Kurds sought to bring their new messages home to the villages in eastern Turkey, they often met with a cool, even hostile response. Kurds for centuries had been divided along clan lines; now a new rift was opening between urban and rural Kurds.[10] But was that the principal gap? A majority of the Kurds who migrated to Turkish cities and to Europe were men. So it was to increasingly feminized village societies that these freshly politicized nationalist men returned. Did this urban/rural gender gap encourage those men to imagine women in ways akin to Pierre Vallières's image of his non-nationalist mother? If they did, the likely corollary has been a reaffirmed sense among politicized male Turkish Kurds that masculinity is the most reliable launchpad for nationalized political consciousness.

The postmobilization period of any nationalist movement—whether it succeeds or fails at creating a state or carving out new areas of political autonomy—is a time of lesson-fashioning and mythmaking. Women as well as men have to live with those lessons and myths. They will form the bases of national identity and of strategies for sustaining gains or recouping losses. Most of the lessons and myths are fraught with gendered memories.

Woman-as-traitor—or as a potential traitor—is a common postmobilization icon. Contemporary Iranian nationalist cosmology assigns an important place to women as vulnerable to foreign materialist allures. It is precisely because women are relied on to be the bearers of culture that they are so suspect in many nationalists' eyes. If Iranian women succumb to (are seduced by?) Western materialism, as they allegedly were during the prerevolutionary reign of the Shah, the entire national project would be jeopardized.[11]

In a more self-critical spirit, male Brazilian cultural nationalists are beginning to reassess their earlier attitudes toward the singer, dancer, and film star Carmen Miranda. Caetano Veloso has recently admitted that perhaps they were wrong when, in the 1960s, he and his fellow Brazilian nationalist intellectuals charged Miranda with selling out to North American money, cheapening authentic Brazilian song and dance in the process. Carmen Miranda might have been more a source of nationalist pride for her popularization and creative development of national traditional forms.[12]

Similarly, the condemnation of La Malinche, the Indian woman who was given by her tribe to the Spanish conquistador Cortés and who later acted as his translator and his mistress, was used by nineteenth-century Mexican male intellectuals as a brick in their new edifice of Mexican identity. La Malinche was popularized not only as a traitor to her nation but also as a source of humiliation because of her sexual subjugation.[13]

Mary Robinson, the Irish feminist lawyer who was elected president of Ireland in 1991, is an example of a woman who has had to walk a very fine—often treacherously fine—line. As president, in a largely ceremonial post, she has attempted both to meet popular expectations that she will symbolically represent the nation as it exists in Irish citizens' minds and, at the same time, to subtly redefine the very meaning of the Irish nation. In trying to accomplish the latter, Mary Robinson has risked becoming an Irish Malinche. For she has made gestures—such as visiting AIDS patients in the hospital, offering solice to a gay male partner at his lover's funeral, and asking feminists to tea—that announce that this president imagines the boundaries of the Irish nation as including within it people whom many Irish nationalist politicians and the state's current legal system presume are not only outside the nation but actually present a real threat to it.[14] Thus far, Robinson appears to be winning the symbolic contest because so many Irish women and men—even those who oppose her positions on divorce and abortion because they believe that either would undermine Irish nationhood—nonetheless believe she brings to the presidency a kind of visibility and modern style that is winning Ireland new international respect. She is clearly a postcolonial representative of the Irish nation. Moreover, Robinson has reached out to precisely those women who have embraced the patriarchal policies of the Catholic Church and the major parties, explaining that "if feminists don't value the work of women who stay at home, how is society going to value it?"[15] But in the 1990s, as debates over European integration, Irish women's rights in Europe, resolution of the war in Northern Ireland, and domestic laws prohibiting homosexuality, divorce, contraception, and abortion are all merging in a potent nationalist brew, a feminist presidential reinterpretation of Irish identity is a political high-wire act.

When they are represented as sexual partners and as bearers of national traditions, women can either acquire nationalist prestige or lose it. It is precisely because sexuality, reproduction, and child-rearing acquire such strategic importance with the rise of nationalism that many nationalist men become newly aware of their need to exert control over the women. Controlling girls and women becomes a man's way of protecting or reviving the nation. Not a few nationalist women have assisted in those efforts by policing other women. Thus, as is usually the case, relations between nationalist women and men can be understood in part by investigating relations between women themselves. Other nationalist women, however, denounce the myth of woman-as-traitor and its obverse, woman-as-patriotic-mother, as false and oppressive. They have a hard time being heard inside many nationalist movements and have often risked their nationalist credentials—which many of them prize—in speaking out.

Rape and prostitution have been central to many men's construction of the nationalist cause. They have permitted men to hear the feminized nation beckoning them to act as "her" protectors. The external enemy is imagined to be other men, men who would defile or denigrate the nation. Too often missing in this gendered nationalist scenario are the voices of the actual women who have suffered rape or have been compelled to seek an income from prostitution. Thus, Bangladeshi women who had been raped during the war of secession from Pakistan were rarely asked to help build the identity of the new nation, though news of their rapes had the effect of mobilizing the anger of many Bangladeshi men. Likewise today, women who have been raped are more symbols than active participants in countries such as Sri Lanka and Kashmir.

In the early 1990s, Bosnian, Croatian, and Serbian feminists began to alert the international media to rape being wielded in Bosnia as an instrument of militarized, masculinized nationalism. "We have orders to rape the girls," a young Bosnian Muslim woman named Mirsada was told by a Serbian soldier who abducted her from her village of Brezovo Polje in June 1992. Telling her story to an American newspaper reporter two months later (a story afterward confirmed by other sources), Mirsada told of forty village women who were abducted and raped by Serbian male soldiers. A gynecologist who treated the survivors said that she believed the rapes were intended to humiliate the Muslim women: "They were raped because it was the goal of the war."[16] A European

Community investigation team estimated that twenty thousand Muslim women were raped in Bosnia between April 1992 and January 1993.[17]

Rape has been part of many wars, not all of them nationalist. We cannot completely understand any war—its causes, its paths, its consequences—unless male soldiers' sexual abuse of women on all sides is taken seriously, described accurately, explained fully, and traced forward as well as backward in time. Thus, in Bosnia we need to consider what the rapes and reports of rapes reveal about the masculinization and militarization of Serbian nationalism, Bosnian Croatian nationalism, and Bosnian Muslim nationalism. Neither masculinization nor militarization of any ethnic group's nationalist consciousness is automatic. We need to be more curious. We need to figure out what the experience of rape did to each one of the Serbian male soldiers who took part in the assault of Brezovo Polje.

One Serbian soldier, Borislav Herak, told an American journalist that he had been close to his Muslim brother-in-law during his years in Sarajevo before the war. He had done poorly in school, drank heavily, physically intimidated his father, and grumbled about his dead-end job pushing a cart in one of the city's textile factories. But he had not thought of the Muslims in his extended family or his neighborhood as the source of his unhappiness. And while he had wished for girlfriends he didn't have and stored stacks of pornographic magazines in his room at home, he had had no history of sexual assault on women. It was only after being recruited into one of the several Serbian nationalist militias in 1992 that Borislav Herak's unstable mix of alienation and anger was turned into the stuff of which a militarized nationalist rapist could be made. He recalled what a revelation it had been to him when older Serbian men in his militia explained to him and other new recruits how Muslims, since the Ottoman Empire, had been the cause of Serbian misfortune. He also confessed to the reporter that it was while serving as a fighter in the militia that for the first time in his life he could acquire things that he felt had heretofore been beyond his reach: videos, television sets, and women. This was the young man, then, who didn't think to question his commander's order to rape Muslim women whom his militia was holding captive in a motel outside the Bosnian town of Vogosca. His commander's explanation made sense to Borislav Herak: raping Muslim women was, he was told, "good for raising the fighters' morale." And he presumed that his commander meant him and his colleagues to murder each of the women after they had raped her. He followed the implicit orders.[18]

Another Bosnian woman, a non-Muslim, Marianna, became pregnant as a result of being raped by male soldiers for twenty-four hours in a Serbian-controlled camp. "Never. I will never give birth," she asserted. She by then was seeking refuge and an abortion across the border in Croatia.[19] What she did not realize was that Croatia's male-led regime had outlawed abortion in the name of Croatian nationalism. In fact, in 1992, a coalition of Croatian, Swiss, and British feminists were calling on women's rights advocates to mount an international campaign to protest the Croatian regime's proposed legislative program to control women's work and reproduction for the sake of what the regime called the "Renewal of the Republic of Croatia." Such a renewal was required, the proposal's nationalist backers argued, because while the rate of natural population growth in Croatia at the end of 1990 was 0.7 percent, by the end of the civil war it was projected to drop to "around minus 3 or 4 percent."[20] If the wartime losses were factored into the forecasts, they claimed, "the situation for the biological continuation of the nation will be alarming." Given that a majority of Croatian families in 1992 had two or fewer children, the nation was on the road "to certain extinction of the population." To reverse this trend, the nationalist lawmakers called for the passage of a package of laws aimed at restructuring the family so that more Croatian children would be born and cared for. As translated first by a Swiss feminist and then by a British feminist, the provisions included the following:

- It is urgent and necessary to eliminate all errors and infiltrations of an Anti-Life-Mentality from medicine, school books, television and the print media, and to remove the prescriptions which stem from the times of the communist partyline. Schoolbooks even today continue to teach Croatian children about the "population explosion," and this at a time when the natural population growth in Croatia has sunk to zero.

- Linking of Croatia with Europe and America (USA): We want to link Croatia with similar Pro-Natality movements in Europe and America and to work out a programme of revitalization. The issue of the Croatian family shall be linked with that of the European and the American family, and vice versa.

- For the demographic renewal it is necessary that the creator of the programme for renewal of Croatia give first priority to the following issues: (a) Extension of small family economies; (b) The production of healthy, natural food (for Europe!); (c) Investment in and extension of family tourism (the return of the population to the islands).

- The Republic of Croatia must draft legislation and safeguard conditions which will ensure that the highest profession in the Republic will be that of the mother as educator of children.

- Increase and stimulate extension of child benefits. . . . We should apply the child benefit policy of Germany, Switzerland and France.

- Remove working mothers with children from factories and from other places of heavy work which are unsuitable for them. In this way thousands of work places in Croatia would become vacant. The women—mothers—shall be freed from factory work and receive benefits and a salary for mothers as educators.

- Fighting Non-womanhood: The demographic situation is aggravated by a further evil: late marriages between the ages of 35 and 50, whereby one child or even no child at all is born in these marriages. The new tax policy of Croatia will not support this Non-Woman-hood; it will stimulate the family and couples with children.

- Licenses for private enterprises, employment and diverse other functions shall, other conditions being equal, be granted preferentially to families with several children.

- Fight against pornography, child prostitution and pandering; control private cinemas and video clubs.

- Tighten criteria for the divorce of marriages with children.
- Child care facilities shall be reduced to a minimum and gradually eliminated.
- Setting up youth clubs and societies, in which Croatian history, literature, the virtue of soldiers, sports and arts etc. shall be explored.[21]

Thus at the same time that the nationalist ideals of the manly Serb fighter were being constructed in Bosnia, efforts were being made to reconstruct the woman-as-mother in Croatia. The point here is, however, that these two processes were not moving along merely parallel tracks. The nationalist wars in the former Yugoslavia were being fought in such a way as to make these patriarchal political processes merge in the lives of women.

The post–Cold War era's feminist politics have responded to this merger in new forms of international campaigns. In addressing the militarization of Croatia, Serbia, Bosnia and, most recently, Macedonia, local feminists have developed skills in compensating for the loss of independent local media outlets by forging new links to European and North American media, not just those of the mainstream but also the alternative press outlets interested in human rights, peace movements, and the conditions of women. They also have sought to enter the growing international debate over what should be included as internationally recognized "human rights" and "war crimes." The negotiations by which any condition is assigned such a designation are ideologically complex and bureaucratically tedious. A primary reason why forms of violence against women, not just rape, but also domestic violence and prostitution, have been kept off the international legal agenda is that so many governments, the principal players in United Nations human rights and war crime tribunal negotiations, are opposed to any outside agency being given authority to intervene in any activity deemed to be related to the "family." The family is held up in international law, as currently written in UN documents, as the basic unit of the sovereign nation-state and thus as sacrosanct.[22] Consequently, as feminists try to raise rape to the status of a violation of human rights and as a punishable war crime, they will be faced with two challenges: first, they must overcome government officials' long-standing refusal to accept United Nations jurisdiction in any area those officials define as a "family" matter; second, and equally important, they must prevent nationalist men of one ethnic group turning their outrage over the rapes of their "own women" into a self-serving justification for escalating the militarization of masculinity and for imposing more restrictions on women in the name of their safety.[23]

.   .   .   .   .

Until it was closed in November 1992, the U.S. naval base at Subic Bay inspired a wave of Filipino nationalism. Here again, women's sexuality was the object of intense nationalist discussion. The thousands of women working in the discos and massage parlors providing sexual services to American sailors had stood at the center of a nationalist mural of humiliation. But nonfeminist nationalist organizers in the Filipino anti-base movement differed markedly from their feminist nationalist compatriots. The former relied on the women in prostitution as symbols, but didn't ask the women themselves how they analyzed their poverty, their parenting choices, and their often rocky relationships with Filipino men. In contrast, Filipina feminists in the movement envisioned a nationalism that required that they organize with the prostitutes and listen to them in order to make sense of the bases and thus of the costs and attractions of neocolonization in the 1990s.[24]

Popular culture, a topic treated with growing seriousness, is playing a gendered role we can scarcely yet define in the making—and unmaking—of national consciousness. Raphael Samuels has made a start with his ambitious, three-volume archeological dig into popular culture's historic part in constructing "English" patriotism. His effort is all the more valuable for its feminist contributions analyzing mythical heroines, popular health discourse, and children's fairy tales.[25] Elsewhere in the world, there is anecdotal evidence that the American film *Rambo* has been used to build the morale of insurgent men in the Philippines and Chile, but we know little about the masculinist meanings that insurgents have derived from their clandestine video viewings, or how these meanings have shaped their relationships with women inside and outside of their national communities. Close on the heels of (or perhaps out in front of) the "global film" industry, pornography has also become internationalized and industrialized. Yet we are virtually uninformed about pornography's contribution to the dreams of nations. What consequences do portrayals of Asian women wrestling have for Latin American or Middle Eastern men's constructions of femininity within the framework of their own national identities? During the Gulf War, when white American men and African-American men both pinned up the calendar specially produced for the war (and sold in the Pentagon's own bookstore), which featured white women draped in nothing more than cartridge belts, did it have identical implications for their respective senses of masculinity in this post–Cold War world?

We have been learning in recent years to assign more weight to oral and literary genres as we trace the evolutions of distinctive collective identities. We shouldn't imagine, however, that it is only publishers' candidates for Booker Prize (Britain's top literary award) that help to shape men's and women's politicized sense of belonging—or of alienation. Videos, advertisements, sports, comics, toys, and calendars also help construct the gendered nation.

$$\bullet \quad \bullet \quad \bullet \quad \bullet \quad \bullet$$

Conquerors' mistresses, wartime rape victims, military prostitutes, cinematic soldier-heroes, pin-up models on patriotic calendars—these are only some of the indications, not only that nationalism is often constructed in militarized settings, but that militarization itself, like nationalist identity, is gendered. To put it more simply, no person, no community, and no national movement can be militarized without changing the ways in which femininity and masculinity infuse daily life.

Much of our research in the 1960s and 1970s focused on civil wars— some we labeled as revolutionary, and others portrayed as mere insurgencies. They seemed to offer opportunities to explore changing consciousness, national versus class versus ethnic loyalties, the processes of social mobilization and party building, state fragility, and state expansion. But as I recall, thinking about civil wars did not prompt us to think about—or even conceptualize—militarism. States had militaries; that's how you could tell they *were* states. And certain levels of alienated mobilization seemed naturally to take the form of armed insurgency. But as for militarism—a distinctive set of beliefs and structures—and militarization—a particular societal process entrenching these beliefs and structures—we looked to neither concept to generate questions, to make us stop in our intellectual tracks. So we made militarization of any society appear simpler than, in fact, it was.

When I think back now to the 1960s, I wonder why I didn't pause, why I found it so easy to accept armed nationalist conflicts as, if not inevitable, at least not very surprising. At some level I did not see nationalist warfare as problematic. True, I did puzzle over state elites' use of their militaries—and police forces—to respond to ethnic or anti-imperialist challenges. I did wonder how civilian nationalists came to their decisions to take up armed resistance and whether they would succeed in controlling the military forces they had created. And I did try to understand how relatively unpoliticized people caught in the crossfire would piece together their own strategies for coping with escalating conflict. All this hard questioning notwithstanding, I think I assumed that militarization of any nationalist conflict wasn't difficult to accomplish. It only required, I naively presumed, the state's deployment of military units and the insurgents' acquisition of weapons and recruits and policies to bring both sides into an encounter.

In those days I didn't give much thought to what sorts of mental transformations had to occur in order for national identities to become militarized. Now I am more and more convinced that the militarization of any nationalist movement occurs through the gendered workings of power. It is neither natural nor automatic. Militarization occurs because some people's fears are allowed to be heard, and to inform agendas, while other people's fears are trivialized or silenced. Slovak nationalism, reemerging today; Québecois nationalism, now in its third decade of development; Lithuanian nationalism, successful in its achievement of statehood—none have (as yet) been militarized.

Within other nationalist movements, by contrast, there has been ambivalence and even explicit conflict over militarization. Thus, within
contemporary Russian nationalism, U.S. black nationalism, Canadian
Indian nationalism, South African black nationalism, German nationalism, and Serb, Croatian, and Bosnian nationalism, there have been debates over social changes that would legitimize particular militaristic
tendencies. In each of these processes of national formation, the struggle
today remains inconclusive. It is impossible to make sense of how nationalist ideologies and organizations emerge, grow, wither, or disappear
altogether unless we chart these *internal* debates over militarization.
Who supports militarizing strategies, and who offers alternatives? Do the
supporters and their critics look different in their gender, region, generation, class, or political experience?

Principal among militarizing transformations are changes in ideas
about manliness—manliness as it supports a state, and manliness as it
informs a nation. If I had given more (or any!) thought to how the
meaning assigned to being a man changed as a state deployed its forces
in the name of "national security" or in the name of creating a new, more
authentic nation, or as a nationalist movement mobilized its force, then
I might have noticed that changes in ideas about masculinity do not
occur without complementary transformations in ideas about what it
means to be a woman.

For instance, I might have paid attention to a state's policies regarding
rape: were soldiers given instructions to avoid sexual assaults on women
in the contested regions? Were reported assaults treated seriously by
superior officers, or glossed over? I might have given more analytical
weight to evidence that insurgent male leaders deliberately excluded or
included women, that they tried to prevent sexual liaisons within their
units, that they encouraged most women to serve the now-militarized
cause in roles compatible with concepts of femininity preexisting in the
community. And by paying attention I might have caught sight of the
contradictions that thread their way through most instances of militarization.

For militarization is a process that is not greased with natural inclinations and easy choices. It usually involves confusion and mixed messages. On the one hand, it requires the participation of women as well as men. On the other hand, it is a social construction that usually privileges masculinity. It is the first of these two conditions that makes many women who have become nationalists willing to support militarization: their participation as women becomes valuable, and they often gain new space in which to develop political skills. During the Intifada, Palestinian women began to run more of the West Bank community institutions as the Israeli military closed down older institutions as security risks, and as hundreds of Palestinian men were imprisoned. During the eight-month Iraqi military occupation, Kuwaiti women, having lost their Asian maids, likewise gained a new sense of their political value; actions such as obtaining food, carrying information, and caring for torture victims took on new, nationalist connotations. Similarly, Iraqi women who identify themselves as nationalists by virtue of participation in the ruling Baathist Party's Women's Federation today speak of the earlier Iran-Iraq war as a time when the state was compelled to take women's talents seriously, as it replaced conscripted men with women in hosts of official positions.

Yet because it is a process riddled with gendered contradictions, the militarization of any nationalist movement is usually contested. It is often precisely where one can observe the formal and informal political struggles between women and men. In these debates over militarization, women and men are divided, not simply over priorities on the political agenda, but also over what constitutes this amorphous thing, "the nation."

Peace movements that emerge within militarizing nationalist movements are typically treated as though they are hopeless and/or analytically trivial. The militarization of our own curiosity often takes the form of treating the most militarized tendencies—such as the formation of mostly male militias—as the most analytically interesting.

For example, there is a Serbian Women's Party. Going by the acronym ZEST, it was founded by a small group of women in November 1990, on the eve of the Serbian elections—elections suffused with nationalist

Fig. 11. In Belgrade, a Serbian woman protests the conscription of her sons into the Serb-led federal army fighting in Bosnia. (AP/Wide World Photos)

rhetoric. Within two months ZEST had five hundred enrolled members. Its leaders explained in the party's manifesto why they were moved to launch a Women's Party at this crucial juncture in the decline of Communism and the emergence of Serbian nationalism, within what then still remained a Yugoslav state. Their goal was "to expose the authoritarian consciousness and behavior of those Serbs who hardly care for the genuine democratization of those Serbs who lust for power."[26] These women weren't mincing their words.

The Women's Party called for respect for cultural diversity within Yugoslavia. It reached out to non-Serbian women. It published reports to show women that they were discriminated against in the Yugoslav work force more on the basis of their gender than of their ethnicity. The mobilization of ever-more-intolerant nationalist organizations, they argued, would not assure that women's labor would be fairly valued. Thus, the party's activists became increasingly skeptical that violence was justified in the name of communal progress. They joined other Serbian antimilitarist groups composed of both men and women to create the Belgrade Center for Anti-War Action. Serbian Women's Party members swelled peace marches, decrying policies which were resulting in Serbians' being "trapped in a meaningless war which most of the citizens do not want."[27]

Thus, Serbian militarization, like any nation's militarization, has not been a foregone conclusion. It has been gendered in ways that have sometimes slowed or even halted its progress. When a community's politicized sense of its own identity becomes threaded through with pressures for its men to take up arms, for its women to loyally support brothers, husbands, sons, and lovers to become soldiers, it needs explaining. How were the pressures mounted? What does militarization mean for women's and men's relationships to each other? What happens when some women resist those pressures?

What if we took seriously the women-led peace efforts inside Serbia and Croatia in 1991? What if we treated as intellectually significant the current mothers' peace movement inside Sri Lanka's Tamil and Sinhalese communities? What if we paid more attention to Russian women's anticonscription movement? What if we integrated into our analyses the concerns of black South African women about the impact of the return from exile of many men who have spent years training as guerrilla fighters? What if we listened, as students of nationmaking, to the Québecois women who spoke out against one man's murder of women engineering students he claimed had used feminism to push him to the margins of Quebec society? In the aftermath of the December 1989 "Montreal massacre," Québecois writers called on all Québecois to explore the misogyny in their daily lives.[28]

My hunch is that we would be compelled to rethink nationalism. We would have to see the making of nations as a process of struggle between women and men. This struggle cannot be portrayed simple-mindedly as all the women being lined up on one side and all the men on the other, in a war-of-the-sexes standoff. Rather, we can bestow significance on those pressures and divisions, employing gender to fashion a national community in somebody's, but not everybody's, image. If we took seriously these intracommunal, women-led efforts to forestall or roll back militarization, we also would have to ask more acute questions about what has actually been required to militarize any particular community's national consciousness. We would discover power in its full array of forms.

In the post–Cold War 1990s it may be less fashionable than it was in Berkeley in the mid-1960s to celebrate nationalism—or its product, the nation-state. But if one casts a wary eye toward nationalism today *without* a feminist understanding of its inner workings and its consequences, one might simply revise patriarchy so that it can thrive in new forms fit for a post–Cold War world.

Chapter Nine

Conclusion:
When Is Postwar Postpatriarchy?

A best-selling postcard at Amsterdam's big 1992 International Feminist Book Fair came from Britain. Soon after the fair, scores of women on far-flung continents must have found this message waiting for them in their mailboxes: "I'll be a post feminist in post patriarchy."[1]

Any postwar time is fraught with questions. These post–Cold War years are no different. The first always is: what has changed? Since 1989, a lot. Any schoolchild could make a list. But a lot has not changed, and it is not at all clear what needs to be put on that list.

It remains unclear, for example, whether the end of the superpower rivalry and the collapse of Communist-led regimes in Eastern Europe have so reduced the appeal of militarism that the very concept of manliness has been transformed. Have the changes witnessed in Eastern Europe, the Persian Gulf, Central America, Southeast Asia, and Southern Africa demilitarized masculinity? If so, then a principal ingredient of patriarchal culture will have been eliminated. If so, then women will relate to men differently, and the state will expect new attitudes from both. If so, the state itself and international diplomacy between states won't look the same. If the Cold War is really over and the militarism it depended upon is truly on the wane, then those endings should be showing up in the politics of femininity and masculinity.

The morning after is always an ambiguous moment. What just happened? Who benefited? It is not always crystal-clear that today, the day growing out of the morning after, is a fresh, new day.

In fact, the present morning, after the formal ending of the superpower rivalry, doesn't yet look like the dawning of a brand-new day in the ongoing evolution of sexual politics. We are still living in a post–Cold War period, a time when grand politics and the politics of everyday life continue to be defined in large part by the anxieties and aspirations of the Cold War. This continuity is especially evident in the reluctance of governments and of many ordinary citizens to make their militaries less central to their gendered notions of security and even identity.

But militarism never was "natural" or monolithic. Even at the height of Cold War paranoia, militarism couldn't have survived without constant tending, coaxing, and manipulating. Today, as yesterday, militarism cannot be perpetuated merely by drawing on raw civilian masculinity; it has always required drill sergeants. Militarism couldn't rely on men from different countries to get along in allied armies simply because they shared masculinity; it required joint maneuvers and training courses designed to translate diverse masculinities into standardized soldiering for the sake of an alliance. Militarism couldn't get along with just men's willingness to earn their manhood credentials by soldiering; it required women to accept particular assumptions about mothering, marriage, and unskilled work. And if women began to question either the naturalness or the wisdom of such ideas, then militarism relied on public policies to limit women's ability to act on their skepticism.

The militarism that was legitimated when mutual superpower hostilities were at their fiercest had to be fed by enormous infusions of public funds, distorting whole economies in both large countries and small. But even then, militarism couldn't live on money and weaponry alone. It depended upon policies to ensure certain sorts of sexual relations: male bonding that stopped short of sexuality; men's sexual liaisons with foreign women that stopped short of the affection that might reduce militarized racism; misogyny that stopped short of a domestic violence that might undermine discipline and morale; wives' and lovers' sexual fidelity that stopped short of their having any sense of entitlement.

These conditions weren't easy to sustain. The Cold War never was

free of internal tensions and contradictions. Without deliberate decisions
by policymakers—some made so quietly and so far down the chain of
accountability that most citizens didn't even realize they were official
decisions—the peculiar relations between women and men necessary to
perpetuate the Cold War might have crumbled long before 1989. Only
by digging deep into the bureaucratic archives, opening file drawers far
below those holding the treaties and defense budgets, can one bring these
decisions—and thus the fragility of the Cold War's workings—to light.
Only by looking closely at the minutiae of ordinary people's lives wher-
ever the Cold War's brand of militarism prevailed can one explain why
it began, why it didn't end earlier, and why it is so hard to terminate
now. The exploration cannot be confined to the lives of those women
and men whose governments were allied in NATO or in the Warsaw
Pact; it must consider the gendered politics in both Koreas, in Chile, in
Guyana, in Vietnam, in Egypt, in South Africa, and in Tahiti. Exploring
the Cold War must take our curiosity everywhere that presumptions
about Communism and anti-Communism, and the significance of each
for international politics, relied on the complementary militarization of
both femininity and masculinity. Nowhere was that militarization inevitable. Nowhere was it accomplished without official help.

Similarly, today's construction of a post–Cold War world is happening at multiple levels of political life simultaneously. For example, Kuwait held its first postwar parliamentary election on October 6, 1992. It
had been six years since the ruling Al-Sabah family had closed down the
previous National Assembly. However, only 81,400 of the country's
606,000 citizens were allowed to cast ballots: those male citizens over
twenty-one who could trace their Kuwaiti roots back to 1921.[2] Women
were excluded from voting. Nor could women stand for one of the fifty
parliamentary seats. Nonetheless, women, and the relationships between
women and men, between women and the state, and between secularized
and fundamentalist men, were very much in the foreground of this
postwar political contest. Some women had been active in the Kuwaiti
women's suffrage movement before the Iraqi invasion. Others had
become politicized and newly confident of their abilities to act in public

roles because of their activities during the wartime resistance or in exile. Male candidates from all six of the secular and religious opposition blocs were pressed by women suffragists to commit themselves to votes for women, should they win seats. For the first time in Kuwait's history women turned out for candidates' campaign meetings, though they remained separated by a curtain from the male voters. They asked rhetorically: why were we honored during the war for our sacrifices, but not now?

On election day an estimated one hundred women traveled to various polling stations. There they marched silently and were sometimes arrested by Kuwaiti police. Women suffragists made clear what they expected of winning candidates. They carried banners that read "With You in 1996" and "The Voice of the Women is in the Nation's Interest."

The opposition won a surprising majority—thirty-one seats—of the total of fifty in the revived National Assembly. Yet the implications of these results for women and thus for Kuwait "national security" remained uncertain. The Islamic opposition blocs together won nineteen of the thirty-one opposition seats. And while some Islamic bloc delegates came out in favor of women's right to vote, others made the imposition of a conservative version of Islamic law—including the forced veiling of women—their legislative priority. Thus, we can look forward to a decade of Kuwaiti politics marked by debates over who is to blame for Kuwait's past military vulnerability and over whether Kuwait's postwar security is best ensured by closer cooperation with the American military. These debates will be conducted in terms that shape discussions over Kuwaiti women's relationships not only to men but to the state.

Danish women shocked the political classes of Western Europe in June 1992 when they provided the margin of victory for the "no" votes in their country's referendum on the European Community's Maastricht treaty, the agreement moving the twelve countries in the EC the next steps along on the path toward political and economic integration. These steps would also open the way for Eastern European post-Communist regimes to normalize their relations with the rest of Europe. Wider European unity is seen by most political elites around the world as a crucial building block for post–Cold War politics. No one had given the Danish women much thought. Thus, it came as a rude surprise to many EC proponents to wake up the morning after the referendum to find that not only had a majority of Danes voted to reject the Maastricht treaty, but women had provided the single largest bloc of votes for the "no" side. Only in the hurriedly called post mortem sessions did commentators begin to imagine that Maastricht might be gendered, that it looked forward to a post–Cold War Europe that appeared to many Danish women as if it contained too many hallmarks of Cold War Europe.

In particular, these women told anyone who would listen that they were wary of the militarizing trends within the EC—trends that might turn the Western European Union into the principal vehicle for ensuring future European security. They had other ideas about what constituted genuine security. They held up their own hard-won Danish social security system, one which had provided Danish women with more emancipation and less dependence on the men in their lives than was enjoyed by most other women in the world. When many Danish women voters compared that package of policies and structures with what the men running the EC envisioned as a new European standard for social security, they found the latter wanting. Voting for European post–Cold War integration as spelled out at Maastricht, many concluded, would lower, not increase, Danish women's actual security. On the eve of the election, two-thirds of Danish women between the ages of thirty and forty-nine told pollsters that they intended to vote against Maastricht.[3]

In each country of Europe the relationships between women, men, the state, and militarism are different. Thus, Danish women's rejection of the blueprint for European security was not emulated in Ireland, France, or Greece. But the Danish vote served as a sharp reminder that this four-legged relationship cannot be taken for granted—that it can be reimagined and even challenged.

The post–Cold War world is being fashioned in part out of new—or freshly painted—ideas about what is natural and right for men and what is natural and good for women. Salvadoran women ex-guerrillas are being urged to remove their IUDs in the name of peace. Canadian women and their Mexican sisters are being told that joining in a continentalist trade triangle with the U.S. as the pivot will provide them with post–Cold War security. Irish women are being told that the only way for them to maintain their Irish identity and still acquire the benefits of the European Community is to forgo other European women's access to abortion and reproductive information.[4] Polish women are being urged to worry less about unemployment in the new, masculinized, post-Communist market economy and to take more satisfaction in bearing children for the sake of nationalist revival.[5] Serbian women are being pressed to ignore data revealing that they are more discriminated against in the work force because of their gender than because of their ethnicity.[6] Angolan women are being urged to put their own needs as women on the political back burner for the sake of keeping afloat the fragile boat of post–Cold War Angolan democratization. American women are being encouraged by some to see professional soldiering as their best chance for acquiring first-class citizenship and by others to leave all but the military's support roles to men in the name of strengthening American family values at a time when their society is threatened by new international economic rivals.

Japanese men are being urged to see remilitarization as an inevitable process in becoming a "mature" international power. Russian men are wondering whether being professional, volunteer soldiers would restore some of the sense of masculine pride lost when the Soviet military was shown to be internally corrupt.[7] By contrast, German men are being asked to extend conscription in exchange for the chance to join French male conscripts in a new European military, free of American control. British men are being pushed to imagine that arms sales to Indonesia or Turkey are their best job insurance now that the British government has less incentive to buy weaponry. Zulu men are being encouraged to see the warrior as the essence of the sort of manhood best suited for postapartheid South African politics. American men are being tempted to imagine that it is only Arab enemy soldiers who sexually assault women.[8]

Many of these women and men may adopt those identities and aspira-

Fig. 12. Women in Luanda lining up to vote in Angola's election to end that country's long civil war. (NYT Pictures)

tions which, together, would perpetuate much of what constituted the international culture of the Cold War. But many may not. We scarcely yet know why they will make the choices they make.

Demilitarization isn't any more automatic than militarization. Indeed, it may be a far stickier process because it goes against the grain of the feminine and masculine conventions and political strategies now prevalent in so many societies. But blocking demilitarization is not that easy, either. It would require each one of these diverse women and men to come to conclusions about their lives that don't necessarily appear reasonable.

As individual women and men are making their own assessments, the people wielding political influence will be creating new militaries and refashioning old ones. The United Nations is now being drawn into more and more wars. This is happening at a time when the upper reaches of the UN's civil service are even more thoroughly masculinized than they were in the late 1980s; for example, the number of women occupying the prestigious post of undersecretary general has dropped from two to zero.[9] In the 1990s, the UN's development, health, and environmental programs can barely get a hearing from members of the Security Council, a body which is increasingly preoccupied with military questions. The Security Council has also been among the most masculinized of the world body's agencies. Perhaps that fact helps explain why its members are more comfortable spending their time and energy on the militarized dimensions of security. Some observers have argued that one test of the Clinton administration's commitment to constructing a genuinely post–Cold War world will be whether it pays up the United States' outstanding UN debt and relies on the United Nations to achieve American foreign policy objectives. But doing so would not be a sufficient test of the Clinton administration's commitment to demilitarization. Any government can rely on that international body in a way that simply militarizes it. The more useful test for any government claiming to be working toward a demilitarized world is whether its foreign policy officials take steps to enhance the UN's nonmilitary capacities for preventing and resolving military conflicts.

United Nations peacekeeping forces, drawn from its members' own militaries, may in fact offer a chance to detach military service from state interests and possibly from the kind of misogynist masculinity that has served state interests for so long. Will a Fijian, Irish, or Indian man who dons a blue helmet conceive of his own manliness differently from the way he does when he wears his own state's flag on his sleeve? Will American women, men, and children licking ice-cream cones and watching a parade along Main Street cheer American soldiers returning from UN peacekeeping service with as much pride as they have cheered their Vietnam and World War II veterans? Perhaps effective UN soldiering will call for a new kind of masculinity, one less reliant on misogyny, less insecure about heterosexual credentials. Perhaps. We will know only if we ask.

Georgia, Lithuania, Latvia, Estonia, Ukraine, Iraqi Kurdistan, Slovenia, Croatia, and Bosnia are just a few of the nations in the process of designing new militaries in the morning after the Cold War. As each citizenry and its officials create their new military, they will be making choices—about prostitution, homosexuality, marriage, nursing, and combat. Exactly what they decide, why, and with what results could surprise us.

Simultaneously, Kuwait, South Africa, Russia, Angola, Ethiopia, El Salvador, and Cambodia are remaking existing militaries. While it is not a foregone conclusion, the weight of patriarchal militarized convention will lean toward the repetition of past formulas. For instance, already the African National Congress (ANC) has sent three thousand of its guerrillas overseas for officer training in a program designed to prepare the ANC for participating in South Africa's new, post-apartheid military. Not a single woman was sent.[10]

The United States Department of Defense is on the brink of making deep cuts in its military "manpower" at a time when more American women—both white women and women of color—see soldiering as a job option. It is a time when more gay men see military service as a means of gaining public respect, when more black young men consider military service as a possible exit from inner-city despair. But the military is an active player; it is not simply a target for pressures. Its several agencies will be taking steps to shape gender, racial, and class expectations for the next decade so that it gets the personnel it thinks will best serve its mission after the Cold War. BBDO, one of Madison Avenue's biggest advertising agencies, won a $19 million contract in mid-1992 from the U.S. Navy to promote the navy's recruiting strategy in coming years.[11] It is a "morning after" advertising mandate. How will BBDO's copy writers address the Tailhook scandal? Will white men be featured on the television ads and post office brochures? Will protecting Iraqi Kurds and supporting UN food distribution in Somalia be part of the appeals to young American men?

In each country someone will be making calculations about how masculinity and femininity can best serve national security. This someone may be casual, confused, or ambivalent, but he or she will be making those decisions. This is a postwar period crowded with gendered decisions.

In the 1990s many people are still trying to make sense of the wartime and postwar periods of a generation ago. There is a new wave of French films that reexamine the behavior of French men and French women in 1930s Vietnam and 1950s Algeria. Women from Singapore, Korea, the Philippines, Japan, Taiwan, and Malaysia met recently in Seoul to share information about and analyses of the Japanese military's World War II "comfort women" policy fifty years after the events.[12] Young American women who never imagined that World War II had relevance for their own lives are asking their mothers and grandmothers new questions about Rosie the Riveter, thanks to Madonna's cinematic outfielding in "A League of Their Own." We are living in a new postwar period without having resolved the questions of earlier postwar periods. The morning after can last a long time.

Notes

Introduction

1. This account is drawn from Julie Light's "Salvadoran Women Plan for Peace," *Ms.*, July 1992, 13.

2. Ibid.

3. Jeffrey Schmalz, "Clinton Carves a Wide Path Deep into Reagan Country," *New York Times,* November 4, 1992.

4. ABC Network data derived from exit polls taken on November 3, 1992. I am grateful to Prof. John Blydenburgh of Clark University, ABC's chief polling consultant, for sharing these data with me.

5. Youssef M. Ibrahim, "Iraqis Left Coarse Scars on the Psyche of Kuwait," *New York Times,* August 4, 1992; Chris Hedges, "Foreign Women Lured into Bondage in Kuwait," *New York Times,* January 3, 1992.

6. Louise do Rosario, "Japan: Men's Magazines: Proliferation Shows Shift in Lifestyle," *Far Eastern Economic Review,* August 6, 1992, 27–28.

7. Joni Seager, *Earth Follies: Coming to Feminist Terms with the Global Environmental Crisis* (New York: Routledge, 1993). The book uses a feminist approach to reveal why militaries are the single biggest institutional polluter of the environment.

Chapter 1

1. Rosamund Shreeves, "Mothers against the Draft: Women's Activism in the USSR," *Report on the USSR,* September 21, 1990, 3–9.

2. "Soldier Boy," part of the series *Comrades,* was shown on the American Public Broadcasting Service (PBS) program "Frontline," aired in Boston on WGBH, May 28, 1988.

3. Shreeves, "Mothers against Draft."

4. "Regional Update," *Pacific Research,* August 1991, 19.

5. "Mothers Cause Disruption," a report from *Izvestiya,* October 15, 1991, summarized in *Foreign Broadcast Information Service,* October 17, 1991, 43. For an unusual direct transcript of a meeting in which women identifying themselves as mothers of soldiers publicly challenged local party secretaries for allowing their soldier sons to be deployed in domestic interethnic clashes, see "Stavropol Women Protest Troop Call-Up," *Foreign Broadcast Information Service—Soviet Union,* January 22, 1990, 90. I am grateful to Keith Severin for sharing this report with me.

6. Carole L. J. Collins, "Women as Hidden Casualties of the Cold War," *Ms.,* November 1992, 14.

7. The connection between militarized anti-Communism and domestic violence is revealed in a descriptively detailed and analytically rich study of women's changing definitions of issues during the course of mobilizing to install a democracy: Sonia Alvarez, *Engendering Democracy in Brazil: Women's Movements in Transitional Politics* (Princeton, NJ: Princeton University Press, 1990).

8. An imaginative new study of the gendered dynamics that shaped the U.S. civil defense policies of the Cold War era is Laura McEnaney, *Civil Defense Begins at Home: Gender and Family Politics in the Making of the Cold War* (Ph.D. diss., Department of History, University of Wisconsin, Madison, forthcoming). See also Elaine Tyler May, *Homeward Bound: American Families in the Cold War Era* (New York: Basic Books, 1988).

9. Lillian Faderman provides a thought-provoking look at the sexual politics of America's McCarthy era in chapter 6 of her book *Odd Girls and Twilight Lovers* (New York: Columbia University Press, 1991).

10. In early 1992, President George Bush appointed a member of Phyllis Schafly's Eagle Forum, Elaine Donnelly, to his fifteen-member Presidential Commission on the Assignment of Women in the Armed Forces. She became one of the commission's proponents of sustaining the ban on women in combat positions. See Stephen Power, "Panel on Women in Military under Fire," *San Francisco Examiner,* August 4, 1992. For a discussion of the still-unratified Equal Rights Amendment and its implications for the status of women in the U.S. military, see Judith Hicks Stiehm, *Arms and the Enlisted Woman* (Philadelphia: Temple University Press, 1989), 111–13.

11. Vaclav Havel, "Letter to Dr. Gustav Husak," in *Vaclav Havel: Living in Truth,* ed. Jan Vladislav (London: Faber and Faber, 1987), 11. See also Vaclav Havel, *Letters to Olga* (New York: Henry Holt, 1988).

12. Barbara Wolfe Jancar, *Women under Communism* (Baltimore, MD: Johns Hopkins University Press, 1978); Sharon L. Wolchik and Alfred G. Meyer, eds., *Women, State, and Party in Eastern Europe* (Durham, NC: Duke University Press, 1985).

13. Yugoslav feminist Slavenka Drakulić thinks back on her own Cold War Barbie yearnings in her essay "A Doll That Grew Old," in Slavenka Drakulić, *How We Survived Communism and Even Laughed* (New York: Norton, 1991), 55–65.

14. Luise White, *The Comforts of Home: Prostitution in Colonial Nairobi* (Chicago: University of Chicago Press, 1990).

15. Victoria De Grazia, *How Fascism Ruled Women: Italy, 1922–1945* (Berkeley: University of California Press, 1992).

16. Theoretical accounts of masculinity include R. W. Connell, *Gender and Power* (Stanford, CA: Stanford University Press, 1988); Jeff Hearn and David Morgan, eds., *Men, Masculinities and Social Theory* (London: Unwin Hyman, 1990); Mark E. Kann, *On the Man Question: Gender and Civic Virtue in America* (Philadelphia: Temple University Press, 1991). See also Jeff Hearn, *Men in the Public Eye* (London: Routledge, 1992); David Morgan, *Discovering Men* (London: Routledge, 1992); *Manful Associations: Masculinities in Britain since 1800,* ed. Michael Roper and John Tosh (London: Routledge, 1991). Case studies include Christopher Browning, *Ordinary Men: Reserve Police Battalion 101 and the Final Solution in Poland* (New York: Harper-Collins, 1992); Klaus Theweleit's study of the German Freikorps during World War I, *Male Fantasies,* vols. 1 and 2 (Minneapolis: University of Minnesota Press, 1989).

17. Sandra Whitworth, "Feminism, Gender and the International Labor Organization," in *International Organization* (forthcoming). See also Whitworth's *Gender in the IPPF and the ILO: A Feminist Analysis of International Relations* (Ph.D. Diss., Carlton University, Ottawa, Ontario, 1991).

18. Among the most prominent of these feminist analyses of international relations are the following: J. Ann Tickner, *Gender in International Relations* (New York: Columbia University Press, 1992); Rebecca Grant and Kathleen Newland, eds., *Gender and International Relations* (Bloomington: Indiana University Press, 1991); Christine Sylvester, *Feminist Theory and International Relations in a Postmodern Era* (Cambridge: Cambridge University Press, forthcom-

ing); V. Spike Peterson, ed., *Gendered States: Feminist (Re)Visions of International Relations Theory* (Boulder, CO: Lynne Rienner, 1992).

19. For analyses of Eastern European women's oppositional organizing leading up to the 1989 revolutions, see Drakulić, *How We Survived Communism;* Barbara Schaeffer-Hegel, "Makers and Victims of Unification: German Women and the Two Germanies," *Women's Studies International Forum* 15, no. 1 (1992), 101–11; Irene Dolling, "Between Hope and Helplessness: Women in the GDR after the 'Turning Point,'" *Feminist Review* 39 (Winter 1991), 3–15; Barbara Einhorn, "Where Have All the Women Gone? Women and the Women's Movement in East Central Europe," *Feminist Review,* 39 (Winter 1992), 16–36; Julia Szalai, "Some Aspects of the Changing Situation of Women in Hungary," *Signs* 17, no. 11 (1991), 152–170; Yudit Kiss, "The Second 'No': Women in Hungary," *Feminist Review* 39 (Winter 1991), 49–57; Renata Siemienska, "Dialogue: Polish Women and Polish Politics since World War II," *Journal of Women's History* 3, no. 1 (Spring 1991), 108–130. Linda Racioppi and Kathleen O'Sullivan See, two social scientists at Michigan State University, have conducted extensive interviews with Russian women active in Moscow women's groups—some of whom have ties to the former Communist regime—who are creating new, autonomous, and consciously feminist local organizations. Many of these women are among the newly unemployed, highly educated women who were laid off from their public institute jobs in the first year of the post-Gorbachev era. Racioppi and See were also told by their Russian interviewees that the label "lesbian" has been wielded against women attempting to mobilize an independent Russian women's movement. Racioppi and See reported these findings in discussion at the Women and Democratization Panel at the annual meeting of the International Studies Association—Midwest, East Lansing, Michigan State University, November 21, 1992.

20. The description that follows of feminists in East Germany before and after unification is drawn from the account presented by Barbara Schaeffer-Hegel in "Makers and Victims."

21. Marina Beyer, "The Situation of East German Women in Post Unification Germany," in Duchen, ed., "Continent in Transition," 114.

22. Mira Janova and Mariette Sineau, "Women's Participation in Political Power in Europe," in Duchen, ed., "Continent in Transition," 117.

23. Jolanta Plakwicz, "Between Church and State: Polish Women's Experience," in *Superwomen and the Double Burden: Women's Experience of Change in Central and Eastern Europe and the Former Soviet Union,* ed. Chris Corrin (Toronto: Second Story Press, 1992).

24. For examples of the sexualization of East European cultures, see Dra-kulić, *How We Survived Communism;* Yelena Khanga, "No Matryoshkas Need Apply," *New York Times,* November 25, 1991; Andrew Meier, "The Big Bride Swap," *Moscow Magazine,* February/March 1992: 28–34; Melinda Hen-neberger, "Mail Order of Russian Bride Results in Bitter Exchanges," *New York Times,* October 28, 1992.

25. Conversation with a former Czech environmental official, Madison, Wis-consin, October 29, 1992.

26. Jean-Claude Pomonti, "Caught between Dogma and Liberalization," originally published in *Le Monde,* January 29, 1992, reprinted in the *Guardian Weekly,* February 9, 1992, 16.

27. Ibid.

28. Ibid.

29. Stan Sesser, "Report from Cambodia," *New Yorker,* May 18, 1992, 43.

30. I am grateful to an anonymous Africa specialist in the U.S. State Depart-ment for offering this policy interpretation in a phone conversation on October 16, 1992.

31. A new study of girls in U.S. public schools found that "Black males in particular, and Hispanic males to a lesser extent, express a much greater interest in the military than do whites, even when controlling for SES [socioeconomic status] or test scores." American Association of University Women, *How Schools Short-Change Girls* (Washington, DC: AAUW Educational Foundation, 1992), 36.

32. Baarveld-Schlaman, *The Role of Women in the Armed Forces.* Docu-ment 1267 (London: Western European Union, 1991).

33. Fernando Marques, "Women Enlist for the War of the Sexes," originally published in *Publico* (Lisbon), reprinted in *The Guardian* (London), March 20, 1992.

34. "Female Cadets a First for Japan," *Boston Globe,* April 5, 1992.

35. For a more detailed discussion of gay and lesbian military politics, see chapter 3.

36. The best investigation of the tension between these two feminist under-standings as they are displayed in the American political context is Mary Katzen-stein's new book *Liberating the Mainstream* (forthcoming).

37. Paola Bono and Sandra Kempt, eds., *Italian Feminist Thought: A Reader* (Oxford, England: Basil Blackwell, 1991).

38. I am grateful to Nishkala Suntharalingam, an international legal researcher, for providing me with a copy of a summary of this interview with an anonymous member of the UN peacekeeping staff in September 1992; correspondence, October 6, 1992.

39. Sandra Whitworth, an international relations researcher at York University in Toronto, Canada, is currently posing some of these questions. Her gendered analysis of the UN peacekeeping force will complement her already completed gendered analysis of the International Labor Organization and International Planned Parenthood, *Gender in the IPPF and ILO.*

40. Clyde Farnsworth, "Canadian Troops to Pull Out of Europe by '94," *New York Times,* February 27, 1992.

41. Flora Lewis, "Gurkhas Can Solve the U.N.'s Problem," *New York Times,* February 8, 1992.

42. A feminist study of the British military's policies to control relations between Nepali women and the Nepali husbands who serve in the Gurkhas is Seira Tamang, "Nepali Women as Military Wives" (Honors thesis, Department of Government, Clark University, Worcester, MA, 1992).

Chapter 2

An earlier version of this chapter appeared as "Feminists Thinking about War, Militarism and Peace," in *Analyzing Gender: A Handbook of Social Science Research,* ed. Beth B. Hess and Myra Marx Ferree (Beverly Hills, CA: Sage Publications, 1987).

1. This experience was described to me by Rajini Sarma Balachandran, an Indian international security scholar, during a symposium at Rutgers University, March 1991.

2. Among the classic texts on capitalism and militarism are Seymor Melman, *The Permanent War Economy* (New York: Simon and Schuster, 1974); Mary Kaldor, *The Baroque Arsenal* (New York: Hill and Wang, 1981); Paul Kostinen, *The Military Industrial Complex: An Historical Perspective* (New York: Praeger, 1980). A recent report by the Air Force Association which argues against the dismantling of the American military-industrial complex describes its economic workings as benign or even healthy: Air Force Association, *Lifeline Adrift: The Defense Industrial Base in the 1990s* (Arlington, VA: 1991). See also Roger Lotchin, *Fortress California, 1910–1961: From Warfare to Welfare* (New York: Oxford University Press, 1992).

3. Stockholm International Peace Research Institute, *World Armaments and Disarmament: The 1992 SIPRI Yearbook* (Oxford: Oxford University Press, 1992). In early 1993, the European Community's top five arms producers were, in descending order of sales, British Aerospace, the French electronics manufacturer Thomson-CSF, Britain's General Electric Company, France's DCN, and Daimler Benz, the famous German manufacturer. Andrew Marshall, "What Happened to the Peace Dividend?" *The Independent* (London), January 3, 1993.

4. "The 1991 Gulf War," *Campaign Against Arms Trade Newsletter* 117 (October 1992), 7. The Campaign Against Arms Trade is a group which keeps especially close watch on arms sales and seeks to organize Britons to protest against weapons sales shows and government promotion of defense companies' interests abroad. Their newsletter and other educational materials are available from CAAT, 11 Goodwin Street, London 4 3HQ, Great Britain.

5. "Japan's Defense Industry: At War with the Budget," *The Economist*, October 31, 1992, 72.

6. For a description of a pilot project to convert Martin, a tank-producing region of Slovakia, to civilian production, see Mary Kaldor, "Martin: Facing Conversion," *Helsinki Citizens Assembly Newsletter* 5 (Fall 1992), 16–17.

7. For an example of the eagerness to sell arms, see John Tagliabue, "Czechoslovaks Find Profit and Pain in Arms Sales," *New York Times*, February 19, 1992. Tagliabue also discusses Czechoslovak internal efforts to convert arms factories and opposition to those efforts. See also Christine Bohlen, "Arms Factory Can Make Bricks, But, Russia Asks, Is That Smart?" *New York Times*, February 24, 1992. A meeting of European groups campaigning for an end to arms exports deliberately sited their meeting in Bratislava, Slovakia, in recognition of that region's heavy dependence on arms production and exports: *Campaign Against Arms Trade Newsletter* 112 (December 1991): 7. For more on Slovakia's arms factories, see Yahia Said, "New Challenges for Conversion: The Martin Project," *Helsinki Citizens Assembly Newsletter* 6 (Winter 1993): 25. In 1992, Russia's principal arms buyers were China, Iran, Syria, and Turkey. On this and continuing efforts by Russian officials to sell arms abroad, see Steven Erlanger, "Moscow Insists It Must Sell the Instruments of War to Pay the Costs of Peace," *New York Times*, February 3, 1993.

8. Nicole Ball, *Pressing for Peace: Can Aid Induce Reform?* (Washington, DC: Overseas Development Council, 1992), 27.

9. Peter Hall and Ann R. Markusen, "The Pentagon and the Gun Belt," in *The Pentagon and the Cities*, ed. Andrew Kirby, Urban Affairs Annual Review,

vol. 40 (Newbury Park, CA: Sage Publications, 1992), 60. See also Ann Markusen and Joel Yudken, *Dismantling the Cold War Economy* (New York: Basic Books, 1992).

10. Hall and Markusen, "The Pentagon," 61.

11. Jacklyn Cock, *Women and War in South Africa* (London: Open Letters Press, 1992).

12. "High-Tech Employment Patterns in Silicon Valley, 1990," *Global Electronics* 116 (October 1992), 2. *Global Electronics* is published by the Pacific Studies Center, 222B View St., Mountain View, CA 94041.

13. Elizabeth Mueller, "The Other Side of the Defense Build Down," *Positive Alternatives*, Summer 1992, 4. Published by the Center for Economic Conversion, 222 View St., Mountain View, CA 94041.

14. Jean Alonso, "In the Belly of the Beast," *Women's Review of Books* 8, no. 10–11 (July 1991), 12–13. For interviews with some of the men and women working at Raytheon's Patriot missile plant in Massachusetts during the Gulf War, see "At a Missile Maker, Pride and Relief," *New York Times,* Jan. 28, 1991; Barbara Carton, "Pride in the Patriot," *Boston Globe,* January 26, 1991.

15. One of the most famous "whistle-blowers," A. E. Fitzgerald, has described how he himself was socialized into this militarizing behavior of bureaucratic allegiance and what eventually prompted him to violate the unwritten rules of American civil service life. His book is *The High Price of Waste* (New York: Norton, 1972). See also Gordon Adams, *The Iron Triangle: The Politics of Defense Contracting* (New York: Council on Economic Priorities, 1981); Sisela Bok, *Secrets* (New York: Vintage, 1984); Michael Klare, *The American Arms Supermarket* (Austin: University of Texas Press, 1984). A recent analysis of a U.S. federal bureaucratic agency that is especially invested in government spending for military research is Nance Goldstein, "The Defense Advanced Research Projects Agency as the National Agent for Technological and Industrial Change—DARPA Support for Software and AI Technologies," *Defense Analysis,* vol. 8:1 (Summer 1992): 61–80.

16. International Economic Conversion Conference, *Proceedings* (Chestnut Hill, MA: Boston College, 1984); "Women and Economic Conversion," *Plowshares* 10, no. 3 (1985); Hilary Wainwright, "The Women Who Wire Up the Weapons," in *Over Our Dead Bodies,* ed. Dorothy Thompson (London: Virago, 1983).

17. Katherine DeFoyd, "Rosie the Riveter Revisited: Women Face Dead End Jobs in Defense Industry," *Plowshare Press* 10, no. 3 (Summer, 1985), 1. For a

detailed description of how women at a peace camp set up near an aerospace defense contractor, Boeing, learned to build relationships with women employees, see Puget Sound Women's Peace Camp participants, *We Are Ordinary Women,* (Seattle: Seal Press, 1985).

18. "Economic Conversion: An Emerging U.S. Issue," *AFSC Women's Newsletter,* 6, no. 1 (1985), A3.

19. "Defence Industry: Attacked on All Sides," *The Economist,* February 22, 1992, 52.

20. Ibid. The rise in incidents of domestic violence around Groton, Connecticut, home of General Dynamics Corporation's submarine-building plant, is reported by Kirk Johnson, "Winning the Cold War and Losing a Job," *New York Times,* February 3, 1993.

21. This quotation and the information that follows are from Nicholas D. Kristof, "Potent Office Weaves Web in China Arms," *New York Times,* August 21, 1991.

22. Using sources from the Stockholm International Peace Research Institute, the International Institute for Strategic Studies, NATO, and WEU, Elisabetta Addis, professor of economics at the University of Rome, arrived at this composite figure in "The Reality and the Image: Women and the Economic Consequences of Being a Soldier" (paper presented at the conference on Women at War: Images of Women Soldiers, European University Institute, Florence, November 15–16, 1991), 6.

23. For examples of the overwhelmingly male character of the military, see John Keegan, *The Face of Battle* (New York: Vintage, 1977); Mark Baker, *Nam* (New York: Berkeley Books, 1984); John Ellis, *The Sharp End of War: The Fighting Man in World War II* (London: Corgi, 1982); Wallace Terry, *Bloods: An Oral History of the Vietnam War by Black Veterans* (New York: Ballantine Books, 1984); John McPhee, *La Place de la Concorde Suisse* (New York: Farrar Straus Giroux, 1984).

24. Before I understood the value of feminist analysis, I investigated the relations between men of different ranks and ethnic and racial groups in Enloe, *Ethnic Soldiers: State Security in Divided Societies* (London: Penguin Books; Athens, GA: University of Georgia Press, 1980). Several recent case studies graphically describe efforts to bind officers and men of different ethnic and racial groups: Joseph T. Glatthaar, *Forged in Battle: The Civil War Alliance of Black Soldiers and White Officers* (New York: Meridian, 1991); Tom Holm, "Patriots and Pawns: State Use of American Indians in the Military and the Process of

Nativization in the United States," in *The State of Native America,* ed. M. Annette Jaimes (Boston: South End Press, 1992); "Nepalis in Uniform" (special issue), *Himal,* July–August 1991; N. F. Dreisziger, ed., *Ethnic Armies* (Waterloo, Ontario: Wilfred Laurier University Press, 1990); Alexander Alexiev, *Inside the Soviet Army in Afghanistan* (Santa Monica, CA: Rand Publication Series, 1988).

25. For a glimpse of the popular debate over American men's responses to conscription during the Vietnam War as it played itself out during the 1992 presidential primaries, see Walter A. McDougall, "What We Do For Our Country," *New York Times,* February 17, 1992; Jonathan S. Gellman, Letter to the Editor, *New York Times,* March 9, 1992.

26. These quotations are from white South African men interviewed by Jacklyn Cock for her book *Women and War,* 73.

27. Ibid., 76.

28. Robert Bly, *Iron John* (New York: Vintage, 1990). A collection of feminist essays responding not only to Bly but to the men's groups he has helped spawn is Kay Hagen, ed., *Women Respond to the Men's Movement* (San Francisco: Harper-Collins, 1992).

29. Conversation with a woman U.S. Air Force officer, Cambridge, MA, March 7, 1992. I am indebted to Mary Katzenstein, of Cornell University, who allowed me to sit in on this conversation, part of her research for her forthcoming study of American women's lobbying inside the U.S. military, entitled *Liberating the Mainstream.*

30. Nancy Hartsock, *Sexuality and Politics: The Barracks Community in Western Political Thought* (New York, Longman's, 1983).

31. The U.S. Army official figures, as quoted in Carolyn Becraft, *Women in the Military, 1980–1990,* commissioned and published by the Women's Research and Education Institute (Washington, DC: 1990), 9. (Women's Research and Education Institute, 1700 18th St. N.W., Washington, DC 20009.)

32. This episode is described in more detail in Cynthia Enloe, *Does Khaki Become You? The Militarization of Women's Lives* (London: Pandora / Harper Collins, 1988).

33. Military recruitment brochures can provide some surprising insights into a country's definitions of femininity and masculinity. For the U.S. Army's complete list of its jobs, with stars beside those closed off to women as of 1988, see its recruiting brochure, "Turn Two Years of College into a Head Start on the Future" (Washington, DC: U.S. Government Printing Office, 1988). This bro-

chure can be read as the outcome of the women-versus-the-army struggle of 1983. More struggles are to come; they will require ongoing revision of recruiting brochures.

34. Becraft, *Women in the Military,* 5–6.

35. Susan Brownmiller, *Against Our Will: Men, Women and Rape* (New York: Bantam Books, 1976); Daniel Lang, *Casualties of War* (New York: McGraw-Hill, 1969).

36. Amnesty International, *Rape and Sexual Abuse: Torture and Ill Treatment of Women in Detention* (New York: Amnesty International, 1992).

37. One hesitates even to start a list of works on women's experiences of World War I and II, but among the most enlightening are Ben Bousquet and Colin Douglas, *West Indian Women at War: British Racism in World War II* (London: Lawrence and Wishart, 1991); White, *Comforts of Home,* 147–184; De Grazia, *How Fascism Ruled Women;* Gail Braybon and Penny Summerfield, *Out of the Cage: Women's Experiences in Two World Wars* (London: Pandora, 1987); Steven C. Hause with Anne R. Kenney, *Women's Suffrage and the Social Politics in the French Third Republic* (Princeton, NJ: Princeton University Press, 1984); Judy Barrett Litoff and David C. Smith, eds., *Since You Went Away: World War II Letters from American Women on the Home Front* (New York: Oxford University Press, 1991); Sarah Fishman, *We Will Wait: Wives of French Prisoners of War, 1940–1945* (New Haven: Yale University Press, 1991); William J. Breen, "Black Women and the Great War: Mobilization and Reform in the South," *The Journal of Southern History* 44, no. 3 (August, 1978), 421–440; Charity Adams Early, *One Woman's Army: A Black Officer Remembers the WAC* (College Station, Texas A&M Press, 1989); John Costello, *Virtue under Fire: How World War II Changed Our Social and Sexual Attitudes* (Boston: Little, Brown, 1985); Margaret Randolph Higonnet, Jane Jenson, Sonya Michel, and Margaret Collins Weitz, eds., *Behind the Lines: Gender and the Two World Wars* (New Haven, CT: Yale University Press, 1987); Claudia Koonz, *Mothers in the Fatherland* (New York: St. Martin's Press, 1987); Karen Anderson, *Wartime Women* (Westport, CT: Greenwood Press, 1981); D'Ann Campbell, *Women at War with America* (Cambridge, MA: Harvard University Press, 1984); Susan Hartman, *The Home Front and Beyond* (Boston: Twayne Publishers, 1982); Penny Summerfield, *Women Workers in the Second World War* (New York: Routledge, 1984); Amy Kesselman, *Fleeting Opportunities: Women Shipyard Workers in Portland and Vancouver during World War II and Reconversion* (Albany, NY: SUNY Press, 1990); Maureen Honey, *Creating Rosie the Riveter: Class, Gender and Propaganda during World War II* (Amherst: Univer-

sity of Massachusetts Press, 1984); Ryoko Kurihara, "The Japanese Woman Suffrage Movement," *Feminist Issues* 11, no. 2 (Fall, 1991), 81–100; Women's Division of the Sokka Gakkai, *Women against War: Personal Accounts of Forty Japanese Women* (Tokyo: Kodansha, 1986).

38. As a start in this investigation of postwar militarization, one can turn to Mandana Hendessi's report, *Armed Angels: Women in Iran,* International Reports: Women and Society, Report no. 16, issued in 1990 by Change (P.O. Box 824, London SE24 9JS); also Grace Akello, *Self Twice-Removed: Ugandan Woman,* Report 8, rev. ed. (London: Change, 1990). Also providing a window on postwar women's lives is Irene Staunton, ed., *Mothers of the Revolution: The War Experiences of Thirty Zimbabwean Women* (Bloomington: Indiana University Press, 1990). For a description and analysis of the conflicting postwar interpretations of the anticolonial war by Zimbabwe's ex-guerrilla women and rural women who stayed in their villages, see Sita Ranchod-Nilsson, "Gender Politics and National Liberation: Women's Participation in the Liberation of Zimbabwe," Ph.D. diss., Northwestern University, 1992.

39. Among the most influential feminist writings on peace are Brigit Brock-Utne, *Educating for Peace: A Feminist Perspective* (Oxford: Pergamon Press, 1985); L. Caldecott and S. Leland, eds., *Reclaim the Earth* (London: Women's Press, 1983); Cambridge Women's Peace Collective, *My Country Is the Whole World* (London: Pandora Press, 1984); "Special Peace Issue," *Helicon Nine* 12–13 (Summer 1985); Feminism and Non-Violence Group, *Piecing It Together: Feminism and Non-Violence* (Spencer, NY: J. Tiffany, 1983); "Women and Peace" (special issue), *Frontiers* 8, no. 2 (1985); Christa Wolf, *Cassandra* (London: Virago Press, 1984).

40. Barbara Taylor, *Eve and the New Jerusalem* (New York: Pantheon Books, 1984).

41. Debates among British feminists over the political implications of taking all forms of violence against women in peace organizing are described vividly in Alice Cook and Gwyn Kirk, *Greenham Women Everywhere* (Boston: Southend Press, 1983); Barbara Harford and Sarah Hopkins, editors, *Greenham Common: Women at the Wire* (London, Women's Press, 1984); *Breaching the Peace* (London: Onlywomen Press, 1983); Jill Liddington, *The Long Road to Greenham: Feminism and Anti-Militarism in Britain since 1820* (Syracuse, NY: University of Syracuse Press, 1990); Anne Wiltshire, *Most Dangerous Women: Feminist Peace Campaigners of the Great War* (London: Pandora Press, 1985).

42. Deborah Corbett, "Women in Iraq," in *Saddam's Iraq: Revolution or Reaction?* ed. Committee against Repression and for Democratic Rights in Iraq (London: Zed Books), 120–137.

43. Some of these investigations by Third World women are available in DAWN, *Alternatives,* vols. 1 and 2, Rio de Janeiro, Editora Rosa Dos Tempos, 1991 (distributed by Change: International Reports: Women and Society, P.O. Box 824, London SE24 9JS, England). DAWN is an international network of Third World feminist researchers concerned with devising alternative, nonsexist strategies for development. See also *Subha,* a feminist Pakistani journal, published by Shirkat Gah, 1 Bath Island Road, Karachi 75530, Pakistan; Blanca Figueroa and Jeanine Anderson Velasco, *Women in Peru,* rev. ed. (London: Change, 1990); Khin Thitsa, *Providence and Prostitution: Women in Buddhist Thailand,* rev. ed. (London: Change, 1990); R. Vanita, "The 1984 Elections: United We Fall—Into the Trap of Manipulators," *Manushi: Journal about Women and Society* 26 (1985); Ximena Bunster, "Surviving beyond Fear: Women and Torture in Latin America," in *Women and Change in Latin America,* ed. June Nash and Helen Safa (South Hadley, MA: Bergin and Garvey, 1986), 297–325; "Women and Militarism" (special issue), *Connexions* 2 (Winter 1984).

Chapter 3

An earlier version of this chapter appeared as "Beyond Steve Canyon and Rambo: Feminist Histories of Militarized Masculinity" in John R. Gillis, ed., *The Militarization of the Western World* (New Brunswick, NJ: Rutgers University Press, 1989).

1. Milton Caniff, *Steve Canyon* (Princeton, NJ: Kitchen Sink Press, 1985); Bobbie Ann Mason, *In Country* (New York: Perennial Books, 1986).

2. Cortez F. Enloe, conversations with the author, Annapolis, Maryland, from February 1987 to January 1992; David Enloe, correspondence with the author, February 1987; Harriett Goodridge Enloe, diaries, 1915–1982 (unpublished).

3. Philip Taubman, "Russians Strike Back with a Rambo of Their Own," *New York Times,* July 24, 1986.

4. James Fenton, "The Snap Revolutions," *Granta,* (London: Penguin, 1986); Steven D. Stark, "Ten Years into the Stallone Era," *New York Times,* February 22, 1987; Philippa Brewster, conversation with the author, London,

October 1986. See also Susan Jeffords, *The Remasculinization of America: Gender and the Vietnam War* (Bloomington: Indiana University Press, 1989). See also *From Hanoi to Hollywood: The Vietnam War in American Film,* ed. Linda Dittmar and Gene Michaud (New Brunswick, NJ: Rutgers University Press, 1991), and Elliott Gruner, *Prisoners of Culture: Representations of the Vietnam P.O.W.* (New Brunswick: Rutgers University Press, 1993).

5. Useful cross-national collections of feminist analyses of militarized gender are Eva Isaksson, editor, *Women and the Military System* (London: Harvester-Wheatsheaf, 1988); Sharon McDonald, Pat Holden, and Shirley Ardener, eds., *Images of Women in Peace and War: Cross-Cultural and Historical Perspectives* (Madison: University of Wisconsin Press, 1988); Jean Bethke Elshtain and Sheila Tobias, eds., *Thinking about Women, Militarism and War: Essays in History, Politics and Social Criticism* (New York: Rowman and Allenheld, 1989).

6. I have spelled out how militaries hide their dependence on women in more detail in Enloe, *Does Khaki Become You?*

7. The roles played by American professional psychologists in World War II in ensuring American male soldiers' morale and the psychologists' incentives for willingly playing these roles are explored in Ellen Herman, "The Public Uses and Political Consequences of American Psychology, 1940–1970" (unpublished Ph.D. diss., Department of History, Brandeis University, 1993).

8. I am indebted to Georgia State University geographer Melissa Gilbert and Clark University international development researcher Octavia Taylor for sharing with me their findings from studies of Vietnamese immigrant communities in Worcester, Massachusetts. Gilbert's study, which includes an analysis of Vietnamese-American low-income women, is "Ties to People, Bonds to Place: The Urban Geography of Low Income Women's Survival Strategies" (Ph.D. diss., Clark University, in progress.) Taylor's work analyzing the gendered and bureaucratized politics of health in the Vietnamese community of Worcester is a 1992 master's thesis available from the International Development Program, Clark University, Worcester, MA: "Funding Frailties: The Vietnamese Refugee Experience with Bureaucracy in Worcester, Massachusetts." See also Seth Mydens, "Old Soldiers: The Last Refugees Free to Leave Vietnam," *New York Times,* September 14, 1992.

9. Elizabetta Addis, Italian feminist economist and military critic, in conversation with the author, Cambridge, MA, November 1986.

10. Isaksson, *Women and the Military System.*

11. Theweleit, *Male Fantasies,* vol. 1. See also Koonz, *Mothers in the Fatherland.*

12. Kathleen Mihalisko, "Defense and Security Planning in Ukraine," *Report on the USSR,* December 6, 1991, 15–19; "Army without a Country, Countries without an Army," *The Economist,* January 25, 1992, 43.

13. Philip Shenon, "Japanese Sun Again Rises Overseas," *New York Times,* September 27, 1992. Typically, home office editors, not the reporter in the field, choose an article's headline. For a sampling of Japanese male officers' reactions to being sent to Cambodia, see "Voices from the SDF," *AMPO: Japan-Asian Quarterly Review* 24, no. 1 (1993): 19–22.

14. Tai Ming Cheung, "Self-Defense and Beyond," *Far Eastern Economic Review,* July 30, 1992, 27; Virginia Woolf, *Three Guineas* (New York: Harcourt Brace Jovanovich, 1938).

15. Yumi Iwai, conversations with the author, Worcester, MA, November 1985; Kano Mikiyo, "Remolding Tennoism for Modern Japan," *AMPO* 19, nos. 2–3 (1986).

16. Enloe, *Ethnic Soldiers,* 25–33. Progressive Nepali scholars and activists are taking the lead in rethinking just what sorts of nineteenth- and twentieth-century government-to-government agreements and political economies it took to usher so many Nepali men into the British-controlled Gurkha regiments: see "Nepalis in Uniform," a special issue of the Nepali journal *Himal.* A unique analysis of British policies toward Gurkha wives and of those Nepali women's adaptations to those policies is Seira Tamang's "Nepali Women as Military Wives."

17. Dewitt Ellinwood, ed., *India in World War I* (New Delhi: South Asia Books, 1978).

18. *The Dawn,* no. 5 (1889), no. 22 (1893), no. 27 (1895), and no. 30 (1896), published in London by the British, Continental and General Federation for the Abolition of the State Regulation of Vice. New research is now being done on the wives of the famed Gurkhas: see Tamang, "Nepali Women as Military Wives."

19. Bousquet and Douglas, *West Indian Women at War.*

20. David E. Sanger, "Japan Admits It Forced Koreans into Its Brothels," *New York Times,* January 14, 1992.

21. Chris Hedges, "The Runaway Army Is Back, But Standing at Ease," *New York Times,* January 14, 1992.

22. A young Vietnamese peasant woman's attempts to negotiate between French, Moroccan, American, ARVN, and nationalist militarized masculinities are recounted in Le Ly Hayslip's autobiography, *When Heaven and Earth Changed Places* (New York: Plume/Penguin, 1989).

23. Addis, "Reality and the Image," 11–13. Addis uses data from a report from the London-based International Institute of Strategic Studies, *Military Balance, 1990–91*, to reveal that none of the militaries of the Warsaw Pact had a significant number of women in their uniformed ranks.

24. Baarveld-Schlaman, *Role of Women in the Armed Forces*. See also Addis, "Reality and the Image."

25. Baarveld-Schlaman, *Role of Women in the Armed Forces*.

26. John Lancaster, "Does Anyone Allow Gays to Serve in the Military?" *Washington Post Weekly Edition*, December 7–13, 1992, 4. For a report on the media and parliamentary debate over whether the Israeli military discriminates against gay soldiers, see Clyde Habermann, "Homosexuals in Israeli Army: No Official Discrimination, But Keep It Secret," *New York Times*, February 21, 1993. See also Sally Jacobs, "Canada to Let Gays Serve in Forces; Impact Eyed on U.S. Ban," *Boston Globe*, October 28, 1992.

27. Clyde H. Farnsworth, "Canada Ending Anti-Gay Army Rules," *New York Times*, October 11, 1991.

28. Jacobs, "Canada to Let Gays Serve in Forces"; "National Notes: Gays and Arms," *MacLean's*, November 9, 1992, 81. See also "Little Trouble in Canada When Its Gay Ban Ended," *New York Times*, January 31, 1993.

29. House of Commons, *Special Report from the Select Committee on the Armed Forces Bill*.

30. "Anger as Parliament Backs Chief of Staff," *Carrier Mail* (Brisbane, Australia), June 19, 1992.

31. Ibid.; Margo Kingston, "Government to Note Canadian Example on Homosexual Ban," *The Age* (Melbourne, Australia), July 7, 1992; Amanda Meade, "Caucus to Review Military Gays Ban," *Sydney Morning Herald* (Australia), June 24, 1992. Hugh Smith, a senior lecturer at the Australian Defense Academy, has written an informative article providing context for the 1992 debate among Australians on homosexuals in the military: "Blind-Eye Approach," *Canberra Times* (Australia), June 30, 1992. See also "Army Reinstates Lesbian Officer," *The Age*, August 4, 1992; Wendy Pryor, "RSL Warns of Violence over Gays in Forces," *West Australian*, September 19, 1992; Michael O'Connor, "No Sex Please, We're Soldiers," *The Australian*, September 21,

1992; Amanda Meade, "Lifting of Gay Ban Disgusting—Forces," *Sydney Morning Herald,* September 19, 1992; Tom O'Connors, "Cabinet to Lift Services Ban on Gays within Week," *Canberra Times,* September 19, 1992.

32. Allan Berube, *Coming Out under Fire* (New York: Plume/Penguin, 1990); Mary Ann Humphrey, *My Country, My Right to Serve* (New York: Harper/Collins, 1990); Kate Dyer, ed., *Gays in Uniform: The Pentagon's Secret Reports* (Boston: Alyson Publications, 1990). A special series of articles on gay men and lesbians in the military and a discussion of the implications of the Gulf War are available in *Outlook: National Lesbian and Gay Quarterly* 13 (Summer 1991): 14–29. See also Jacobs, "Canada to Let Gays Serve in Forces." Finally, a case study of evolving U.S. government policy and conceptualizations of homosexuality in the military is Gary Lehring's Ph.D. dissertation, *Difference as Identity, Difference and Identity: Strategies in American Public Policy* (Department of Political Science, University of Massachusetts, Amherst, 1993).

33. Robert Sullivan, "Postcard from Oregon: Revolution Number Nine," *New Yorker,* November 9, 1992, 67–79; Timothy Egan, "Oregon G.O.P. Faces Schism over Agenda of Christian Right," *New York Times,* November 14, 1992. As reported by Egan, on November 3, 1992, the reputedly liberal voters of Oregon defeated the Christian Right–backed referendum denying homosexuals protection under state law by only 56 to 44 percent. The state chairman of the Oregon Republican Party, who publicly argued against passage of Ballot Measure 9, sent out letters to Republican leaders in other states warning that their party was on the brink of being taken over by the organized Christian Right.

34. Jeffrey Schmaltz, "Gay Politics Goes Mainstream," *New York Times Magazine,* October 11, 1992, 41.

35. Thomas L. Friedman, "Clinton to Open Military's Ranks to Homosexuals," *New York Times,* November 12, 1992.

36. Eric Schmitt, "Challenging the Military," *New York Times,* November 12, 1992.

37. Quoted in John H. Cushman, "Top Military Officers Object to Lifting Homosexual Ban," *New York Times,* November 14, 1992.

38. Ibid.

39. Scott Simon, "Weekend Edition," National Public Radio, November 14, 1992.

40. Eric Schmitt, "Military's Gay Subculture: Off Limits but Flourishing," *New York Times,* December 1, 1992.

41. "The Gay Question," *MacLean's,* February 15, 1993, 12.

42. Larry Rohter, "Open Hostility to Homosexuals outside Navy Base," *New York Times,* January 31, 1993.

43. Jeffrey Schmaltz, "Homosexuals Wait to See a Referendum: It's on Them," *New York Times,* January 31, 1993.

44. Ibid.

45. Schmitt, "Challenging the Military." The National Organization for Women interpreted earlier Defense Department figures as showing that between 1974 and 1983, "overall, women are three times more likely than men to be discharged for homosexuality; in the Marine Corps, the rate for women is 8 times that of men." These figures were included in a combined fact sheet and letter from Molly Yard, then NOW's president, to NOW members: "Lesbians in the Military," (Washington, D.C.: National Organization for Women, 1990). Ten days after Eric Schmitt's article appeared in the *New York Times,* the paper's editorial board ran an editorial arguing that the United States was out of step with its own military allies in continuing to ban homosexuals from its military. The editors noted that a congressionally authorized report on homosexuals in the military completed by the government's General Accounting Office in June, 1992 had shown that not only did Spain, Sweden, Austria, Denmark, Japan, the Netherlands, and France permit gays and lesbians in their militaries, but so did Israel, a country whose military places a high premium on discipline and morale—precisely those values many senior U.S. military officers have claimed would be jeopardized if the antihomosexual ban were lifted. "Editorial: Gay Soldiers Cut the Mustard Abroad," *New York Times,* November 22, 1992. For the GAO report, see U.S. General Accounting Office, *Defense Force Management: DOD's Policy on Homosexuality* (Washington: U.S. General Accounting Office, 1992). For a description of the subtle discrimination that accompanies official tolerance in the Israeli military, a discrimination that provoked national discussion in early 1993, see Ethan Bronner, "Gays in the Military: Israeli Model Has Limits to Equality," *Boston Globe,* February 2, 1993; Clyde Haberman, "Homosexuals in Israeli Army: No Official Discrimination, But Keep It Secret," *New York Times,* February 21, 1993.

46. Schmaltz, "Clinton Carves Wide Path"; Jeffrey Schmaltz, "Gay Areas Are Jubilant over Clinton," *New York Times,* November 5, 1992. For a detailed account of the steps during his election campaign by which Bill Clinton came to an awareness of discrimination against gay men and lesbians in the military, see Chris Bull, "And the Ban Played On," *The Advocate,* March 9, 1993, 37–42.

47. The most focused, though not necessarily the most profound, forum for this national debate was the hearings held by the Senate Armed Services Committee; those hearings began on March 29, 1993. The Senate committee was chaired by Senator Sam Nunn, a conservative Democrat from Georgia, who made clear that he supported the ban on homosexuals. The committee as a whole looked remarkably like the Senate Judiciary Committee that oversaw the nomination hearings of Clarence Thomas, accused of sexual harassment by Anita Hill: both committees were all white and all male. The more diverse House of Representatives Armed Services Committee had equal jurisdiction over military personnel issues, but following its new black, liberal chair, Ronald Dellums, Democrat from California, it shied away from holding its own hearings on the ban, thus leaving the political playing field to its more conservative counterpart. Michael R. Gordon, "Senate Hearings Open on Homosexuals in the Military," *New York Times,* March 30, 1993; Eric Schmitt, "Calm Analysis Dominates Panel Hearing on Gay Ban," *New York Times,* April 1, 1993; Gary Lehring, "Gaze in the Military," typescript, Department of Government, Clark University, Worcester, MA, April, 1993.

48. Carol Cohn, "Clean Bombs and Clean Language," in *Women, Militarism, and War: Essays in History, Politics, and Social Theory,* ed. Jean Bethke Elshtain and Sheila Tobias (Savage, MD: Rowman and Littlefield, 1990), 33–55.

49. William Broad, *Star Warriors* (New York: Simon and Schuster, 1987).

50. Richard Rhodes, *The Making of the Atomic Bomb* (New York: Simon and Schuster, 1986).

51. Hilary Wainwright, "Women Who Wire."

52. Mercedes Charles C., "After Pinochet," *Connexions,* 39 (1992): 32–33. This article originally appeared as "La Mujer chilena en el proceso de transición democrática," in *Fem,* the Mexican feminist monthly, no. 99 (March 1991).

Chapter 4

Parts of this article were originally published as "Bananas, Bases and Patriarchy," in *Radical America* 19, no. 4 (1985): 7–23.

1. I have attempted a more complete analysis of the gendered politics of the international banana industry in Enloe, *Bananas, Beaches and Bases: Making Feminist Sense of International Politics* (Berkeley: University of California Press, 1990).

2. Sistren and Honor Ford Smith, *Lionheart Gal* (London: Women's Press, 1986).

3. Ximena Bunster and Else Chaney, *Sellers and Servants* (New York: Praeger, 1985). Other descriptions of women's work in Latin America and Central America include Laurel Bossen, *The Redivision of Labor: Women and Economic Choice in Four Guatemalan Communities* (Albany: SUNY Press, 1984) and Audrey Bronstein, *The Triple Struggle* (Boston: South End Press, 1983). See also a statistical overview of selected Latin American and Caribbean countries published by the Women and Development Section of the U.S. Agency for International Development (Washington, DC: 1984).

4. Rigoberta Menchú's autobiography has been published as *I, Rigoberta Menchú: An Indian Woman in Guatemala,* (New York: Verso, 1983). See also *You Can't Dream the Fire: Latin American Women Writing in Exile* (Philadelphia: Cleis Press, 1989). Among the reports of Menchú's Nobel Prize is that by Tim Golden, "Guatemalan Indian Wins the Nobel Prize," *New York Times,* October 17, 1992.

5. Interviews with West Indian women working in Canada as domestic workers are included in Makeda Silvera's *Silenced* (Toronto: Williams-Wallace, 1983).

6. Tom Barry, Beth Wood, and Deb Preusch, *The Other Side of Paradise* (New York: Grove Press, 1984), 85.

7. Lynne Bolles, "Kitchens Hit by Priorities: Employed Working Class Jamaican Women Confront the IMF," in *Women, Men, and the International Division of Labor,* ed. June Nash and Maria Patricia Fernandez Kelly (Albany, NY: SUNY Press, 1983). Recent feminist analyses of women's responses to the international debt crisis include United Nations Non-Governmental Liaison Service, Department of Public Information, *Beyond the Debt Crisis* (New York: United Nations 1990); Kathy McAfee, *Storm Signals: Structural Adjustment and Development Alternatives in the Caribbean* (Boston: South End Press, 1992).

8. The information on offshore office work in Barbados comes from Carla Freeman's report on her field work in Barbados: "From Tourism to Typing: Barbadian Women in the Global Network," *Listen Real Loud* 11, no. 1 (1991): 12–13 (published by the American Friends Service Committee, Philadelphia, PA). A complete report on this work will be available in Carla Freeman's dissertation (Department of Anthropology, Temple University, Philadelphia, PA). My own efforts to think about the implications of Carla Freeman's findings

can be found in Cynthia Enloe, "Silicon Tricks and the Two Dollar Woman," *New Internationalist* (special issue on feminism), no. 227 (January 1992), 12.

9. *Boston Globe,* September 15, 1985.

10. Conversation with the author, September 1985.

11. The American Friends Service Committee provided just such an opportunity for Americans to understand how their bases affect other women when it organized a tour of twenty women from countries whose governments had signed base agreements with Washington. Women on the tour not only talked to American audiences, giving them a sense of how U.S. bases had affected their lives, but also talked to each other. A report on the tour can be obtained in American Friends Service Committee, National Women's Program, "Voices of Hope and Anger: Women Speak Out for Sovereignty and Self-Determination" (special issue), *Listen Real Loud* 10, no. 1–2 (1990).

12. Lucy Kosimar, "White Slavery in Honduras?" *Honduras Update* 3, no. 11 (1985).

13. In Uganda, during that country's winding down of its long civil war, women made rape by both sides a political issue, refusing to write it off as merely a natural element of warfare. Ugandan women lawyers and politicians, together with Amnesty International, reported that the new regime of the National Resistance Movement (NRM), though publicly committed to human rights reforms, had neither charged nor punished NRM soldiers who had committed more than a dozen rapes during routine security checks in 1991, the first year of NRM rule. They also held the opposition United Christian Democratic Army responsible for actions by its soldiers, who raided the Sacred Heart Girls' School in Gulu and raped forty-three of its students. "Uganda: Security for Whom?" *Ms.,* November 1992, 10.

14. Michael McClintock, *The American Connection* (London: Zed Press, 1985) 2:245.

15. Bunster, "Surviving beyond Fear," 297–325.

16. The best cross-national comparative source on women's diverse conditions in the 1980s is Joni Seager and Ann Olson's *Women in the World: An International Atlas* (New York: Simon and Schuster, 1986).

17. For details of the Salvadoran peace agreement, see *New York Times,* January 1, 1992; Mike Prokosch, "El Salvador Pact Raises Hopes," *Central America Reporter,* January-February 1992, 1, 9.

18. "Morning Edition," National Public Radio, January 16, 1992.

19. Shirley Christian, "Salvadorans Demobilize, with Verbal Sniping," *New York Times,* July 26, 1992.

20. Shirley Christian, "New Salvadoran Police Force Is Off to a Slow Start," *New York Times,* February 11, 1992.

21. Emilie Smith-Ayala, *The Granddaughters of Ixmucane: Guatemalan Women Speak* (Toronto: Women's Press), 118.

22. Amnesty International, *Rape and Sexual Abuse.*

23. "U.S. Nun Returns to Guatemala to Tell of Rape," *New York Times,* April 10, 1992. See also Smith-Ayala, *Granddaughters of Ixmucane,* 108–10.

24. See, for instance, *Women, Violence and Human Rights,* published by the Center for Women's Global Leadership, 27 Clifton Avenue, Douglass College, Rutgers University, New Brunswick, NJ 08903, 1992.

25. These demands were spelled out in a circular urging women in different countries to lobby their own governments before the Vienna conference. The letter, "Alert for Action," dated September 18, 1992, was distributed by the France-based Muslim feminist organization, Women Living Under Muslim Laws, Box 23—34790 Grabels, France.

26. Tim Golden, "Salvador Rebels Back U.N. Plan, But Say Cristiani Must Agree Too," *New York Times,* October 29, 1992.

27. Information on the land redistribution process comes from Tim Golden, "Both Sides in El Salvador Back Land Program," *New York Times,* October 18, 1992.

28. Shari Turitz, "Guatemala: Torture of a Nation," *Resist Newsletter* 242 (January 1992): 4.

29. For details on the Chamorro government's new antigay legislation, opposed unsuccessfully by the Sandinista legislators, see Shirley Christian, "Newest Storm in Nicaragua: Anti-Gay Law," *New York Times,* July 10, 1992; David L. Wilson, Letter to the Editor, *New York Times,* July 30, 1992. For a description of postwar gay and lesbian organizing in Nicaragua, see Margaret Randall, "Coming Out in Nicaragua," *Sojourner,* June 1992, 4–5. In early 1993, three years after the UNO coalition's victory over the Sandinistas at the polls, many men are persisting in militaristic actions, both as government soldiers accused of assassinations and as reactivated contra insurgents: Shirley Christian, "Democracy in Nicaragua Polluted by Killings and Political Feuding," *New York Times,* February 16, 1993.

30. Isabel Letelier, "Women and Democracy in Chile," *Let the Other Half Speak: Newsletter of the Third World Project* 1, no. 2 (Fall 1991): 3 (published by the Institute for Policy Studies, Washington, DC). Other analyses of Chilean women and demilitarization include Patricia M. Chuchryk, "Feminist Anti-Authoritarian Politics: The Role of Women's Organizations in the Chilean Transition to Democracy," in *The Women's Movement in Latin America: Feminism and the Transition to Democracy,* ed. Jane Jaquette (Boulder, CO: Westview Press, 1991); Adriana Muñoz Dalbora, "The Women's Movement in Chile: A Desired Reality," in *Alternatives,* vol. 2, *Women's Visions and Movements,* ed. DAWN (Rio de Janeiro: Editora Rosa Dos Tempos, 1991; distributed by Change, London); Nancy Saporta Sternbach, Marysa Navarro-Aranguran, Patricia Chuchryk, and Sonia E. Alvarez, "Feminisms in Latin America: From Bogota to San Bernardo," *Signs,* Winter 1992. I have also benefited from ongoing conversations with one of the active participants in Chile's democratization process, the feminist anthropologist Ximena Bunster. For a description of the dilemmas that faced Brazilian women activists when male political party leaders recaptured the political stage as the military regime faltered, see Alvarez, *Engendering Democracy.*

31. Barbara J. Steitz, "From Home to Street: Women and Revolution in Nicaragua," in *Women Transforming Politics,* ed. Jill M. Bystdzienski (Bloomington: Indiana University Press, 1992), 172. See also Helen Collinson, ed., *Women and Revolution in Nicaragua* (London: Zed Books, 1990).

32. Lois Wessel, "Reproductive Rights in Nicaragua: From the Sandinistas to the Government of Violeta Chamorro," *Feminist Studies* 17, no. 3 (Fall 1991): 547. See also the work of Karen Kampwirth, a political scientist at the University of California, Berkeley, on Nicaraguan women's organizing since the Sandinistas' defeat: "The Revolution Continues: Women's Organizing under the UNO," paper presented at the annual meeting of the American Political Science Association, Chicago, September 1992.

33. "Nicaragua: Standing Room Only," *Ms.,* March/April 1992, 10. See also Margaret Randall, *Gathering Rage: The Failure of Twentieth-Century Revolutions to Develop Feminist Agendas* (New York: Monthly Review Press, 1992).

34. Marjorie Griffin Cohen, *Free Trade and the Future of Women's Work,* published in 1987 by the Canadian Centre for Policy Alternatives, 251 Laurier Ave. West, Ottawa. The Free Trade Agreement's impact on Canadian women is being monitored by the National Action Committee, 606 Shaw Street, Toronto, M6G 3L6, Canada.

35. For commentaries by Mexican, Canadian, and U.S. women active in this continental feminist network, see *Correspondencia* 12 (Winter 1991 / Spring 1992), published by Interchange/Woman to Woman, 1305 North Flores, San Antonio, TX 78212.

36. For a report on Tennessee garment workers' response to learning that their employer, the Mercade Group of New York, had received subsidies to open an assembly plant in El Salvador, see Michael deCourcy Hinds, "Workers Say Program Took Their Jobs," *New York Times,* October 19, 1992.

37. I'm grateful to Jane Collins of the University of Wisconsin, a feminist analyst of agribusiness in northeast Brazil, for this insight: conversation with the author, Madison, Wisconsin, October 28, 1992.

38. Kurt Petersen, *The Maquiladora Revolution in Guatemala,* Occasional Paper Series, no. 2 (New Haven, CT: Orville H. Schell Center for International Human Rights, Yale Law School, Yale University, 1992).

39. A reported sixty thousand women from the Dominican Republic were working as prostitutes by early 1992. Most were young, rural women who felt they could not survive on the land but believed that neither factory work nor domestic service offered livable wages. The majority of these women's customers were male tourists from abroad. Some of the Dominican women were sent overseas to work in brothels in the Netherlands, Greece, Haiti, and Suriname. Howard W. French, "For the World's Brothels, Caribbean Daughters," *New York Times,* April 20, 1992.

40. Petersen, *Maquiladora Revolution,* 14.

41. Ibid., 40–41.

42. Ibid., 46.

43. Stephen Coats, "Phillips Van Heusen Workers Organize," *Central America Reporter* 3 (1992), 12.

44. Smith-Ayala, *Granddaughters of Ixmucane,* 145–148. See also "U.S./ Guatemala Labor Education," *Resist Newsletter* 2, no. 1 (January 1993): 9–10.

Chapter 5

An earlier version of this chapter appeared as an introductory essay in Saundra Sturdevant and Brenda Stoltzfus, *Let the Good Times Roll: The Sale of Women's Sexual Labor around U.S. Military Bases in the Philippines, Okinawa and the Southern Part of Korea* (New York: New Press, 1992). This is a wonderful collection of oral histories by Filipina and Korean women working as prostitutes around U.S. bases in the Philippines, South Korea, and Guam.

1. Letter from a former CIA analyst and Defense Department consultant, August 20, 1991.

2. Beth Bailey and David Farber, *The First Strange Place: The Alchemy of Race and Sex in World War II Hawaii* (New York: Free Press, 1992), 95.

3. Ibid., 102–3. The material that follows is based on Bailey and Farber, 95–107.

4. Ibid., 102–3.

5. The information on Belize is contained in a manuscript by Stephanie C. Kane, "Prostitution and the Military: Planning AIDS Intervention in Belize" (Department of American Studies and African-American Studies, State University of New York at Buffalo, 1991); information on the Gurkhas is from correspondence from Stephanie Kane, December 11, 1991.

6. Tamang, "Nepali Women as Military Wives."

7. "Troops Want to Stay in Belize," *Carib News* (New York), March 17, 1992.

8. The information on Subic Bay and Clark bases is derived from Anne-Marie Cass, "Sex and the Military: Gender and Violence in the Philippines" (Ph.D. diss., Department of Sociology and Anthropology, University of Queensland, Brisbane, Australia, 1992), 206–209; and Saundra Sturdevant and Brenda Stoltzfus, *Let the Good Times Roll: The Sale of Women's Sexual Labor around U.S. Military Bases in the Philippines, Okinawa and the Southern Part of Korea* (New York: New Press, 1992).

9. For descriptions and analyses of the lives of Filipino women and men who have migrated to Japan, including many women who went there for exploitative work in the entertainment industry catering to male customers—see Randolf S. David, "Filipino Workers in Japan: Vulnerability and Survival," *Kasarinlan: A Philippine Quarterly of Third World Studies* (Quezon City: University of the Philippines) 6, no. 3 (1991): 9–23; Rey Ventura, *Underground in Japan,* London, Jonathan Cape, 1992.

10. Rigoberto Tiglao, "Open for Offers," *Far Eastern Economic Review,* October 15, 1992, 62–63.

11. I am grateful to Suzaina Abdul Kadii, of the University of Wisconsin political science graduate program, for her analysis of the U.S.–Singaporean basing agreement process: conversation with the author, Madison, Wisconsin, October 29, 1992.

12. Sturdevant and Stoltzfus, *Let the Good Times Roll.*

13. Cass, "Sex and the Military," 210.

14. Ibid., 205.

15. Ibid., 215.

16. The most complete account of the Thai military's role in Thailand's prostitution industry is Thanh-Dam Truong, *Sex, Money and Morality: Prostitution and Tourism in Southeast Asia* (London: Zed Press, 1990). I am also indebted to Alison Cohn for sharing her as yet unpublished research in Thailand with me at Clark University, Worcester, MA, February–April, 1992. For an investigation of Indonesia's prostitution business, a system which is not organized around either foreign tourists or foreign soldiers but is deeply affected by Indonesia's militarized national politics, see Saraswati Sunindyo's forthcoming Ph.D. dissertation (Department of Sociology, University of Wisconsin, Madison). Saraswati Sunindyo has also written a collection of poetry, entitled *Yakin* (typescript, 1992), which describes some of her own responses to conducting research in a coastal town's government-owned hotel, which was shared by a number of Indonesian women working as prostitutes servicing Indonesian military officers, civil servants, businessmen, farmers, and schoolboys.

17. Cass, "Sex and the Military."

18. Nakahara Michiko, "Forgotten Victims: Asian and Women Workers on the Thai-Burma Railway," *AMPO: Japan-Asia Quarterly* 23, no. 2 (1991): 21–25; Yoshiaki Yoshimi, "Japan Battles Its Memories" (Editorial), *New York Times,* March 11, 1992; Sanger, "Japan Admits"; David E. Sanger, "History Scholar in Japan Exposes a Brutal Chapter," *New York Times,* January 27, 1992.

19. Sanger, "History Scholar."

20. Ibid. See also: George Hicks, "Ghosts Gathering: Comfort Women Issue Haunts Tokyo as Pressure Mounts", *Far Eastern Economic Review,* February 18, 1993, 32–37.

21. Rita Nakashima Brock, "Japanese Didn't Invent Military Sex Industry" (Letter to the Editor), *New York Times,* February 23, 1992.

22. Truong, "Sex, Money and Morality."

23. Cass, "Sex and the Military," 210.

24. Sturdevant and Stoltzfus, *Let the Good Times Roll.* In a slide and tape show produced by Sturdevant and Stoltzfus, Filipinas describe being ashamed at having to perform demeaning acts. "Pussy Cat III," 726 Gilman St., Berkeley, CA 94710.

25. Anne-Marie Cass, "Sexuality, Gender and Violence in the Militarized Society of the Philippines" (Paper presented at the annual conference of the Australian Sociological Association, Brisbane, December 12–16, 1990), 6.

26. Donald Goertzen, "Withdrawal Trauma," *Far Eastern Economic Review,* January 30, 1992, 10.

27. Pat Ford, "Weekend Edition," National Public Radio, March 21, 1992.

28. I am grateful to Lauran Schultz for bringing to my attention the *Philippine Journal of Public Administration* 34, no. 4 (October 1990), a special issue devoted to articles on the current conditions of Filipina women, including women as migrants. See, in particular, Bievenda M. Amarles, "Female Migrant Labor: Domestic Helpers in Singapore," 365–389; Prosperina Domingo Tapales, "Women, Migration and the Mail-Order Bride Phenomenon: Focus on Australia," 311–322.

29. American Friends Service Committee Peace Education Division and the Alliance for Philippine Concerns, *Swords into Plowshares: Economic Conversion and the U.S. Bases in the Philippines* (Philadelphia, PA: American Friends Service Committee, 1991). See also Sheila Coronel, "With Hope and Tears, U.S. Closes Philippine Base," *New York Times,* November 25, 1992; P. N. Abinales, "Searching for the Philippine Eden—the Post-Bases Era," *Kasarinlan: A Philippine Quarterly of Third World Studies* 7, no. 4 (1992): 8–12.

Chapter 6

Parts of this chapter appeared in earlier versions in *Collateral Damage,* ed. Cynthia Peters (Boston: South End Press, 1992); "Womenandchildren," *Village Voice,* September 25, 1990; "Tie a Yellow Ribbon 'round the New World Order," *Village Voice,* February 19, 1991; "Tailhookers and Draftdodgers," *Village Voice,* October 13, 1992.

1. Reports on the abuse of Asian women working as domestic servants in Kuwait include Raymond Bonner, "Report from Kuwait: A Woman's Place," *New Yorker,* November 16, 1992, 55–56; "Kuwait: Alert Update: Liberated to 'Abuse,' " *Ms.,* November-December 1992, 10. Four months after Bonner's report, Chris Hedges of the *New York Times* reported that there were one hundred thousand foreign domestic servants in Kuwait. Approximately five hundred Filipina maids remained in the Philippines embassy in Kuwait City, all accusing their Kuwaiti employers of abuse but unable to leave the country, either because their employers held their passports or because they owed money to the agencies that recruited them originally. Another estimated one hundred Asian

women working as domestic servants were taking refuge at the Indian, Sri Lankan, and Bangladeshi embassies. A Kuwaiti official seeking to explain the seeming epidemic of abuse speculated that "Kuwaitis, especially those who remained here during the Iraqi occupation, have become more aggressive. . . . Tempers are more volatile and people are more prone to being abusive." Chris Hedges, "Foreign Maids in Kuwait Fleeing by the Hundreds," *New York Times,* February 24, 1993.

2. Chris Hedges, "Voters in Kuwait Elect Legislators," *New York Times,* October 6, 1992; Chris Hedges, "Kuwaiti Opposition Wins Legislative Election," *New York Times,* October 7, 1992. Michael Sullivan, of National Public Radio, also reported on Kuwaiti women's election activities for "All Things Considered," October 5, 1992. See also Mary Ann Tetreault, "Democratization and Women in Kuwait," paper presented at the Annual Meeting of the International Studies Association—Midwest, East Lansing, Michigan, November 21, 1992.

3. "American Military Women Can't Drive in Saudi Arabia," *Minerva's Bulletin Board,* December 2, 1992, 6.

Chapter 7

An earlier version of this paper was presented at the European University Institute's Conference on Women at War: Images of Women Soldiers, Florence, Italy, November 15–16, 1991. The proceedings of the conference will be edited by Valeria Russo, Lorenza Sebesta, and Elizabetta Addis and are scheduled for publication in 1993 in *Women at War: Images of Women Soldiers* (London: Macmillan, forthcoming).

1. Carolyn Becraft, *Women in the U.S. Armed Services: The War in the Persian Gulf,* published by the Women's Research and Education Institute (1700 18th Street N.W., Suite 400, Washington, DC 20009), March 1991, 1. See also "Women in the Military: What Role Should Women Play in the Shrinking Military?" *Congressional Quarterly* 2, no. 36 (September 25, 1992), 842.

2. Two recent explorations into the specifically American history of militarized thinking about citizenship are Linda K. Kerber, "May All Our Citizens Be Soldiers and All Our Soldiers Citizens: The Ambiguities of Citizenship in the New Nation," in *Women, Militarism, and War: Essays in History, Politics, and Social Theory,* ed. Jean Bethke Elshtain and Sheila Tobias (Savage, MD: Rowman and Littlefield, 1990), and Kann, *On the Man Question.*

3. One of the best cross-national collections is Isaksson, *Women and the Military System.* Other cross-national comparisons can be found in McDonald,

Holden, and Ardener, *Images of Women;* Elshtain and Tobias, *Women, Militarism, and War;* and *Female Soldiers—Combatants or Noncombatants?,* ed. Nancy Loring Goldman (Westport, CT: Greenwood Press, 1982). A useful bibliography of journal articles published in English from 1980 to 1990 on women and militaries appears as "Bibliographies: Military/War" in *Journal of Women's History* 3, no. 1 (Spring 1991): 141–58. A detailed case study of U.S. military debates over strategies to maximize the use of women in the country's World War II military without violating popular beliefs about femininity is offered in Leisa D. Meyer, "Creating G.I. Jane: The Regulation of Sexuality and Sexual Behavior in the Women's Army Corps during World War II," *Feminist Studies* 18, no. 3 (Fall 1992): 581–601.

4. A cultural analysis of the Private Benjamin image came out of an international conference of European, Israeli, and North American women, the results of which are contained in Wendy Chapkis, ed., *Loaded Questions: Women in the Military* (Amsterdam: Transnational Institute, 1981).

5. Annette Fuentes, "Equality, Yes—Militarism, No," *Nation,* October 28, 1991, 516.

6. That military planners deliberately recruited women to avoid disproportionate enlistment by African-American men is a hypothesis and has not yet been confirmed by detailed research. I have spelled it out in more detail in *Does Khaki Become You?*

7. For descriptions and oral histories of American women who served in the U.S. military in Vietnam, see Kathryn Marshall, *In the Combat Zone* (New York: Penguin Books, 1987); Keith Walker, *A Piece of My Heart* (New York: Ballantine Books, 1985); Lynda Van Devanter, *Home before Morning* (New York: Beaufort Books, 1983).

8. The World War II and immediate postwar ups and downs of U.S. military attention to, and harassment of, lesbians and gay men are charted in Berube's *Coming Out under Fire.*

9. A provocative account of the demands on military wives and especially daughters during the 1960s and 1970s to conform to those standards of femininity that best served current American needs has recently been published by a journalist who herself grew up as a military daughter: Mary Wertsch, *Military Brats: The Legacy of Childhood inside the Fortress* (New York: Crown, 1991).

10. Committee on Armed Services of the U.S. House of Representatives, *Women in the Military: Hearings before the Military Personnel and Compensation Subcommittee, March 20, 1990* (Washington, DC: U.S. Government Printing Office).

11. The book coming out of this conference of civil rights leaders and defense officials is Edwin Dorn, ed., *Who Defends America? Race, Sex, and Class in the Armed Forces* (Washington, DC: 1989).

12. Although the Women's Equity Action League (WEAL) died for lack of funding in the late 1980s, copies of its valuable newsletter are available at the Schlesinger Library of Women's History, Radcliffe College, Cambridge, MA. Carolyn Becraft, the guiding spirit of WEAL's Women in the Military Project and one of Washington's most skilled lobbyists, has recently revived this project within the Women's Research and Equity Institute, 1700 18th Street N.W., Washington, DC 20009.

13. The first serious feminist analysis of DACOWITS is Mary Fainsod Katzenstein's "Feminism within American Institutions: Unobtrusive Mobilization in the 1980s," *Signs* 16, no. 1, 27–34. Her full-length book comparing feminists inside the U.S. Defense Department with feminists inside the American Catholic Church is forthcoming. Mary Katzenstein is a professor of government at Cornell University, Ithaca, New York. A report describing DACOWITS' engagement with a liberal feminist research organization and with Israeli and South African feminists more critical of militarism is: *Women in the Military,* ed. Anne J. Stone (Washington, D.C.: Women's Research and Education Institute, 1992).

14. For detailed accounts of the Tailhook scandal, see Eric Schmitt, "Dozens of Women Sexually Assaulted at Pilots Meeting, Navy Finds," *New York Times,* May 1, 1992; Eric Schmitt, "Wall of Silence Impedes Inquiry into a Rowdy Navy Convention," *New York Times,* June 14, 1992; John Lancaster, "Navy Officer Tells of Pilots' Attack on Her in Vegas," *International Herald Tribune,* June 25, 1992; Eric Schmitt, "Now at Navy's Bridge, Engaging Sexism," *New York Times,* July 4, 1992; Ellen Goodman, "The 'Friendly Fire' of Sexual Assault," *Boston Globe,* July 5, 1992; Eric Schmitt, "Officials Say Navy Tried to Soften Report," *New York Times,* July 8, 1992; Eric Schmitt, "Harassment Questions Kill 2 Admirals' Promotions," *New York Times,* July 18, 1992; "Pentagon Given Film of Harassment, Report Says," *New York Times,* July 30, 1992; Jim Drinkard, "Navy Failed to Act against Harassment, Admiral Says," *Boston Globe,* July 31, 1992; Eric Schmitt, " 'People's Admiral' is Buffeted in Storm over Ethics," *New York Times,* August 1, 1992; Eric Schmitt, "The Military Has a Lot to Learn about Women," *New York Times,* August 2, 1992; "The Tailhook Scandal," *Minerva's Bulletin Board,* Summer 1992, 5–8.

15. Edwin Dorn, "Integrating the Military: Comparing the Experiences of Blacks and Women" (Statement delivered at a hearing held by the Defense Policy

Panel and the Subcommittee on Military Personnel and Compensation, House Armed Services Committee, Washington, DC, July 29, 1992), 6.

16. U.S. Department of Defense, Office of Inspector General, *Tailhook 91, Part 1: Review of the Navy Investigations* (Washington, DC: Department of Defense, 1992), 15.

17. Ibid., 16. Descriptions of internal obstacles put in the way of three women soldiers who complained of assault or harassment and the conflicts of interest often denied by supervisory male officers in three different branches of the American military are included in John Lancaster's detailed article "In the Military Harassment Cases, His Word Outranks Hers," *Washington Post,* November 15, 1992. This article also appeared as "Military Macho: Harassment of Women in the Armed Services Often Means One Thing: She Asked for It," *Washington Post Weekly Edition,* November 23–29, 1992, 10–12.

18. For a detailed account of U.S. intramilitary debates over the definition of combat and thus over positions in which only men could serve, see Stiehm, *Arms and the Enlisted Woman.*

19. Some of these opinions are articulated in the House of Representatives hearings on "Women in the Military." They are also voiced regularly in the independent but widely circulated military weeklies, *Army Times, Navy Times,* and *Air Force Times.*

20. Eric Schmitt, "Many Women in Army Favor Ending Combat Ban," *New York Times,* September 11, 1992.

21. Fuentes, "Equality, Yes," 517.

22. In late 1992, under the glare of media lights following the Tailhook affair, the U.S. Defense Department's General Counsel initiated a review of the Pentagon's magazine distribution policy for bases. One navy commander had already unilaterally decided that his post store would no longer carry sexually explicit literature. See "Sex-Explicit Magazines to Face Pentagon Review," *New York Times,* October 16, 1992.

23. See article by Ann Wright, a major in the U.S. Army, entitled "The Roles of U.S. Army Women in Grenada," *Minerva: Quarterly Report on Women and the Military* 2, no. 2 (Summer 1984), 103–113. *Minerva* is the best journal covering U.S. and other militaries' use of women. Its address is 1101 South Arlington Ridge Rd., #210, Arlington, VA 22202.

24. For coverage of American women in the Panama invasion, see "Women in Arms: What Happened in Panama," *Defense Media Review* (Boston University) 4, no. 1 (May 31, 1990); "Army and Air Force Women in

Action in Panama," *Minerva's Bulletin Board,* Spring 1990; "Combat Controversy Destroyed Her Career, Says Linda Bray," *Minerva's Bulletin Board,* Summer 1991.

25. Becraft, *Women in the Military,* 8. Hispanic women constituted 3.0 percent of all active-duty U.S. Army enlisted women; Asian-American, Native American, and Pacific Island women together constituted 4.4 percent. Altogether, women of color made up 54.0 percent of all the army's active-duty enlisted women. By contrast, men of color made up only 38.1 percent of all the army's active-duty enlisted men. Although they constituted 47.0 percent of all army enlisted women, black women comprised only 19.1 percent of the army's women of officer rank; all women of color combined were likewise underrepresented in the army's officer corps, making up only 24.7 percent.

26. Rhonda Cornum, *She Went to War: The Rhonda Cornum Story* (Novato, CA: Presidio Press, 1992); Elaine Sciolino, "Women in War: Ex-Captive Tells of Ordeal," *New York Times,* June 29, 1992. Major Cornum expressed similar sentiments when interviewed on NBC's "Dateline," July 21, 1992, and on "Fresh Air," National Public Radio, August 7, 1992.

27. I have discussed in more detail the relationships between Saudi women's politics and U.S. military women's politics in "The Gendered Gulf," in *Collateral Damage,* ed. Cynthia Peters (Boston: South End Press, 1992).

28. Eric Schmitt, "Senate Votes to Remove Ban on Women as Combat Pilots," *New York Times,* August 31, 1991.

29. Power, "Panel on Women in Military." I am indebted to Dan Brook for showing me this article.

30. The recommendations of the Presidential Commission on the Assignment of Women in the Armed Services (1992) can be obtained from the Public Affairs Office of the U.S. Department of Defense, Washington, DC.

31. Michael R. Gordon, "Panel Is against Letting Women Fly in Combat," *New York Times,* November 4, 1992. Another male member of the commission, Newton N. Minow, a former chair of the Federal Communications Commission, said afterwards that his vote in favor of ending women's exclusion from combat positions was also affected in part by being the father of daughters: "My wife and I have three daughters and three grandchildren (two are granddaughters). We do not want any of them in military combat. But . . . all six are eligible someday to become president of the United States and thus commander in chief. Why should our country be deprived of the talent and commitment all six could

contribute to keeping our nation safe and free?" Newton N. Minow, "Less Brawn, More Brains," *Washington Post National Weekly Edition,* November 23–29, 1992, 29.

32. Gordon, "Panel Is Against Letting Women Fly."

33. Ibid.

34. For a summary of the recommendations of the Presidential Commission on the Assignment of Women in the Armed Services, see "News Briefs," *Minerva's Bulletin Board,* Winter 1992, 3–6.

35. See a special issue of the gay and lesbian journal *Outlook* devoted to post–Gulf War commentary: no. 13 (Summer 1991). See also Adam Clymer, "War Foe to Oversee Military in House," *New York Times,* December 24, 1992; Michael Gordon, "Aspin Overhauls Pentagon to Bolster Policy Role," *New York Times,* January 28, 1993. Unofficial reports that Defense Secretary Les Aspin might select a woman, Sheila E. Widnell (an aerospace scientist and provost at the Massachusetts Institute of Technology), to be the new civilian secretary of the air force provoked "a mixture of angst and culture shock" among Defense Department careerists. Paul Quinn-Judge, "M.I.T. Provost Considered for Air Force Secretary," *Boston Globe,* February 13, 1993.

Chapter 8

An earlier version of this chapter was presented at the annual meeting of the American Anthropological Association in Chicago, November 1991, and is reprinted in Constance Sutton, *Feminism, Nationalism, and Militarism* (published jointly by the Association of Feminist Anthropologists and the International Women's Anthropology Conference, 1993; distributed by the American Anthropological Association, Washington, DC). I appreciate the intellectual energy of Constance Sutton, June Nash, and Linda Basch in organizing the special session.

1. By "my own work" I mean specifically *Multi-Ethnic Politics: The Case of Malaysia* (Berkeley: Center for Southeast Asian Studies, University of California, 1970); *Ethnic Conflict and Political Development* (Boston: Little, Brown, 1973); *Ethnic Soldiers: State Security in Divided Societies* (London: Penguin, 1980); and *Police, Military, and Ethnicity* (New Brunswick, NJ: Transaction Press, 1980).

2. Tamang, "Nepali Women as Military Wives."

3. Benedict Anderson, *Imagined Communities* (New York: Verso), 127.

4. Pierre Vallières, *White Niggers of North America* (New York: Monthly Review Press, 1971). For a feminist history of Quebec, see the Clio Collective, *Quebec Women: A History,* Toronto, Women's Press, 1987.

5. Michele Jacqueline Lamothe, Marie Lavigne, and Jennifer Stoddart, "Nationalism and Feminism in Quebec: The 'Yvettes' Phenomenon," in *The Politics of Diversity: Feminism, Marxism and Nationalism,* ed. Roberta Hamilton and Michele Barrett (London: Verso, 1987), 322–342.

6. One of the best places to start an exploration of feminism's uneasy relationship to nationalism is with Kumari Jayawardena's *Feminism and Nationalism in the Third World* (London: Zed Press, 1986). Distributed in the U.S. by Biblio Distribution Center, Totowa, N.J.

7. Nira Yuval-Davis, ed., *Unholy Orders: Women against Fundamentalism* (London: Virago, 1992). Women Against Fundamentalism has published two issues thus far of their journal, by the same name, the most recent being no. 2 (July 1991). Their address is BM Box 2706, London WC1, 3XX, United Kingdom. Also see case studies detailing women's ambivalent relationships to nationalism collected by Nira Yuval-Davis and Floya Anthias, eds., in *Woman, Nation, State* (London: Macmillan, 1989).

8. I am grateful to Beverly Grier, of Clark University, an active participant in these conversations between African-American women, for giving me a sense of how the meetings evolved.

9. The entire advertisement, together with the full list of signatories, is now available from Kitchen Table: Women of Color Press, P.O. Box 908, Latham, NY 12110. An abridged version is reprinted in a book edited by the staff of *The Black Scholar, Court of Appeal: The Black Community Speaks out on the Racial and Sexual Politics of Thomas vs. Hill* (New York: Ballantine, 1992), 291–292. Another collection of essays by African-American writers, including several women who signed the *New York Times* advertisement, is Toni Morrison, ed., *Race-ing Justice, En-gendering Power: Essays on Anita Hill, Clarence Thomas, and the Construction of Social Reality* (New York: Pantheon, 1992). For more information on the group that created and published the advertisement, contact African American Women in Defense of Ourselves, 317 S. Division St., Suite 199, Ann Arbor, MI 48104.

10. David McDowall, *The Kurds* (London: Minority Rights Group, 1989).

11. Eliz Sanararian, *The Women's Rights Movement in Iran* (New York: Praeger, 1982).

12. Caetano Veloso, "Caricature and Conqueror, Pride and Shame," *New York Times,* October 20, 1991.

13. Jean Franco, *Plotting Women: Gender and Representation in Mexico* (New York: Columbia University Press, 1991).

14. For a fuller Irish feminist analysis of Mary Robinson's surprising electoral victory and her uses of the presidency, see Ailbhe Smyth, "Hail Mary—A President of Women," *Trouble and Strife* 23 (Spring 1992), 4–7.

15. Andrew Phillips, "A Woman of Substance," *MacLean's,* October 19, 1992, 46–47.

16. "Bosnia and Herzegovina: 'Only Following Orders,' " *Ms.,* November 1992, 11. Other accounts of rapes of Bosnian women are given in Slavenka Drakulić, "Rape after Rape after Rape," *New York Times,* December 13, 1992; "Rape Goes to War," *The Economist,* January 23, 1993, 46; "Dispatches from Bosnia and Herzegovina: Young Survivors Testify to Systematic Rape," *Ms.,* January-February 1993, 12–13.

17. "Team Cites Signs of Thousands of Rapes in Former Yugoslavia," *Boston Globe,* February 13, 1993.

18. John F. Burns, "A Serbian Fighter's Trail of Brutality," *New York Times,* November 27, 1992.

19. "Bosnia and Herzegovina: 'Only Following Orders,' " 11.

20. The "Renewal of the Republic of Croatia" proposal was distributed in typescript in February, 1993 by Rights of Women, a British legal advocacy group. Their address is 52–54 Featherstone St., London EC14 8RT, United Kingdom.

21. Ibid.

22. I am especially grateful to Vasuki Nesai, a Sri Lankan feminist and human rights activist at Harvard Law School, for introducing me to the new debates among international legal experts and feminists about the barriers preventing various forms of violence against women from being recognized by the United Nations as violations of human rights. I am also indebted to Stanlie M. James of the department of Afro-American studies at the University of Wisconsin, Madison, for sharing with me the draft of her 1993 essay, "Challenging Patriarchal Privilege through the Development of Human Rights." Materials containing an analysis of the justification for including prostitution among the UN-recognized violations of human rights are available from the Coalition Against Trafficking in Women, Calder Square, P.O. Box 10077, State College,

PA 16805. Information on the campaign to introduce feminist legal theory into the UN's 1993 World Conference on Human Rights can be obtained from the Sisterhood is Global Institute, Department of Politics, University of Waikato, Hamilton, New Zealand.

23. Ivana Balen, "Using Women for War Propaganda: Responding to Wartime Rapes," *Helsinki Citizens Assembly Newsletter* 6 (Winter 1993): 12–13.

24. See Sturdevant and Stoltzfus, *Let the Good Times Roll.*

25. *Patriotism: The Making and Unmaking of National Identity,* ed. Raphael Samuels (London and New York: Routledge, 1989), vols. 1–3.

26. The entire Women's Party manifesto is published in Cynthia Cockburn's "A Women's Political Party for Yugoslavia: Introduction to the Serbian Feminist Manifesto," *Feminist Review* 39 (Winter 1991): 155–60.

27. Quoted in "Anti-War Movement in Yugoslavia," *Overseas* 18, 1992, 13. The journal's address is Vilbeler Str. 36, 6000 Frankfurt, Germany.

28. *The Montreal Massacre,* ed. Louis Malette and Marie Chalough (Charlottetown, Prince Edward Island: Gynergy Books, 1991).

Chapter 9

1. This postcard is published by Leeds Postcards, P.O. Box 84, Leeds, England, U.K.

2. The account of the Kuwaiti election is based on Michael Sullivan, report from Kuwait, "All Things Considered," National Public Radio, October 5, 1992; Hedges, "Voters in Kuwait"; Hedges, "Kuwaiti Opposition"; "Arabia's Slow Presser Cooker," *The Economist,* October 10, 1992, 47; "Kuwait: Commoner," *The Economist,* October 24, 1992, 47–48. Mary Ann Tetreault, a political scientist at Old Dominion University in Norfolk, Virginia, is engaged in what may be the first systematic investigation of the gendered politics of Kuwaiti democratization. Some of her findings, based on interviews conducted during the 1992 election campaign, are presented in her unpublished paper "Democratization and Women in Kuwait," presented at the annual meeting of the International Studies Association—Midwest, Michigan State University, East Lansing, November 21, 1992. Tetreault concludes that women's suffrage already has widespread public support in Kuwait and is likely to be introduced within the next few years. Far more controversial among Kuwaitis and less likely to be permitted is allowing women to run for the legislature and to serve in the judiciary. Seen as far more radical than giving women the vote, allowing women

to hold office is imagined by many patriarchal Kuwaitis as upsetting public/private gendered dichotomies: as legislators or judges, women would have authority over men, and women would have to be able to come and go everyday as if they were autonomous individuals, not defined by their family status.

3. Jan Jenkins, "Danish Women Vow to Give Delors a Jolt," *Sunday Times* (London), May 31, 1992; Sean Flynn, "Late Swing to Treaty Takes Drama out of Danish Poll," *Irish Times,* June 2, 1992; Joe Carroll, "Danish Women Voted Heavily against European Union," *Irish Times,* June 6, 1992. In the weeks before Denmark's second vote on the Maastricht treaty on May 18, 1992, most commentators continued to analyze Danish voters along left-right party lines, ignoring gender. Thus commentators noted that the EC leaders' willingness to allow Denmark to opt out of any future defense plans might win over the Danish voters who earlier saw Maastricht as a step toward militarization. Still these observers asked no questions about women's specific objections to militarism. See William E. Schmidt, "Left in Denmark Shifts on Europe," *New York Times,* February 17, 1993.

4. The June 1992 Maastricht treaty referendum held in Ireland provided a wealth of information on the government's presumption's about Irish femininity within post–Cold War Europe. It also provided Irish feminists room for some public discussion—although it was scarcely open—of the costs to women of joining the EC under the current protocol attached to Maastricht at the Irish government's request. For reporting on both, see daily issues of the *Irish Times,* the *Irish Independent,* and the *Cork Examiner* throughout June 1992. For a feminist account of how the government's policy-making processes worked to insure that abortion rights would not come with EC membership, see Emily O'Reilly, *Masterminds of the Right* (Dublin: Attic Press, 1992).

5. See, for instance, the report by Jill Benderly, "Eastern European Feminism: No Room of One's Own," *Issues* 24 (Fall 1992), 40–44; Hanna Janlowska, "Abortion, Church and Politics in Poland," *Feminist Review* 39 (Autumn 1991), 174–81; Mita Castle-Kanerova, "Czechoslovakia: Interview with Alena Valterova," *Feminist Review* 39 (Autumn: 1991), 161–165.

6. Cockburn, "A Women's Political Party."

7. According to Mark Kramer of Harvard University's Russian Research Center, in Russia and the republics that were joined with it in the Commonwealth of Independent States a mere 17 percent of the men who were called up for the draft in mid-1992 responded. This, plus the impression that the U.S. military's performance in the Gulf War made on many Russian observers, have led the Russian parliament to introduce a new military personnel system that

would consist half of volunteers and half of conscripts, a dramatic move away from the past conscript-dependent formula. I am grateful to Zena Sochor of Clark University, who is also a scholar at the Russian Research Center, for sharing Mark Kramer's observations in correspondence, July 28, 1992.

8. For an argument for why we need more empirical research on masculinity in order to reveal when and how it translates into men's power over women, see Caroline Ramazanoglu, "What Can You Do with A Man? Feminism and a Critical Appraisal of Masculinity," *Women's Studies International Forum* 15, no. 3 (1992), 339–350.

9. Responding to women's advocates alarmed at this trend, UN Secretary-General Boutros Boutros-Ghali promised to raise the number of women in senior secretariat posts to 50 percent by 1995: "UN Leader Vows to Put Women in Half of Top Posts," *Boston Globe,* November 7, 1992.

10. Jacklyn Cock, in discussion, cited in Stone, *Women and the Military,* 77.

11. "U.S. Navy Account Is Won by BBDO," *New York Times,* August 18, 1992.

12. Robin Bulman, "Japan's Wartime 'Comfort Women' Decried," *Washington Post,* August 12, 1992. Chinese survivors of the Japanese Imperial Army's prostitution program have also begun to tell their stories publicly: see "China: More 'Comfort Women' Speak Out," *Ms.,* November-December, 1992, 10.

Select Bibliography

Abinales, P. N. "Searching for the Philippine Eden—The Post-Bases Era," *Kasarinlan: A Philippines Quarterly of Third-World Studies* 7, no. 4 (1992): 8–12.

Adams, Gordon. *The Iron Triangle: The Politics of Defense Contracting.* New York: Council on Economic Priorities, 1981.

Addis, Elizabetta, "The Reality and the Image: Women and the Economic Consequences of Being a Soldier." Paper presented at conference on Women at War: Images of Women Soldiers, European University Institute, Florence, November 15–16, 1991.

Air Force Association. *Lifeline Adrift: The Defense Industrial Base in the 1990s.* Arlington, VA: 1991.

Akello, Grace. *Self Twice-Removed: Ugandan Woman.* Rev. ed. London: Change International Reports, 1990.

Alexiev, Alexander. *Inside the Soviet Army in Afghanistan.* Santa Monica, CA: Rand Publication Series, 1988.

Alonso, Jean. "In the Belly of the Beast," *Women's Review of Books* 8, nos. 10–11 (July 1991): 12–13.

Alvarez, Sonia. *Engendering Democracy in Brazil: Women's Movements in Transitional Politics.* Princeton: Princeton University Press, 1990.

Amarles, Bievenda M. "Female Migrant Labor: Domestic Helpers in Singapore," *Philippine Journal of Public Administration* 34, no. 4 (October 1990): 365–89.

American Association of University Women. *How Schools Short-Change Girls.* Washington, DC: AAUW Educational Foundation, 1992.

American Friends Service Committee. National Women's Program. "Voices of

Hope and Anger: Women Speak out for Sovereignty and Self-Determination" (special issue). *Listen Real Loud* 10, nos. 1–2, 1990.

American Friends Service Committee. Peace Education Division and the Alliance for Philippine Concerns. *Swords into Plowshares: Economic Conversion and the U.S. Bases in the Philippines*. Philadelphia: American Friends Service Committee, 1991.

Amnesty International. *Rape and Sexual Abuse: Torture and Ill Treatment of Women in Detention*. New York and London: Amnesty International, 1992.

Anderson, Benedict. *Imagined Communities*. New York: Verso, 1983.

Anderson, Karen. *Wartime Women: Sex Roles, Family Relations, and the Status of Women during World War II*. Westport, CT: Greenwood, 1981.

"Army and Air Force Women in Action in Panama." *Minerva's Bulletin Board*. Spring 1990.

"Anti-War Movement in Yugoslavia." *Overseas* 18 (1992): 13.

"Army without a Country, Countries without an Army." *The Economist*. January 25, 1992, 43.

Baarveld-Schlaman. *The Role of Women in the Armed Forces*. Report submitted to the Assembly of the Western European Union, London, 1991. Document 1267.

Bailey, Beth, and David Farber. *The First Strange Place: The Alchemy of Race and Sex in World War II Hawaii*. New York: Free Press, 1992.

Baker, Mark. *Nam*. New York: Berkeley Books, 1984.

Balen, Ivana. "Using Women for Propaganda: Responding to War-Time Rapes." *Helsinki Citizens Assembly Newsletter* 6 (Winter 1993): 12–13.

Ball, Nicole. *Pressing for Peace: Can Aid Induce Reform?* Washington, DC: Overseas Development Council, 1992.

Barry, Tom, Beth Wood, and Deb Preusch. *The Other Side of Paradise: Foreign Control in the Caribbean*. New York: Grove, 1984.

Becraft, Carolyn. *Women in the Military, 1980–1990*. Washington, DC: Women's Research and Education Institute, 1991.

———. *Women in the U.S. Armed Services: The War in the Persian Gulf*. Washington, DC: Women's Research and Education Institute, 1991.

Benderly, Jill, "Eastern European Feminism: No Room of One's Own," *Issues* 24 (Fall 1992): 40–44.

Berube, Allan. *Coming Out under Fire*. New York: Plume/Penguin, 1990.

Beyer, Marina. "The Situation of East German Women in Post-Unification Germany." In "A Continent in Transition: Issues for Women in Europe in the 1990s," edited by Claire Duchen (special issue). *Women's Studies International Forum* 15, no. 1 (1992): 114–23.

"Bibliographies: Military/War." *Journal of Women's History* 3, no. 1 (Spring 1991): 141–59.

The Black Scholar, eds. *Court of Appeal: The Black Community Speaks out on the Racial and Sexual Politics of Thomas vs. Hill.* New York: Ballantine, 1992.

Bly, Robert. *Iron John.* New York: Vintage, 1990.

Bok, Sissela. *Secrets: On the Ethics of Concealment and Revelation.* New York: Vintage, 1989.

Bolles, Lynn. "Kitchens Hit by Priorities: Employed Working Class Jamaican Women Confront the IMF." In *Women, Men, and the International Division of Labor,* edited by June Nash and Maria Patricia Fernandez Kelly. Albany, NY: SUNY Press, 1983.

Bonner, Raymond. "Report from Kuwait: A Woman's Place." *New Yorker,* November 16, 1992, 56–66.

Bono, Paola, and Sandra Kempt, eds. *Italian Feminist Thought: A Reader.* Oxford: Basil Blackwell, 1991.

"Bosnia and Herzegovina: 'Only Following Orders,' " *Ms.,* November-December 1992, 11.

Bossen, Laurel. *The Redivision of Labor: Women and Economic Choice in Four Guatemalan Communities.* Albany, NY: SUNY Press, 1984.

Bousquet, Ben, and Colin Douglas. *West Indian Women at War: British Racism in World War II.* London: Lawrence and Wishart, 1991.

Braybon, Gail, and Penny Summerfield. *Out of the Cage: Women's Experiences in Two World Wars.* London: Pandora, 1987.

Breaching the Peace. London: Onlywomen Press, 1983.

Breen, William J. "Black Women and the Great War: Mobilization and Reform in the South." *Journal of Southern History* 44, no. 3 (August 1978): 421–40.

Broad, William. *Star Warriors.* New York: Simon and Schuster, 1987.

Brock-Utne, Brigit. *Educating for Peace: A Feminist Perspective.* Oxford: Pergamon, 1985.

Bronstein, Audrey. *The Triple Struggle: Latin American Peasant Women.* Boston: South End, 1983.

Browning, Christopher. *Ordinary Men: Reserve Police Battalion 101 and the Final Solution in Poland.* New York: Harper-Collins, 1992.

Brownmiller, Susan. *Against Our Will: Men, Women and Rape.* New York: Bantam Books, 1976.

Bull, Chris. "And the Band Played On." *The Advocate,* March 9, 1993, 37–42.

Bunster, Ximena. "Surviving Beyond Fear: Women and Torture in Latin America." In *Women and Change in Latin America,* edited by June Nash and Helen Safa. South Hadley, MA: Bergin and Garvey, 1986, 297–325.

Bunster, Ximena, and Else Chaney. *Sellers and Servants.* New York: Praeger, 1985.

Burns, John F. "A Serbian Fighter's Tale of Brutality." *New York Times.* December 1, 1992.

Caldecott, S., and S. Leland, eds. *Reclaim the Earth.* London: Women's Press, 1983.

Cambridge Women's Peace Collective. *My Country is the Whole World.* London: Pandora, 1984.

Campbell, D'Ann. *Women at War with America.* Cambridge: Harvard University Press, 1984.

Caniff, Milton. *Steve Canyon.* Princeton, NJ: Kitchen Sink Press, 1985.

Cass, Anne-Marie. "Sex and the Military: Gender and Violence in the Philippines." Ph.D. diss., Department of Sociology and Anthropology, University of Queensland, Brisbane, Australia, 1992.

Castle-Kanerova, Mita. "Czechoslovakia: Interview with Alena Valterova." *Feminist Review* 39 (Autumn 1991): 161–65.

Center for Women's Global Leadership. *Women, Violence, and Human Rights.* New Brunswick, NJ: Center for Women's Global Leadership, Rutgers University, 1992.

"China: More Comfort Women Speak Out." *Ms.,* November-December 1992, 10.

Chuchryk, Patricia M. "Feminist Anti-Authoritarian Politics: The Role of Women's Organizations in the Chilean Transition to Democracy." In *The Women's Movement in Latin America: Feminism and the Transition to Democracy,* edited by Jane Jaquette. Boulder, CO: Westview, 1991.

Chapkis, Wendy, ed. *Loaded Questions: Women in the Military.* Amsterdam: Transnational Institute, 1981.

Charles C., Mercedes. "After Pinochet." *Connexions* 39 (1992): 32–33. Originally published as "La Mujer chilena en el proceso de transición democrática." *Fem* 99 (March 1991).

Clio Collective. *Quebec Women: A History.* Toronto: Women's Press, 1987.

Coats, Stephen, "Phillips Van Heusen Workers Organize," *Central America Reporter* 3 (1992): 12.

Cock, Jacklyn. *Women and War in South Africa.* London: Open Letters Press, 1992.

Cockburn, Cynthia. "A Women's Political Party for Yugoslavia: Introduction to the Serbian Feminist Manifesto." *Feminist Review* 39 (Autumn 1991): 155–60.

Cohen, Marjorie Griffin. *Free Trade and the Future of Women's Work*. Ottawa: Canadian Centre for Policy Alternatives, 1987.

Cohn, Carol. "Clean Bombs and Clean Language." In *Women, Militarism, and War: Essays in History, Politics, and Social Theory*, edited by Jean Bethke Elshtain and Sheila Tobias. Savage, MD: Rowman and Littlefield, 1990, 33–56.

Collins, Carole L. J. "Women as Hidden Casualties of the Cold War." *Ms.*, November-December 1992, 14.

Collinson, Helen, ed. *Women and Revolution in Nicaragua*. London: Zed Books, 1990.

Connell, R. W. *Gender and Power*. Stanford, CA: Stanford University Press, 1988.

Cook, Alice, and Gwyn Kirk. *Greenham Women Everywhere*. London: Women's Press, 1983.

Corbett, Deborah. "Women in Iraq." In *Saddam's Iraq: Revolution or Reaction?* edited by Committee Against Repression and for Democratic Rights in Iraq. London: Zed Books, 120–35.

Cornum, Rhonda. *She Went to War: The Rhonda Cornum Story*. Novato, CA: Presidio Press, 1992.

Correspondencia 12 (Winter 1991–Spring 1992). Published by Interchange/ Woman to Woman, 1305 North Flores, San Antonio, TX 78212.

Costello, John. *Virtue under Fire: How World War II Changed our Social and Sexual Attitudes*. Boston: Little, Brown, 1985.

Dalbora, Adriana Muñoz. "The Women's Movement in Chile: A Desired Reality." In *Alternatives*, edited by DAWN. *Vol. 2: Women's Visions and Movements*. Rio de Janeiro: Editora Rosa Dos Tempos, 1991. Distributed by Change International Reports, London.

David, Randolph S. "Filipino Workers in Japan: Vulnerability and Survival." *Kasarinlan: A Philippine Quarterly of Third World Studies* (University of the Philippines, Quezon City) 6, no. 3 (1991): 9–23.

DAWN, eds. *Alternatives*. 2 vols. Rio de Janeiro: Editora Rosa Dos Tempos, 1991. Distributed by Change International Reports, London.

DeFord, Katherine. "Rosie the Riveter Revisited: Women Face Dead End Jobs in Defense Industry," *Plowshares* 10, no. 3 (Summer 1985): 1.

De Grazia, Victoria. *How Fascism Ruled Women: Italy, 1922–1945*. Berkeley: University of California Press, 1992.

"Dispatches from Bosnia and Herzegovina: Young Survivors Testify to Systematic Rape." *Ms.,* January-February 1993, 12–13.

Dittmar, Linda, and Gene Michaud, eds. *From Hanoi to Hollywood: The Vietnam War in American Film.* New Brunswick, NJ: Rutgers University Press, 1991.

Dolling, Irene. "Between Hope and Helplessness: Women in the GDR after the 'Turning Point.'" *Feminist Review* 39 (Winter 1991): 3–15.

do Rosario, Louise. "Japan: Men's Magazines: Proliferation Shows Shift in Lifestyle." *Far Eastern Economic Review,* August 6, 1992, 27–28.

Dorn, Edwin. "Integrating the Military: Comparing the Experiences of Blacks and Women." Typescript. Statement from a hearing of the Defense Policy Panel and the Subcommittee on Military Personnel and Compensation, House Armed Services Committee, Washington, DC, July 29, 1992.

Dorn, Edwin, ed. *Who Defends America? Race, Sex, and Class in the Armed Forces.* Washington, DC: Joint Center for Political Studies, 1989.

Drakulić, Slavenka. *How We Survived Communism and Even Laughed.* New York: Norton, 1991.

———. "Rape after Rape after Rape." *New York Times,* December 13, 1992.

Dreisziger, N. F., ed. *Ethnic Armies.* Waterloo, Ontario: Wilfred Laurier University Press, 1990.

Duchen, Claire, ed. "A Continent in Transition: Issues for Women in Europe in the 1990s" (special issue). *Women's Studies International Forum* 15, no. 1 (1992).

Dyer, Kate, ed. *Gays in Uniform: The Pentagon's Secret Reports.* Boston: Alyson Publications, 1990.

Early, Charity Adams. *One Woman's Army: A Black Officer Remembers the WAC.* College Station: Texas A&M Press, 1989.

"Economic Conversion: An Emerging U.S. Issue." *AFSC Women's Newsletter* 6, no. 1 (1985): A3.

Einhorn, Barbara. "Where Have All the Women Gone? Women and the Women's Movement in East Central Europe." *Feminist Review* 39 (Winter 1992): 16–36.

Ellis, John. *The Sharp End of War: The Fighting Man in World War II.* London: Corgi, 1982.

Elshtain, Jean Bethke, and Sheila Tobias, eds. *Women, Militarism and War: Essays in History, Politics, and Social Theory.* Savage, MD: Rowman and Littlefield, 1990.

Enloe, Cynthia. *Bananas, Beaches and Bases: Making Feminist Sense of Interna-*

tional Politics. London: Pandora/HarperCollins, 1989; Berkeley, University of California Press, 1990.

————. *Does Khaki Become You? The Militarization of Women's Lives.* London: Pandora/HarperCollins, 1988.

————. *Ethnic Conflict and Political Development.* Boston: Little, Brown, 1973.

————. *Ethnic Soldiers: State Security in Divided Societies.* London: Penguin Books; Athens: University of Georgia Press, 1980.

————. *Multi-Ethnic Politics: The Case of Malaysia.* Berkeley: Center for Southeast Asian Studies, University of California, 1970.

————. *Police, Military, and Ethnicity.* New Brunswick, NJ: Transaction Press, 1980.

————. "Silicon Tricks and the Two Dollar Woman." *New Internationalist* (special issue on feminism) 227 (January 1992): 12–14.

Faderman, Lillian. *Odd Girls and Twilight Lovers.* New York: Columbia University Press, 1991.

Feminism and Nonviolence Study Group. *Piecing It Together: Feminism and Nonviolence.* Spencer, NY: J. Tiffany, 1983.

Fenton, James. "The Snap Revolution." *Granta* 18 (1986): 6–45.

Figueroa, Blanca, and Jeanine Anderson Velasco. *Women in Peru.* London: Change International Reports, 1990.

Fishman, Sarah. *We Will Wait: Wives of French Prisoners of War, 1940–1945.* New Haven: Yale University Press, 1991.

Fitzgerald, A. E. *The High Price of Waste.* New York: Norton, 1972.

Franco, Jean. *Plotting Women: Gender and Representation in Mexico.* New York: Columbia University Press, 1991.

Freeman, Carla. "From Tourism to Typing: Barbados Women in the Global Network." *Listen Real Loud* 11, no. 1 (1991) 12–13.

Fuentes, Annette. "Equality, Yes—Militarism, No." *The Nation.* October 28, 1991, 516.

Gavlak, Dale. "Still Suffering Nonsuffrage in 'Liberated' Kuwait." *Ms.,* January-February 1993, 14.

Gillis, John R., ed. *The Militarization of the Western World.* New Brunswick, NJ: Rutgers University Press, 1989.

Glatthaar, Joseph T. *Forged in Battle: The Civil War Alliance of Black Soldiers and White Officers.* New York: Meridian, 1991.

Goldman, Nancy Loring, ed. *Female Soldiers—Combatants or Noncombatants?* Westport, CT: Greenwood, 1982.

Goldstein, Nance. "The Defense Advanced Research Projects Agency as the

National Agent for Technological and Industrial Change—DARPA Support for Software and AI Technologies." *Defense Analysis,* 1992.

Grant, Rebecca, and Kathleen Newland, eds. *Gender and International Relations.* Bloomington: Indiana University Press, 1991.

Gruner, Elliott. *Prisoners of Culture: Representing the Vietnam P.O.W.* New Brunswick, NJ: Rutgers University Press, 1993.

Hagen, Kay, ed. *Women Respond to the Men's Movement.* San Francisco: Harper-Collins, 1992.

Hall, Peter, and Ann R. Markusen. "The Pentagon and the Gun Belt." In *The Pentagon and the Cities,* edited by Andrew Kirby. Urban Affairs Annual Reviews, vol. 40. Newbury Park, CA: Sage Publications, 1992.

Harford, Barbara, and Sarah Hopkins, eds. *Greenham Common: Women at the Wire.* London: Women's Press, 1984.

Hartman, Susan M. *The Home Front and Beyond: American Women in the 1940s.* Boston: Twayne, 1982.

Hartsock, Nancy. *Sexuality and Politics: The Barracks Community in Western Political Thought.* New York: Longman's, 1983.

Hause, Steven C., and Anne R. Kenney. *Women's Suffrage and Social Politics in the French Third Republic.* Princeton: Princeton University Press, 1984.

Havel, Vaclav. "Letter to Dr. Gustav Husak." In *Vaclav Havel: Living in Truth,* edited by Jan Vladislav. London: Faber and Faber, 1987.

———. *Letters to Olga.* New York: Henry Holt and Company, 1988.

Hayslip, Le Ly. *When Heaven and Earth Changed Places.* New York: Plume/Penguin, 1989.

Hearn, Jeff. *Men in the Public Eye: The Construction and Deconstruction of Public Men and Public Patriarchies.* London: Routledge, 1992.

Hearn, Jeff, and David Morgan, eds. *Men, Masculinities and Social Theory.* London: Unwin Hyman, 1990.

Hendessi, Mandana. *Armed Angels: Women in Iran.* London: Change International Reports, 1990.

Herman, Ellen. "The Public Uses and Political Consequences of American Psychology, 1940–1970." Ph.D. diss., Department of History, Brandeis University, 1993.

Hicks, George. "Ghosts Gathering: Comfort Women Issue Haunts Tokyo as Pressure Mounts." *Far Eastern Economic Review.* February 18, 1993, 32–37.

"High-Tech Employment Patterns in Silicon Valley, 1990." *Global Electronics* 116 (October 1992): 2.

Higonnet, Margaret Randolph, Jane Jenson, Sonya Michel, and Margaret Collins Weitz, eds. *Behind the Lines: Gender and the Two World Wars.* New Haven: Yale University Press, 1987.

Holm, Tom. "Patriots and Pawns: State Use of American Indians in the Military and the Process of Nativization in the United States." In *The State of Native America,* edited by M. Annette Jaimes. Boston: South End, 1992.

Honey, Maureen. *Creating Rosie the Riveter: Class Gender and Propaganda During World War II.* Amherst: University of Massachusetts Press, 1984.

Humphrey, Mary Ann. *My Country, My Right to Serve.* New York: Harper-Collins, 1990.

International Economic Conversion Conference. *Proceedings.* Chestnut Hill, MA: Boston College, 1984.

Isaksson, Eva, ed. *Women and the Military System.* London: Harvester-Wheatsheaf, 1988.

Jancar, Barbara Wolfe. *Women under Communism.* Baltimore, MD: Johns Hopkins University Press, 1978.

Janlowska, Hanna. "Abortion, Church and Politics in Poland." *Feminist Review* 39 (Autumn 1991): 174–81.

Janova, Mira, and Mariette Sineau. "Women's Participation in Political Power in Europe." In "A Continent in Transition: Issues for Women in Europe in the 1990s," edited by Claire Duchen (special issue). *Women's Studies International Forum* 15, no. 1 (1992): 117.

"Japan and the PKO" (special issue). *AMPO: Japan-Asian Quarterly Review* 24, no. 1 (1993).

"Japan's Defence Industry: At War with the Budget." *The Economist.* October 31, 1992, 72.

Jaquette, Jane, ed. *The Women's Movement in Latin America: Feminism and the Transition to Democracy.* Boulder, CO: Westview, 1991.

Jayawardena, Kumari. *Feminism and Nationalism in the Third World.* London: Zed Press, 1986.

Jeffords, Susan. *The Remasculinization of America: Gender and the Vietnam War.* Bloomington: Indiana University Press, 1989.

Kaldor, Mary. *The Baroque Arsenal.* New York: Hill and Wang, 1981.

———. "Martin: Facing Conversion," *Helsinki Citizens Assembly Newsletter* 5 (Fall 1992): 16–17.

Kampwirth, Karen. "The Revolution Continues: Women's Organizations under the UNO." Paper presented at the annual convention of the American Political Science Association, September 1992.

Kane, Stephanie C. "Prostitution and the Military: Planning AIDS Intervention in Belize." Unpublished manuscript. Department of American Studies and African-American Studies, State University of New York at Buffalo, 1991.

Kann, Mark E. *On the Man Question: Gender and Civic Virtue in America.* Philadelphia: Temple University Press, 1991.

Kano Mikiyo. "Remolding Tennoism for Modern Japan." *AMPO: Japan-Asian Quarterly Review* 19, nos. 2–3 (1986): 24–29.

Katzenstein, Mary Fainsod. "Feminism within American Institutions: Unobtrusive Mobilization in the 1980s." *Signs* 16, no. 1.

———. *Liberating the Mainstream.* Forthcoming.

Keegan, John. *The Face of Battle.* New York: Vintage, 1977.

Kerber, Linda K. "May All Our Citizens Be Soldiers and All Our Soldiers Citizens: The Ambiguities of Female Citizenship in the New Nation." In *Women, Militarism, and War: Essays in History, Politics, and Social Theory,* edited by Jean Bethke Elshtain and Sheila Tobias. Savage, MD: Rowman and Littlefield, 1990, 89–104.

Kesselman, Amy. *Fleeting Opportunities: Women Shipyard Workers in Portland and Vancouver During World War II and Reconversion.* Albany, NY: SUNY Press, 1990.

Kiss, Yudit. "The Second 'No': Women in Hungary." *Feminist Review* 39 (Winter 1991): 49–57.

Klare, Michael. *American Arms Supermarket.* Austin: University of Texas Press, 1984.

Koonz, Claudia. *Mothers in the Fatherland.* New York: St. Martin's Press, 1987.

Kostinen, Paul. *The Military Industrial Complex: An Historical Perspective.* New York: Praeger, 1980.

Kurihara, Ryoko. "The Japanese Woman Suffrage Movement." *Feminist Issues* 11, no. 2 (Fall 1991): 81–100.

Lamothe, Michele Jacqueline, Marie Lavigne, and Jennifer Stoddart. "Nationalism and Feminism in Quebec: The 'Yvettes' Phenomenon." In *The Politics of Diversity: Feminism, Marxism and Nationalism,* edited by Roberta Hamilton and Michele Barrett. London: Verso, 1987.

Lancaster, John. "Does Anyone Allow Gays to Serve in the Military?" *Washington Post Weekly Edition.* December 7–13, 1992, 14.

———. "Military Macho: Harassment of Women in the Armed Forces Often Means One Thing: She Asked for It." *Washington Post Weekly Edition,* November 23–29, 1992, 10–12.

Lang, Daniel. *Casualties of War.* New York: McGraw-Hill, 1969.

Lehring, Gary. "Difference as Identity, Difference and Identity: Strategies in American Public Policy." Ph.D. diss., Department of Political Science, University of Massachusetts, Amherst, 1993.

"Lesbians at War with the Military" (special issue). *Outlook: National Lesbian and Gay Quarterly* 13 (Summer 1991).

Letelier, Isabel. "Women and Democracy in Chile." *Let the Other Half Speak:*

Newsletter of the Third World Project 1, no. 2 (Fall 1993): 3. Published by the Institute for Policy Studies, Washington, DC.

Liddington, Jill, *The Long Road to Greenham: Feminism and Anti-Militarism in Britain since 1820.* Syracuse, NY: University of Syracuse Press, 1989.

Light, Julie. "Salvadoran Women Plan for Peace." *Ms.*, July 1992, 13.

Litoff, Judy Barrett, and David C. Smith, eds. *Since You Went Away: World War II Letters from American Women on the Home Front.* New York: Oxford University Press, 1991.

Lotchin, Roger. *Fortress California, 1910–1961: From Warfare to Welfare.* New York: Oxford University Press, 1992.

McAfee, Kathy. *Storm Signals: Structural Adjustment and Development Alternatives in the Caribbean.* Boston: South End, 1992.

McClintock, Michael. *The American Connection.* 2 vols. London: Zed Books, 1985.

McDonald, Sharon, Pat Holden, and Shirley Ardener, eds. *Images of Women in Peace and War: Cross-Cultural and Historical Perspectives.* Madison: University of Wisconsin Press, 1988.

McDowall, David. *The Kurds.* London: Minority Rights Group, 1989.

McEnaney, Laura. "Civil Defense Begins at Home: Gender and Family Politics in the Making of the Cold War." PhD. diss., Department of History, University of Wisconsin, Madison. Forthcoming.

McPhee, John. *La Place de la Concorde Suisse.* New York: Farrar Strauss Giroux, 1984.

Malette, Louise, and Marie Chalough, eds. *The Montreal Massacre.* Charlottetown, Prince Edward Island: Gynergy Books, 1991.

Markusen, Ann, and Joel Yudken. *Dismantling the Cold War Economy.* New York: Basic Books, 1992.

Marques, Fernando. "Women Enlist for the War of the Sexes." *The Guardian* (London), March 20, 1992.

Marshall, Andrew. "What Happened to the Peace Dividend?" *The Independent* (London), January 3, 1993.

Marshall, Kathryn. *In the Combat Zone.* New York: Penguin Books, 1987.

Mason, Bobbie Ann. *In Country.* New York: Perennial Books, 1986.

May, Elaine Tyler. *Homeward Bound: American Families in the Cold War Era.* New York: Basic Books, 1988.

Meier, Andrew. "The Big Bride Swap." *Moscow*, February-March, 1992, 28–34.

Melman, Seymour. *The Permanent War Economy.* New York: Simon and Schuster, 1974.

Menchú, Rigoberta. *I, Rigoberta Menchú: An Indian Woman in Guatemala.* Edited by Elizabeth Burgos-Debray. New York: Verso, 1983.

Meyer, Leisa D. "Creating G.I. Jane: The Regulation of Sexuality and Sexual Behavior in the Women's Army Corps during World War II." *Feminist Studies* 18, no. 3 (Fall 1992): 581–601.

Mihalsko, Kathleen. "Defense and Security Planning in Ukraine." *Report on the USSR.* December 6, 1991, 15–19.

Minow, Newton N. "Less Brawn, More Brains." *Washington Post Weekly Edition.* November 23–29, 1992, 29.

Morgan, David N. J. *Discovering Men: Sociology and Masculinities.* London: Routledge, 1992.

Morrison, Toni, ed. *Race-ing Justice, En-gendering Power: Essays on Anita Hill, Clarence Thomas, and the Construction of Social Reality.* New York: Pantheon, 1992.

Mueller, Elizabeth. "The Other Side of the Defense Build Down." *Positive Alternatives.* Summer 1992, 4.

Nakahara Michiko. "Forgotten Victims: Asian and Women Workers on the Thai-Burma Railway." *AMPO: Japan-Asian Quarterly Review* 23, no. 2 (1991): 21–25.

"Nepalis in Uniform" (special issue). *Himal,* July–August, 1991.

"The 1991 Gulf War." *Campaign Against the Arms Trade Newsletter* 117 (October 1992): 7.

O'Reilly, Emily. *Masterminds of the Right.* Dublin: Attic Press, 1992.

Peters, Cynthia, ed. *Collateral Damage.* Boston: South End, 1992.

Petersen, Kurt. *The Maquiladora Revolution in Guatemala.* Occasional Paper Series, no. 2. New Haven: Orville H. Schell Center for International Human Rights, Yale Law School, Yale University, 1992.

Peterson, V. Spike, ed. *Gendered States: Feminist (Re)Visions of International Relations Theory.* Boulder, CO: Lynne Rienner, 1992.

Phillips, Andrew. "A Woman of Substance." *MacLean's,* October 19, 1992, 46–47.

Plakwicz, Jolanta. "Between Church and State: Polish Women's Experience." In *Superwomen and the Double Burden: Women's Experience of Change in Central and Eastern Europe and the Former Soviet Union,* edited by Chris Corrin. Toronto: Second Story, 1992, 75–96.

Pomonti, Jean-Claude. "Caught between Dogma and Liberalization." *Le Monde.* January 29, 1992; reprinted in *Guardian Weekly.* February 9, 1992, 16.

Presidential Commission on the Assignment of Women in the Armed Services. *Report*. Washington, DC: Government Printing Office, 1992.

Prokosch, Mike. "El Salvador Pact Raises Hopes." *Central America Reporter*. January-February 1992.

Puget Sound Women's Peace Camp. *We Are Ordinary Women*. Seattle: Seal, 1985.

Ramazanoglu, Caroline. "What Can You Do With a Man? Feminism and a Critical Appraisal of Masculinity." *Women's Studies International Forum* 15, no. 3 (1992): 339–50.

Ranchod-Nilsson, Sita. "Gender Politics and National Liberation: Women's Participation in the Liberation of Zimbabwe." Ph.D. diss., Department of Political Science, Northwestern University, 1992.

Randall, Margaret. "Coming Out in Nicaragua." *Sojourner*. June 1992, 4–5.

————. *Gathering Rage: The Failure of Twentieth-Century Revolutions to Develop a Feminist Agenda*. New York: Monthly Review Press, 1992.

"Rape Goes to War." *The Economist*. January 23, 1993, 46.

Rhodes, Richard. *The Making of the Atomic Bomb*. New York: Simon and Schuster, 1986.

Roper, Michael, and John Tosh, eds. *Manful Assertions: Masculinities in Britain since 1800*. London: Routledge, 1991.

Russo, Valeria, Lorenza Sebesta, and Elizabetta Addis, eds. *Women at War: Images of Women Soldiers*. London: Macmillan, 1993.

Said, Yahia. "New Challenges for Conversion: The Martin Project." *Helsinki Citizens Assembly Newsletter* 6 (Winter 1993): 25.

Samuels, Raphael, ed. *Patriotism: The Making and Unmaking of National Identity*. 3 vols. London: Routledge, 1989.

Sanararian, Eliz. *The Women's Rights Movement in Iran*. New York: Praeger, 1982.

Schaeffer-Hegel, Barbara. "Makers and Victims of Unification: German Women and the Two Germanies." In "A Continent in Transition: Issues for Women in Europe in the 1990s," edited by Claire Duchen (special issue). *Women's Studies International Forum* 15, no. 1 (1992): 101–11.

Schmaltz, Jeffrey. "Gay Politics Goes Mainstream." *New York Times Magazine*. October 11, 1992.

Schmitt, Eric. "Military's Gay Subculture: Off Limits but Flourishing." *New York Times*. December 1, 1992.

Seager, Joni. *Earth Follies: Coming to Feminist Terms with the Global Environmental Crisis*. New York: Routledge, 1993.

Seager, Joni, and Ann Olson. *Women in the World: An International Atlas.* New York: Simon and Schuster, 1986.

Sesser, Stan. "Report from Cambodia." *New Yorker.* May 18, 1992, 43–58.

Shreeves, Rosamund. "Mothers Against the Draft: Women's Activism in the USSR." *Report on the USSR.* September 21, 1990, 3–9.

Siemienska, Renata, "Dialogue: Polish Women and Polish Politics Since World War II," *Journal of Women's History* 3, no. 1 (Spring 1991): 108–30.

Silvera, Makeda. *Silenced: Talks with Working Class West Indian Women about Their Lives and Struggles as Domestic Workers in Canada.* Toronto: Williams-Wallace, 1983.

Sistren and Honor Ford Smith. *Lionheart Gal.* London: Women's Press, 1986.

Smith-Ayala, Emilie. *The Granddaughters of Ixmucane: Guatemalan Women Speak.* Toronto: Women's Press, 1991.

Smyth, Ailbhe. "Hail Mary—A President of Women." *Trouble and Strife* 23 (Spring 1992): 4–7.

Sokka Gakkai, Women's Division. *Women Against War: Personal Accounts of Forty Japanese Women.* Tokyo: Kodansha, 1986.

"Special Peace Issue." *Helicon Nine* 12–13 (Summer 1985).

Staunton, Irene, ed. *Mothers of the Revolution: The War Experiences of Thirty Zimbabwean Women.* Bloomington: Indiana University Press, 1990.

"Stavropol Women Protest Troop Call-up." *Foreign Broadcast Information Service—Soviet Union.* January 22, 1990, 9.

Steitz, Barbara J. "From Home to Street: Women and Revolution in Nicaragua." In *Women Transforming Politics,* edited by Jill M. Bystdzienski. Bloomington: Indiana University Press, 1992, 162–74.

Sternbach, Nancy Saporta, Marysa Navarro-Aranguran, Patricia Chuchryk, and Sonia E. Alvarez. "Feminisms in Latin America: From Bogota to San Bernardo." *Signs* (Winter 1992).

Stiehm, Judith Hicks. *Arms and the Enlisted Woman.* Philadelphia: Temple University Press, 1989.

Stockholm International Peace Research Institute. *World Armaments and Disarmament: The 1992 SIPRI Yearbook.* Oxford: Oxford University Press, 1992.

Stone, Anne J., ed. *Women in the Military: International Perspectives.* Washington, DC: Women's Research and Education Institute, 1992.

Sturdevant, Saundra, and Brenda Stoltzfus. *Let the Good Times Roll: The Sale of Women's Sexual Labor around U.S. Military Bases in the Philippines, Okinawa, and the Southern Part of Korea.* New York: New Press, 1992.

Sullivan, Robert. "Postcard from Oregon: Revolution Number Nine." *New Yorker.* November 9, 1992, 67–79.

Summerfield, Penny. *Women Workers in the Second World War.* New York: Routledge, 1989.

Sunindyo, Saraswati. *Yakin.* Typescript, 1992.

Sutton, Constance, Ed. *Feminism, Nationalism, and Militarism.* New York: Association of Feminist Anthropologists and International Women's Anthropological Conference, 1993. Distributed by the American Anthropological Association, Washington, DC.

Swerdlow, Amy. "Ladies' Day at the Capitol: Women Strike for Peace versus HUAC." *Feminist Studies* 8, no. 3 (Fall 1982): 493–520.

Sylvester, Christine. *Feminist Theory and International Relations in a Postmodern Era.* Cambridge: Cambridge University Press. Forthcoming.

Szalai, Julia. "Some Aspects of the Changing Situation of Women in Hungary." *Signs* 17, no. 11 (1991): 152–70.

Tamang, Seira. "Nepali Women as Military Wives." Honors thesis, Department of Government, Clark University, Worcester, MA, 1992.

Tapales, Proserpina Domingo. "Women, Migration and the Mail-Order Bride Phemonenon: Focus on Australia." *Philippine Journal of Public Administration* 34, no. 4 (October 1990): 311–22.

Taylor, Barbara. *Eve and the New Jerusalem.* New York: Pantheon, 1984.

Taylor, Octavia Victoria. "Funding Frailties: The Vietnam Refugee Experience with Bureaucracy in Worcester, Massachusetts." M.A. thesis, International Development Program, Clark University, Worcester, MA, 1991.

Terry, Wallace. *Bloods: An Oral History of the Vietnam War by Black Veterans.* New York: Ballantine Books, 1984.

Tetreault, Mary Ann. "Democratization and Women in Kuwait." Paper presented at the annual meeting of the International Studies Association—Midwest, East Lansing, MI, November 20–21, 1992.

Theweleit, Klaus. *Male Fantasies.* 2 vols. Minneapolis: University of Minnesota Press, 1989.

Thitsa, Khin. *Providence and Prostitution: Women in Buddhist Thailand.* London: Change International Reports, 1990.

Tickner, J. Ann. *Gender in International Relations.* New York: Columbia University Press, 1992.

Truong, Thanh-Dam. *Sex, Money and Morality: Prostitution and Tourism in Southeast Asia.* London: Zed Press, 1990.

Turitz, Shari. "Guatemala: Torture of a Nation." *Resist Newsletter* 242 (January 1992): 4.

U.K. Parliament. House of Commons. *Special Report from the Select Committee on the Armed Forces Bill* (session 1990–91). London: HMSO, 1991.

U.N. Non-Governmental Liaison Service. *Beyond the Debt Crisis.* New York: United Nations Department of Public Information, 1990.

"U.S./Guatemala Labor Education." *Resist Newsletter* 2, no. 1 (January 1993): 9–10.

U.S. Congress. House. Committee on Armed Services. *Women in the Military: Hearings before the Military Personnel and Compensation Subcommittee.* Washington, DC: Government Printing Office, 1990.

U.S. Department of Defense. Office of Inspector General. *Tailhook 91. Part 1: Review of the Navy Investigations.* Washington, DC: Department of Defense, September 1992.

U.S. General Accounting Office. *Defense Force Management: DOD's Policy on Homosexuality.* Washington, DC: General Accounting Office, 1992.

Vallières, Pierre. *White Niggers of North America.* New York: Monthly Review Press, 1971.

Van Devanter, Lynda. *Home Before Morning.* New York: Beaufort Books, 1983.

Vanita, R. "The 1984 Elections: United We Fall—into the Trap of Manipulators." *Manushi: Journal about Women and Society* 26 (1985).

Veloso, Caetano. "Caricature and Conqueror, Pride and Shame." *New York Times.* October 20, 1991.

Ventura, Rey. *Underground in Japan.* London: Jonathan Cape, 1992.

"Voices from the SDF." *AMPO: Japan-Asian Quarterly Review* 24, no. 1 (1993): 19–22.

"Voices of Hope and Anger: Women Speak Out for Sovereignty and Self-Determination" (special issue). *Listen Real Loud* 10, nos. 1–2 (1990): 12–13.

Wainwright, Hilary. "The Women Who Wire up the Weapons." In *Over Our Dead Bodies,* edited by Dorothy Thompson. London: Virago, 1983.

Walker, Keith. *A Piece of My Heart.* New York: Ballantine, 1985.

Wertsch, Mary. *Military Brats: The Legacy of Childhood Inside the Fortress.* New York: Crown, 1991.

Wessel, Lois. "Reproductive Rights in Nicaragua: From the Sandinistas to the Government of Violeta Chamorro." *Feminist Studies* 17, no. 3 (Fall 1991): 537–550.

White, Luise. *The Comforts of Home: Prostitution in Colonial Nairobi.* Chicago: University of Chicago Press, 1990.

Whitworth, Sandra. "Feminism, Gender, and the International Labor Organization." *International Organization.* Forthcoming.

———. "Gender in the IPPF and the ILO: A Feminist Analysis of International Relations." Ph.D diss., Carlton University, Ottawa, Ontario, 1991.

Wiltshire, Anne. *Most Dangerous Women: Feminist Peace Campaigners of the Great War.* London: Pandora Press, 1985.

Wolchik, Sharon L., and Alfred G. Meyer, eds. *Women, State, and Party in Eastern Europe.* Durham, NC: Duke University Press, 1985.

Wolf, Christa. *Cassandra.* London: Virago, 1984.

"Women and Economic Conversion," *Plowshares* 10, no. 3 (Summer 1985): 3–4.

"Women and Militarism." *Connexions* 2 (Winter 1984).

"Women and Peace." *Frontiers* 8, no. 2 (1985).

"Women in Arms: What Happened in Panama." *Defense Media Review* (Boston University) 4, no. 1 (May 1990).

"Women in the Military: What Role Should Women Play in the Shrinking Military?" *Congressional Quarterly* 2, no. 36 (September 1992): 842.

Woolf, Virginia. *Three Guineas.* New York: Harcourt Brace Jovanovich, 1938.

Wright, Ann. "The Roles of U.S. Army Women in Grenada." *Minerva: Quarterly Report on Women and the Military* 2, no. 2 (Summer 1984): 103–113.

You Can't Dream the Fire: Latin American Women Writing in Exile. Philadelphia: Cleis Press, 1989.

Yuval-Davis, Nira, ed. *Unholy Orders: Women against Fundamentalism.* London: Virago, 1992.

Yuval-Davis, Nira, and Floya Anthias, eds. *Woman, Nation, State.* London: Macmillan, 1989.

Index

Compositor: ComCom, Inc.
Text: 10.5 Sabon
Display: Sabon
Printer and Binder: Haddon Craftsmen, Inc.